KENYON COLLEGE.

Middleton, Strobridge & C°. Lith. Cin. O.

A

HISTORY

OF

KNOX COUNTY, OHIO,

FROM 1779 TO 1862 INCLUSIVE:

COMPRISING

BIOGRAPHICAL SKETCHES, ANECDOTES AND INCIDENTS OF MEN CONNECTED WITH THE COUNTY FROM ITS FIRST SETTLEMENT:

TOGETHER WITH

COMPLETE LISTS OF THE SENATORS, REPRESENTATIVES, SHERIFFS, AUDITORS, COMMISSIONERS, TREASURERS, JUDGES, JUSTICES OF THE PEACE, AND OTHER OFFICERS OF THE COUNTY, ALSO OF THOSE WHO HAVE SERVED IN A MILITARY CAPACITY FROM ITS FIRST ORGANIZATION TO THE PRESENT TIME.

AND ALSO

A SKETCH OF KENYON COLLEGE,

AND OTHER INSTITUTIONS OF LEARNING AND RELIGION WITHIN THE COUNTY.

BY

A. BANNING NORTON.

COLUMBUS:
RICHARD NEVINS, PRINTER.
1862.

PREFACE.

To write the history of my native county, and to rescue from oblivion the anecdotes and early incidents of its first settlers, has been with me a pleasant pastime. While it has been much labor to gather the material for this work, and to test it by the crucible of truth, my mind has thereby been relieved of much care and of anxious thoughts upon more serious subjects during an exile in my native land; and if I will have been the means of preserving, for the future historian, matters which are within the recollection of but very few now living, my time and toil have been well spent.

Several years ago, when a resident of this place, I collected many of the items which I now produce from memory: such as the captivity of John Stilley, and events of early occurrence within the knowledge of Dr. Timothy Burr, my father, Daniel S. Norton, Col. John Greer, Judge Bevans, Gilman Bryant, Col. Emor Harris, Judge Jesse B. Thomas, Rev. James Scott, and others, who have since deceased. Among my papers in Texas are notes taken by me of conversations with the above recited parties, as also with Samuel H. Smith and William Smith, old residents of Knox, now residing in that State.

I would have delayed the publication of the sketch I give herewith, were it not very uncertain when the present unhappy war may terminate, or what my future may be. Procrastination might prove fatal to the enterprise; hence I have concluded to furnish it to the children of the old settlers, and the public generally in the Ko-kosing country, conscious that it has imperfections, but without the ability, under existing circumstances, of making it more complete. My object is accomplished in putting in this form for preservation much crude material, which I regard as of value to those who may succeed us: I did not undertake it with expectation or purpose of gain.

I may have overlooked some names in putting the manuscript to press, or improperly placed others; but from the most reliable data I have drawn my conclusions and made my statements. I would have been pleased to have extended my genealogical sketches, and to have traced out the various old families in the townships; but, from having met several who were indisposed to give me information, I found this branch must necessarily be partial, and desisted from researches in that way. The reader will take those named as examples of the manner in which I think a history of the county ought to be written, and I would like to have so presented it. Some, whose names may not be found in this book, may find fault with its compilation, as did "Schmidt," the dutch drayman in the city of Austin, whose name he discovered in the Directory spelled "Smith," and exclaimed, "I would not give one tam for the Correctory vot has my name left out of it; for Smith is not Schmidt no how."

Of one thing all may be assured, and that is this: I have set down naught in malice, nor aught extenuated, but endeavored to represent all fairly and correctly. I have no object to do otherwise. I do not intend ever to live among you, nor in your State, and am, therefore, truly independent. I belong to no political or religious party, sect or organization of the present day, nor do I ever expect to. "He is a freeman whom the truth makes free!" Having no interests to subserve—

"no friends to reward, or enemies to punish"—I am, with my best regards to such as have received me kindly and aided me with information, and to the people of Knox individually and collectively,

Their friend,

A. BANNING NORTON.

MOUNT VERNON, O., *July* 1, 1862.

HISTORY OF KNOX COUNTY.

CHAPTER I.

SKETCH OF THE COUNTRY AND SETTLEMENT PRIOR TO ORGANIZATION.—TRAVERSED BEFORE THE TERRITORY OF OHIO WAS NAMED BY ONE OF ITS SUBSEQUENT SETTLERS.—ITS INHABITANT BEFORE THE STATE WAS ORGANIZED.—ITS CITIZENS WHEN FAIRFIELD COUNTY WAS CREATED.—WITH INCIDENTS OF FRONTIER LIFE AND ADVENTURE.

THE country having for its name Ohio was constituted, under General Arthur St. Clair, a territorial government in the year 1788, and he continued as Governor until the adoption of the State Constitution in 1803.

By his proclamation the county of Fairfield was created December 9th, 1800, and the district of which we now treat was included therein until the month of February, 1808, when it was, by enactment of the Legislature, organized into a separate and distinct county, honored with the name of General Henry Knox, a distinguished officer of the revolutionary army, who was subsequently Secretary of War in Gen. Washington's administration.

The first white man known to have viewed this section of country was John Stilley, who, when a captive among the Indians, traversed the White Woman and Owl Creek from its mouth in a northwesterly direction, as early as June, 1779, nine years before the name of Ohio had been given to this territory, and when the savages and wild beasts roamed at will throughout its vast extent.

The first settlers in this district were from Virginia, Maryland, New Jersey and Pennsylvania, and its inhabitants, at every period of its history, have been chiefly from the middle States.

From our research into early statements, we are led to believe that Andrew Craig was the first white man who located within the present county limits. He was, at a very early day, a sort of frontier character, fond of rough and tumble life, a stout and rugged man—bold and dare-devil in disposition—who took delight in hunting, wrestling and athletic sports, and was "hail fellow well met" with the Indians then inhabiting the country. He was from the bleak, broken, mountainous region of Virginia, and as hardy a pine knot as ever that country produced. He was in this country when Ohio was in its territorial condition, and when this wilderness region was declared to be in the county of Fairfield, the sole denizen in this entire district, whose history is now being written, tabernacled with a woman in a rough log hut close by the little Indian Field, about one-half mile east of where Mount Vernon city now exists, and at the point where Centre Run empties into the Ko-ko-sing. There Andrew Craig lived when Mount Vernon was laid out in 1805—there he was upon the organization of Knox county, its oldest inhabitant—and there he continued until 1809. Such a harum-scarum fellow could not rest easy when white men got thick around him, so he left and went to the Indian village—Greentown—and from thence migrated further out upon the frontier, preferring red men for neighbors.

After many years of solitary residence on the beautiful Ko-ko-sing, the solitude of Craig's retreat is broken by the entrance of a lone Jerseyman, who, in the spring of 1803, penetrates some ten miles further into the wilderness, so as not, by too close proximity, to annoy each other, and there raises a little log cabin and settles down. This follower of the trade of Vulcan soon gets in readiness to blow and strike, and sets about supplying the sons of the forest with the first axes they had ever seen, and by making for them tomahawks, scalping knives, etc., he acquires the sobriquet of the "axe-maker," which for more than half a century has attached to Nathaniel Mitchel Young.

A year passes by before any white accession is made to society on Owl Creek. Then a stalwart backwoodsman breaks the silence by the crack of his rifle, and at the spot where James S. Banning now lives, near Clinton, the pioneer, William Douglass, drives his stake.

The skillful navigator plies his oar, and Robert Thompson ascends Owl Creek to where Mount Vernon now stands, and on the rich bottom land, about one mile west, commences another improvement. George Dial, of Hampshire county, Virginia, in another pirogue comes up the creek, and, pleased with the beautiful country about where Gambier now flourishes, pitches his tent at the place now occupied by John Troutman. Old Captain James Walker, from Pennsylvania, settles on the bank of the creek where Mount Vernon now is. John Simpkins wanders from Virginia, with his son Seeley for his capital, and squats about a mile above Douglass, where George Cassel's beautiful farm now exists. While these plain men from Virginia, New Jersey and Pennsylvania are preparing their cabins for comfortable occupation, and making little clearings, a stray Yankee, solitary and alone, with a speculative eye and money-making disposition, is, with pocket compass, taking his bearings through the forest, soliloquizing about the chance of making a fortune by laying out a town and selling lots to those who may come after him into this charming new country. Having, as he thought, found the exact spot for his future operations, he blazes a tree, and wends his way to the nearest town—Franklinton—west of the Scioto, then a place of magnificent pretensions, where he gets chain and compass and paper, and returns and lays out the town of Clinton, in section number four, township seven, range four, United States military district, with its large "public green," its north street and south street, its main street, first, second, third and fourth streets, and one hundred and sixty lots, and, taking his town plat in his pocket, he walks to New Lancaster, being the first white person ever known to have made a journey in that direction from this infant settlement, and before Abraham Wright, Justice of the Peace, acknowledges that important instrument, and on the 8th of December, 1804, places it upon record. Thus Samuel H. Smith, subsequently the first surveyor of Knox county, for many years a resident, its leading business man, and largest land holder, made his entrance into this district.

Shortly afterwards a large accession was made to the population of the country by the emigration from Ten Mile, Washington county, Pa., of John Mills, Henry Haines, Ebenezer and Abner Brown, and Peter Baxter, who settled a short distance south of Owl Creek, where the Beams, Merrits and Lafevers have since lived. This settlement, by the increase of the Leonards, was in 1805 and '6 the largest and best community in the country, and upon the organization of the county, and for several years thereafter, it furnished the leading men.

Ben. Butler, Peter Coyle, and Thomas Bell Patterson, in the spring of 1805, augment the Walker settlement, where Mount Vernon was located shortly thereafter. William Douglass is joined by James Loveridge, who emigrates from Morris county, New Jersey, and with his wife takes quarters on the 6th of July upon the clapboards in the garret of his little log cabin, and is mighty glad to get such a shelter as that to spend the year in. The next year Loveridge starts off, under pretense of hunting a cow, and goes to the land office and enters and pays for the tract of land, where shortly after he erected a dwelling, and has ever since resided. Upon this land there is an uncommon good spring, which caused him to select it, and he tells with much glee the circumstances under which he obtained it. The only Yankee then in the country claimed to have located it, and proposed to sell it to him at a higher price than the government rate, which was then $2 per acre. Concealing his intention from all but his wife, Loveridge slipped off and examined into and purchased it himself from the government, and when he returned with his patent, Bill Douglass laughed heartily at the Jersey Blue overreaching the cunning Yankee. Amoriah Watson, of Wyoming county, Pa., also put up with Douglass, and thus this settlement was made up of Douglass, Smith, Watson and Loveridge, in 1805. The old axe-maker, in the meantime, is followed up by some of his relations and friends, who start what has ever since been known as the Jersey settlement. Jacob Young, Abraham Lyon and Simeon Lyon are the first to settle upon the South Fork of Owl Creek, and are succeeded by Eliphalet Lewis, John Lewis, and James Bryant. The Indians they found very numerous, and through the kind feelings towards the old axe-maker, they were very friendly, and really quite an advantage in ridding the country of wolves, bears, and other varmints.

In the winter of 1805–6, that settlement entered into a written agreement to give nine bushels of corn for each wolf scalp that might be taken, and three of the men caught forty-one wolves in steel traps and pens! The description of these pens, and one of the stories told of their operation, we give in the words of an old settler:—"Wolf pens were about six feet long, four wide, and three high, formed like a huge square box, of small logs, and floored with puncheons. The lid, also of puncheons, was very heavy, and moved by an axle at one end, made of a small, round stick. The trap was set by a figure 4, with any kind of meat except that of wolf's, the animals being fonder of any other than their own. On gnawing the meat, the lid fell and caught the unamiable native. To make sport for the dogs, the legs of the wolf were pulled through the crevices between the logs, hamstrung, and then he was let loose, when the dogs soon caught and finished him. In Delaware county an old man went into a wolf trap to fix the spring, when it sprung upon him, knocking him flat upon his face, and securely caught him as though he were a wolf. Unable to lift up the lid, and several miles from any house, he lay all one day and night, and would have perished but for a hunter, who passing by heard his groans, and came to his rescue."

North, west and east of these embryo settlements all was wilderness for many long miles. A place bearing the name of Newark had been laid out by Gen. W. C. Schenck, but it had not any greater population than these little scattered settlements aforementioned. The principal towns of note to the early settlers were Lancaster, Chillicothe and Zanesville. Neither of them were much larger then than our usual ⋈ roads villages now are. The people were exceedingly neighborly, and performed all manner of "kind chores" for each other, in going to mills, laying in goods, dividing what they had with each other, &c. The nearest mill in 1805, was in Fairfield county. Our old friend James Loveridge informs us of a trip he made to that mill, which was seven miles up the Hockhocking river, from Lancaster. It belonged to Loveland & Smith, and was situated in a little crack between some rocks, and he went down into the mill from on top of the roof. He made the trip there and back, about 125 miles, and brought home with him in his wagon about 900 pounds of flour, one barrel of whisky, and one barrel of salt. How the settlement must have rejoiced at the arrival of the great staples of frontier life, salt, whisky and flour!

CHAPTER II.

CONTINUATION OF THE EARLY OUTLINE.—MORE ABOUT THE FIRST SETTLERS.—QUAKERS FROM MARYLAND FIND THEIR WAY IN 1806.—INCIDENTS CONNECTED WITH THEIR EMIGRATION, AND IN THE MOVEMENTS OF OTHER SETTLERS.—WHO THEY WERE AND WHAT BECAME OF THEM.—THE PRIVATIONS ENDURED AND DANGERS ENCOUNTERED.—MORE TOWNS LAID OUT.—THE FIRST MILLS.—THE SCENE OF AN ENCOUNTER WITH INDIANS.—INCONVENIENCES OF THE COUNTRY.—EFFORTS FOR A NEW COUNTY.—AN EARLY ELECTION.—FAIRFIELD DIVIDED.—THREE NEW COUNTIES CREATED BY ONE BILL.—STRIFE FOR THE SEAT OF JUSTICE OF KNOX.

THE spring of 1806 brought with it a new element into the wilderness region, in the form of the Friends—the forerunners of large numbers of that society, who by their quiet yet industrious ways have contributed very much to the prosperity and peacefulness of our people. The venerable father Henry Roberts may be justly regarded as the head of this emigration from Maryland. In 1805 he left Frederick county, in that State, with his family, and directed his course to the far west, but on reaching Belmont county, found it necessary to winter his family there, and sent his wagon and team back to Maryland with a load of ginseng and snake-root, and on their return with a load of goods, he started with his family and plunder, and on the 7th of April, 1806, he landed at Henry Haines', in the Ten Mile settlement, and after spending a week looking for a good location, on the 14th of that month settled down his family at the little prairie five miles above Mount Vernon, of late widely known as the Armstrong section. The family consisted of his wife, his sons—William, now living at Pekin, Illinois; Isaiah, now residing near Pilot Knob, Missouri; Richard Roberts, of Berlin—and a daughter Massah, who married Dr. Timothy Burr, and died at Clinton, March 9th, 1814. Nine acres of that beautiful prairie were at once broken up and planted in corn. It was very hard work to break the virgin soil with a first rate four-horse plow team, but it paid for that labor by one of the finest crops of corn ever raised in this country. In the fall Wm. Y. Farquhar, a cousin of Henry Roberts, came with his family, and after him came Wm. W. Farquhar with his family. They all stopped with Henry Roberts, and thus composed the first settlement of Friends in this district. From this nucleus came the numerous society of Quakers in Wayne, Middlebury and Berlin, in after years. Shortly after this we find another Quaker, Samuel Wilson, and John Kerr in what subsequently became Wayne township, and John Cook and Jacob Cook just above, in what is now Middlebury township, and Amoriah Watson goes from Douglass' to the tract of land above, where Fredericktown was the next year laid out, and which he subsequently sold to Jacob Ebersole, a place now easy to be identified by all. In the spring of 1806, there were within the after limits of Knox county but fifteen persons who turned out to vote, and but nine liable to per form military duty out to muster.

The first grist mill erected in this county was of

a decidedly primitive character. It was in the Hains, or Ten Mile settlement, and constructed without the sound of the hammer upon iron. It was the joint work of Ebenezer and Abner Brown, assisted by the mechanical skill of the whole neighborhood, and was built on what was called by the early settlers "Big Run," though in later times it is spoken of as the little Lake, through which the road to Granville has since been laid out. The water has almost disappeared—having been in its appearance greatly changed by ditching, and in some parts obliterated by filling up the hollow. The mill stood where Isaac Beam's house now is, and the dam was where the bridge now stands in the lane. It was all of wood—a sugar-trough made its meal-trough—a little box the hopper—the stones were about two feet through, and hooped with elm bark for want of iron. It cracked corn pretty well with a good head on, but the stream was generally dry, and the mill was only able to run when big showers of rain came. The building was about ten feet square, of rough logs—not a nail or a bit of iron could be had when it was made. The stones of this ancient of days are certainly a curiosity—they are yet to be seen, being the property of Moses Farquhar, of Berlin, who since that day has attempted experiments with them. Richard Roberts at one time took a grist to this original mill and had it ground. He was then about seventeen years old, and not much acquainted with the milling business, but he was greatly impressed with its mechanism, and ready to exclaim, with our old friend Hadly, "The works of God are wonderful, but the works of man are wonderfuller!" He thought that it worked first rate, though Henry Hains at that time had got a little hand mill which he claimed was a great improvement on the little wooden mill.

Mr. Roberts recollects of having at one time packed a bag of corn from Tom Butler's down on White-woman home, and from thence to a mill near Newark, and back home again, less a heavy toll. While at the mill he saw Hughes, and from his own lips had a true account about the killing of Indian horse thieves, whom Jack Ratliff and himself had pursued into the Owl Creek country and killed as they came upon them in the bottom just below where Fredericktown now stands. The story runs thus:—"One night in April, 1800, two Indians stole their horses from a little inclosure near their cabins, located in some old Indian fields on the Licking. In the morning, finding their horses gone, and tracks about, they were satisfied of their having been stolen, and started off in pursuit, accompanied by a man named Bland. They followed their trail all day, and camped at night in the woods, and making an early start in the morning, surprised the Indians in their sleep. They drew up their rifles to shoot, when one of the Indians, discovering them, clapping his hands on his breast, as if to ward off the fatal ball, exclaimed in piteous tones, 'me bad Indian!—me no do so more!' Alas! in vain he plead; the smoke curled from the glistening barrels, the report rang in the morning air, and the poor Indians fell dead." Hughes and Ratliff returned home with the horses and plunder taken from the Indians, feeling as well over their little exploit as any men ever did over a great and glorious action. Ellis Hughes, who was known to very many of our old settlers, died near Utica, in March, 1845, and was buried with military honors. He was believed to be the last survivor of the hard fought battle of Point Pleasant. He was a hardy backwoodsman from Western Virginia.

Our old townsman, Wm. Mefford, informs us that when he improved his farm on Mile Run, in Wayne township, he was clearing off ground on which to build his house, and he then plowed up the two Indians killed by Hughes, and also a rusty gun barrel, brass guard, and other pieces of a gun, which had not decayed. This was in 1835; and Jacob Mitchel now has the old relics.

George Conkie gathered up the bones and buried them, and the house was built on the spot—the old Peck place on Mile Run bottom, where Mrs. Acre now lives. In early days there was a favorite camping ground for the Indians about three-fourths of a mile from where these Indians were killed. Three old settlers have informed us that about 1808 they saw at one time more than one hundred and fifty warriors camped there. They have several times seen Old Crane, the Wyandot Chief, the Chief Armstrong, and Captain Pipe, with bands of Indians, roving through this country, and we have gathered some very amusing incidents connected therewith, which the limit we have prescribed for this work compels us to omit in this edition.

The great inconvenience the settlers labored under for want of building material caused William

Douglass, as early as the spring of 1805, to conceive the design of erecting a mill at the seat now known as Banning's Mill. He then commenced digging the race and building the dam. After getting a saw to running, he set to work building a grist mill; being a man of enterprise, he could not brook the thought that the people in that neighborhood should continue to boil and pound their corn when they could not take time to go to the distant mills.

John Kerr, as will be elsewhere noted in this book, erected a little grist mill on the Sullivant track, and laid out the town of Frederick in the first quarter, seventh township, fourteenth range, United States military district, which on the 11th of November, 1807, he acknowledged, in presence of George Chambers, before Wm. W. Farquhar. A full account of the early settlement and progress of this thriving village will be found under the head of Wayne township.

In our investigation of early matters, we find that the settlers of this district were solicitous upon three great points for legislative aid, to wit: the division of Fairfield, the increase of premium upon wolf scalps, and proper encouragement in killing squirrels. The General Assembly, in 1807, passed a bill to encourage killing of squirrels. It went through the popular branch with a rush, but the vote upon the final passage of the bill in the Senate, on the 21st of December, stood 8 ayes to 7 nays. The price for scalping grown wolves was increased, after some time and much petitioning, and the monster Fairfield was dismembered at last. Happy were those old pioneers, at that period of their existence—

> "All then was happy—possessing and possessed—
> No craving void left aching in the breast!"

In looking over the old petitions and beholding the cramped signatures of a number of these hardy yeomen, whose rough specimen marks of cracked and blistered hands in frontier service, clearly bear witness to their whole heart being in the prayers sent up for these measures, we can well imagine how they must have chuckled with delight, as a Christian over his soul's salvation, at the realization of their wishes. In those primitive times their attention was not diverted from the real live issues affecting the welfare of themselves and their families to grand humanitarian schemes for the benefit of any other race or people. The squirrels eat the kernels when the corn was in silken tassels, taking it out of their children's mouths; the wolves prowled about their tracks, destroying their pigs and poultry, and rendered night hideous with their howling, and frightened and endangered the lives of wives and children, so they could not leave home to attend to necessary business at the remote county seat. This was a remarkable epoch in the history of the pioneers of this country.

In 1807, at the October election, the section of country known as Fairfield county cast but 213 votes, all told; and now there is scarcely a township in all this country that does not contain more voters. Then the entire vote cast for Governor in the State, as officially published, was 5,616; and now, after the space of fifty-four years, our own county of Knox polls over 6,000 votes, and the old county as it then existed polled at the last election 40,000!

What a change in the country we have lived to witness! How striking the contrast in manners, customs, education, intelligence, and in political, religious, and social life! In nothing is the alteration more clearly marked than in the dissemination of information in reference to elections and the system of electioneering. Then every man ran on his own hook—his own race—making the best speed he was capable of—fully impressed with the belief that the devil would take the hindmost. The race was won then by personal merit and cleverness. Now party intervenes; caucuses and juntos dictate; conventions and wigwams gather together political carpenters, joiners and jacks of all trades, whose special province it is to make platforms out of vagrant material for weak-kneed and spavined candidates to stand on. Then there were no daily papers, and weekly ones only existed in great cities like Boston, New York and Philadelphia. In fact nine-tenths of the then inhabitants had never seen a newspaper. The official count of the vote of that year shows more fully than any language could convey the state of blissful ignorance prevailing throughout all this now politically crazy country. There were then two candidates running for Governor, to wit: Return Jonathan Meigs and Nathaniel Massie. The former was voted for under nineteen different names, and the latter under five different styles. The various tickets read: For Return J. Meigs, Return J. Meigs, Jun., Jonathan R. Meigs, Jr., Jonathan Return Meigs, Jonathan Return

Meigs, Jr., Return Meggs, Return R. Meags, Jr., Jonathan Meggs, Jonathan R. Meggs, J. Meigs, Jr., Jonathan Meigs, Jonathan J. Meigs, Judge Meigs, John Meigs, Mr. Meigs, J. Maggs, Return Israel Meigs, James Meigs, Johan Meigs. Nathaniel Massie, Nathaniel Massie, Esq., James Massie, Mr. Massie, Daniel Massie. Meigs received 3,299; Massie 2,317; and Return J. Meigs was declared elected Governor by 982 majority. Thomas Kirker, Speaker of the Senate, was then acting Governor.

Meigs had been a colonel in the army, and was appointed judge of the territory of Louisiana in July, 1805, and had resided in that country some six months; his wife and family, however, had remained, during his absence, at Marietta, in this State. Massie contested his election; and on the 30th of December, 1807, the General Assembly, in joint session, by a vote of 24 to 20, decided that Meigs was not eligible. The vote of Fairfield was: For Meigs, 167; Massie, 46. In 1810, Governor Meigs was elected by the people, and served as Governor until 1814. He was a gentleman of education and talent, and Meigs county, upon the Ohio river, will perpetuate his name as long as Ohio exists. At the election of 1807, above alluded to, Elnathan Scofield was elected Senator, and Philemon Beecher and Wm. W. Irwin Representatives.

The singularity of name borne by Governor Meigs is thus accounted for, as narrated to us by George Browning, Esq., a native of Belpre, and resident in this place since 1820. Jonathan Meigs, the father of Return J., was quite celebrated for his bravery in several Indian campaigns, and when out on one of these perilous excursions, during his absence, his wife was in her confinement, and wrought upon by great anxiety for her husband, kept continually crying out in pain: "Return, Jonathan, oh! return, Jonathan, to me." About the time Return Jonathan was born, Jonathan returned, and she was quieted down, and at once the name "Return Jonathan" was given to the new comer.

The great extent of territory comprised within the limits of Fairfield, and the inconveniences resulting to the settlers in the more new portion of the country from their great distance from the county seat, caused them to agitate the question of a division of the county as early as 1806.

At the fifth General Assembly of Ohio, held in Chillicothe, December 1st, 1806, a strong effort was made, and it was "within an ace" of being successful. Elnathan Scofield, Senator, and Philemon Beecher, Representative, of Fairfield county, were particularly friendly to this measure. How near it came to being a success, may be judged of by the following statement upon the Senate Journal, page 115, January 15th, 1807. A message from the House of Representatives, by Mr. Beecher, represented that "the House had passed 'an act for the division of Fairfield county,' in which they desire the concurrence of the Senate." On the 16th, the bill was received and read a second time. On the 20th, page 128, Mr. Scofield laid before the Senate a petition, signed by a number of the inhabitants of Fairfield county, praying for a division thereof, and recommending Mount Vernon as the temporary seat of justice in said contemplated division, and also recommending certain persons as suitable characters for associate judges, and the petition was received and referred to the committee of the whole, to whom is committed the bill for a division of Fairfield county. On the 21st, the said bill was taken up, and considered and amended, and continued till Saturday next.

At the sixth General Assembly, in December, 1807, we find on the 31st several petitions were presented from Fairfield county for a division of said county, which were referred to Messrs. Scofield, McArthur and Bigger.

On the 7th of January, Senate Journal, page 69, Mr. Scofield presented a petition from citizens of Fairfield county living south of the Refugee Tract, whose names are thereunto subscribed, for two counties; the one lying north of Refugee Tract line to be called Center, and the other to be called ——. January 15th, the bill pending in the Senate, page 83, several amendments were presented to the committee of the whole, one of which is: "Strike out in the 1st section and 6th line, after the word 'heathen,' 'from thence west along the south boundary of said military tract, and insert,'" etc. From which it may be inferred that there were heathen about these parts before these later times.

On the 16th of January the bill passed the Senate, and on the 30th of January, 1808, it passed the House and became a law. The second section of the act created the county of Knox. By this bill three of the best counties in the State of Ohio were marked out by metes and bounds, to wit: Licking, Knox and Richland. By the 4th section the temporary seat of justice of Licking was to be at the house of Levi Hays, and of Knox county at Mount Vernon. The 7th section provides "that Richland county shall be under the jurisdiction of Knox until the Legislature may think proper to organize the same." Hence, the reader will observe that in these pages we have incorporated several items of the early history of our younger sister—Richland —as well as some incidents of more particular interest to those dwelling in Licking. For the same reason, we have carried the history of Bloomfield, Chester and Franklin—three of the townships at present belonging to Morrow county, though until 1848 part and parcel of old Knox. The same commissioners who located the seat of justice of Knox county at Mount Vernon, under the joint resolution of February 9, 1808, fixed the seats of justice of Licking and Delaware counties at Newark and Delaware.

On the 14th of February, in joint ballot, the General Assembly chose the first associate judges of Knox county, Wm. W. Farquhar, John Mills and William Gass.

As we have before stated, in the year 1805 some of the inhabitants became desirous of having a town on Owl Creek, and Mount Vernon was laid out accordingly. The proprietors were Benjamin Butler, Thomas B. Patterson, and Joseph Walker. One of the settlers being from the Potomac, and thinking of the consecrated spot on its shores, suggested that, as the stream was so clear and beautiful, the place should bear the sacred name—Mount Vernon—and it was so done.

Clinton—one mile and a half north—located the year before, was by its proprietor named after Governor DeWitt Clinton, of New York, and he also showed his regard for his old friend by giving the name to his son—DeWitt Clinton Smith—who was a member of the sixth Legislature of Texas, and now resides in the Lone Star State. And in 1807 Fredericktown was laid out. Thus there were three towns, having a "local habitation and a name," before the county of Knox was created. Neither of them had advanced very far in the scale of citydom up to 1808; of the number, however, Clinton was the most promising. It had, at that time, more houses, shops and workmen, than either of the others.

Gilman Bryant opened a grocery store in Mount Vernon, on the lot where Buckingham Emporium now stands. It was a little story and a half sycamore cabin, where he kept powder, shot, lead, whisky, etc., for sale to the Indians and the few whites in 1807. Samuel H. Smith had a pretty good stock of goods and traps at Clinton. Of each of these towns we shall speak more fully under their appropriate heads.

Upon the organization of the county, the inhabitants were greatly pleased. Those who had been compelled to travel to New Lancaster to transact county business, were particularly gratified. The proprietors of town sites and holders of lots therein, were superlatively elated.

On the 9th day of February, 1808, James Armstrong, James Dunlap and Isaac Cook were appointed Commissioners to locate the seat of justice.

In pursuance thereof, they proceeded to discharge the duties imposed upon them, and on the 28th day of March, they appeared before John Mills, Justice of the Peace, and were severally sworn to discharge the duties assigned them as Commissioners as aforesaid.

Clinton and Mount Vernon were the principal competitors for the seat of justice. The former place at that time was the larger. It had more goods, more mechanics, more enterprises on foot, more houses, more people, and more hope for the future. It had more of New England families, more of Yankee spirit and shrewdness; and yet, with all their cunning and craftiness—all their money and management—all their efforts and inducements—Clinton lost the selection. Its generals were out-generaled—its managers out-manœuvered—its wits outwitted—its Yankees out-Yankeed by the less showy and pretending men from the Potomac and the Youghiogheny, who had settled at Mount Vernon. The choice of either one for the county seat involved the ultimate ruin of the other. Clinton made a bold effort to keep up against adverse winds. It could not sustain an appeal from the decision of the Commissioners, but still it kept on for several years in its improvements, and until after the war it was ahead of Mount Vernon in many respects. It had the first and only newspaper in the county for two years; it had the first and only church in the county for many years; it had stores, tanyards, shops of various kinds, and greater variety of business than Mount Vernon; but after the war was over it began to decay, and its rival took the lead. The accredited account of the location of the county seat is as follows:—The Commissioners first entered Mount Vernon, and were received with the best cheer at the log tavern of Mr. Butler. To impress them with an idea of the public spirit of the place, the people were very busy at the moment of their entrance and during their stay, at work, all with their coats off, grubbing the streets. As they left for Clinton, all quitted their labor, not "of love;" and some rowdies, who dwelt in cabins scattered round about in the woods, away from the town, left "the crowd," and stealing ahead of the Commissioners, arrived at Clinton first. On the arrival of the others at that place, these fellows pretended to be in a state not comformable to temperance principles, ran against the Commissioners, and by their rude and boisterous conduct so disgusted the worthy officials as to the apparent morals of the inhabitants of Clinton, that they returned and made known their determination that Mount Vernon should be the favored spot. That night there were great rejoicings in town. Bonfires were kindled, stews made and drank, and live trees split with gunpowder.

Such is a plausible account of this matter, which we have often heard related by our old friend Gilman Bryant, who took great pride in rehearsing a fable calculated to give Mount Vernon the manifest advantage in the estimation of moral and temperance men in these later times. But some of those who lived in the county at that early day give an entirely different version to the subject, and even have gone so far as to aver that the Commissioners themselves delighted, as did the rest of mankind, in taking a "wee drap of the cratur," and could not have been "disgusted by rude and boisterous conduct" to which they were accustomed.

And again it is suggested that "the crowd" at that day was not so great in this locality that men who had sense and observation sufficient to be selected for Commissioners, would not have been able to observe and distinguish "the rowdies," and class them where they belonged.

Another old settler, whose partiality at that day was for Clinton, avers that the proprietor of Clinton, Mr. Smith, had been very illiberal in his dealings with those who wished to purchase lots in his town. He had adopted a plan of withholding from market the best lots on the plat, and keeping the corner lots to be enhanced in value by the improvements made by settlers upon inside lots. At this course many of them became dissatisfied, and some of the number who had bought of him collogued with the Mount Vernonites against Clinton. We have been told by another old citizen, that two of the men living north of Mount Vernon, and considered as in the Clinton interest, proposed to Kratzer and Patterson to help secure the location of the county seat at Mount Vernon, in consideration of their receiving two lots apiece in the town, and that their favor and influence went accordingly.

And yet another account of this mooted question as to how the preference came to be Mount Vernon, comes to us in this wise:—

One of the Commissioners was security for Samuel Kratzer, and had become involved on that account. Kratzer had moved to this place from Lancaster, where he had been acting as land tax collector of Fairfield county, in 1805, and reported himself to have been robbed of the public money while upon the road going to make his return. He was a fine looking, large, fleshy man, and wore tight buckskin breeches. They had holes in them which he alleged to have been shot in the encounter, though they bore the appearance of having been cut; his saddle-bags were also exhibited with horrid gashes in them, and making profert of these he petitioned the Legislature for relief, and at the session of 1806, the bill for his relief was lost by a vote of 10 yeas to 17 nays.—H. J., p. 114.

Certain it is, Kratzer lost caste, and broken up and humiliated, he came to the new town site and bought out Patterson's interest in the town of Mount Vernon, and it is represented that one of the Commissioners was counted on by the settlers as certain for said place. He got another of the Board with him, and Mount Vernon came off victor. Subsequently—and as resulting from this judgment—Kratzer, enabled by the rise of property to pay off his debt, did the fair and just thing by the Commissioner.

Mount Vernon at that time was a rough, ragged, hilly spot, with a thick growth of hazel and other bushes, not near so inviting a place as Clinton, where everything appeared enticing to the stranger. Gilman Bryant says that: "The ground north of Butler's Tavern was then almost wholly in woods. Some timber had been chopped down in places.

Main Street was full of stumps, log heaps and trees, and the road up the street was a poor crooked path winding round amongst the stumps and logs." Richard Roberts says that it was very rough and broken where Mount Vernon was located, and was the last spot on God's earth a man would have picked to make a county seat.

Another gentleman residing north of Mount Vernon, and very partial to Fredericktown, thinks that by a little management that place might have been made the permanent seat of justice, when the strife was so great between the other towns. They might have got a strip thrown off of Delaware county, which might have been attached, and then Frederick would have been alike central; but Kerr and his comrades had not their eyes open to the importance of getting that five mile range with Knox, and they were left out of doors when the location was made permanent.

We have thus minutely given all the statements made to us in regard to the selection of a permanent seat of justice, for it will be a matter of far greater interest to future generations than to the present. Our seventh chapter we devote to Ben. Butler's version, which will be read with great interest, as he is the only one of the proprietors of the town now living, and was a prominent actor in that affair. With that we leave this elaborately discussed subject.

CHAPTER III.

KNOX COUNTY ORGANIZED.

THE FIRST TERM OF COMMON PLEAS.—REPORT OF COMMISSIONERS ON SEAT OF JUSTICE.—THE FIRST CRIMINAL TRIALS.—"THE ENFORCEMENT OF THE LAWS" UPON HEDRICK'S BARE BACK.—FORTY STRIPES LAID ON A POOR WHITE MAN'S NAKED SKIN!—THE PUBLIC WHIPPING ON THE PUBLIC SQUARE OF MOUNT VERNON.—ACTION OF THE COUNTY COMMISSIONERS, A. D. 1808.—THE FIRST OFFICERS, AND SOME ACCOUNT OF THEM.—THE FIRST GRAND JURIES AND FIRST PETIT JURIES.—THE FIRST ELECTION.—FIRST LICENSED PREACHERS, MERCHANTS AND TAVERN KEEPERS.—EXTRAORDINARY WOLF SESSION.—RIGID HONESTY AND ECONOMY OF OFFICERS.

ON the first of May, 1808, the faces of old and young, great and small, of the male and female, upon Owl Creek's "stormy banks," were anxiously turned to the south to catch the first glimpse of that august personage, "the Court," then expected to make a first visitation to Mount Vernon. Ben. Butler and Aunt Leah had their house all "in apple-pie order" for their grand reception; Jim Craig, at his house on the corner of Mulberry and Gambier, had laid in a fresh supply of whisky and other refreshments; Gilman Bryant had got a bran new horn for his customers, and had rubbed his little store up until the stock looked as bright as a dollar; and Sheriff Brown had caused the little wagon maker shop of Coyle & Sons to be swept out and supplied with

3

smooth round logs for the jurymen and others in attendance to sit on. Every man and boy that had been fortunate enough to kill his deer had buckskin leggins and a new hunting shirt, and every woman that had a wheel had spun and dyed and made herself and little ones a good homespun garment. Some few who could stand the expense had bought of store calico three to five yards, at seventy-five cents a yard, and fitted themselves with a two or three breadth dress, the third breadth made into gores, so as to be wider at the bottom, as their ability enabled; for in those days there were no fashionable women to parade the streets with fifteen to eighteen yards in a dress, and no disposition for extravagant displays of wearing apparel. The Court traveled on horse-back—handed the saddle-bags to "Knuck Harris," and, after rest and refreshment, bright and early on the morning of the 2d of May "opened" and proceeded to business. The whole population—men, women and children—were out in their best rig, to witness this great event; and we give the following faithful transcript of the entire proceedings:

FIRST COURT OF COMMON PLEAS IN KNOX COUNTY.

" *The State of Ohio, to wit:*

"Agreeable to an act of the General Assembly of the State of Ohio, passed on the 17th day of February, 1808, for establishing and organizing the county of Knox:

"Be it, therefore, remembered and known, that we, William Wilson, President, John Mills and Wm. Gass, Associate Judges for said county of Knox, did on this day, to wit: Monday, the second day of May, in the year of our Lord 1808, meet at Mount Vernon, the temporary seat of justice for the county aforesaid, and proceeded to the appointment of a clerk for the said county, whereupon it was declared by the Court that Chas. Loffland was duly elected *pro tempore*, who came into Court and was duly qualified as the law directs.

"Samuel H. Smith, Esq., was duly elected surveyor of Knox Co.

"Present: William W. Farquhar, gentleman."

"*The State of Ohio* vs. *Wm. Hedrick*—Felony.—William Wallace, William Bowen and Joseph Cherry Holmes entered into recognizance of $100 each to appear at the next Court of Common Pleas and testify against William Hedrick.

"James Armstrong, James Dunlap and Isaac Cook, gentlemen, who was appointed by the Legislature on the 9th of February last for fixing the county seat in the county of Knox, made their report to the Court of Common Pleas for the county aforesaid that Mount Vernon should be the seat of justice for said county.

"WILLIAM WILSON."

Such is the beginning of the minutes of the first Court. The "Report" reads as follows:

"*To the Hon. William Wilson, Esq., President, and John Mills, William Gass and Wm. W. Forker, Esqs., Associate Judges of the Court of Common Pleas in and for the County of Knox, in the State of Ohio:*

"May it please your Honors, In conformity to an act of the Legislature of the State of Ohio, passed the 28th of March, 1803, entitled an act establishing seats of justice, we, the subscribers, were appointed by a Resolution of both Houses of the Legislature, passed on the 9th of February, 1808, commissioners for fixing the Parmanent seat of justice in and for s'd county of Knox. We do hereby make report to your Honors, that, Having Met and attended to the duties of our s'd appointment in s'd county on the 28th of the present Inst., and Having paid due Regard to the centre, Extent of population, Quality of soil, as well as the General convenience, we Hereby declare that the Town of Mount Vernon is the most suitable place for the Courts of s'd county to be held at, and we do hereby declare the said Town of Mount Vernon the parmanent seat of Justice in and for s'd county of Knox. Given under our hands and seals this 29th day of March, 1808.

"JAMES ARMSTRONG, [SEAL.]
"JAMES DUNLAP, [SEAL.]
"ISAAC COOK, [SEAL.]
"*Commissioners.*

"*The first Grand Jury Impanneled.*—Matthew Merrit, foreman, John Herrod, Samuel H. Smith, James Walker, Jr., David Miller, Joseph Walker, Gilman Bryant, James Walker, Sen., William Douglass, Ziba Leonard, Stephen Chapman, Benj. Butler, Jonathan Hunt, Ichabod Nye.

"*Fighting cases first disposed of.*—*State of Ohio* vs. *John Williamson.*—For fighting yesterday with William Herrod. The Court do assess him in a breach of the peace, &c., in the sum of $1.60 and costs. *State of Ohio* vs. *William Herrod.* For fighting John Williamson yesterday. Fine $1.60 and costs.

"*Preachers next in order.*—William Thrift, a Baptist minister, is authorized to solemnize marriages.

"*Traders Licensed.*—Samuel Kratzer and Stephen Chapman are authorized to retail goods, wares and merchandize in Mount Vernon, on paying into the treasury $5.

"*Tavern-keepers Licensed.*—Samuel Kratzer is licensed to keep a house of entertainment in the town of Mount Vernon for one year, on paying $6. Daniel Ayres is licensed to keep in Fredericktown, on paying $5.

"*First Will admitted to Probate.*—The last will and testament of William Leonard was proven.

"*The First Trial by Jury.*—*State of Ohio* vs. *William Hedrick.*—Indicted for stealing a watch from William Bowen. Plea—Not guilty.

"*Jury.*—James Loveridge, Henry Smith, Aaron Brown, James Smith, Benjamin Brown, John Beam, William Nash, Daniel Demick, Michael Brown, Peter Baxter, Archibald Gardner, and Levi Herrod. Verdict—Guilty.

"*Judgment.*—Fine $5, pay the owner, William Bowen, $15, *and be whipped on his naked back ten stripes,* imprisoned one month, pay the cost, and stand committed until the sentence is complied with.

"*Second Trial.*—*State of Ohio* vs. *William Hedrick.*—Indictment for stealing bay mare, property of William Wallace.

"*Jury.*—John Baxter, William Herrod, William Biggs, Daniel Ayres, Nicholas Kyle, John Shinabery, James Craig, James Smith, Thomas Merrill, Dorman Lofland, James Pell, and Thompson Mills.

"*Judgment.*—Prisoner be whipped 20 lashes on his naked back, and pay a fine of $20, and be imprisoned one month, and pay the owner $70, the value of the mare, pay the cost, and stand committed, &c.

"*Third Trial.—State of Ohio* vs. *William Hedrick.*—Indictment for stealing one pair over-alls, the property of Joseph Cherry Holmes.

"*Jury.*—James Loveridge, Henry Smith, Aaron Brown, James Smith, Benjamin Brown, John Beam, William Nash, Daniel Demick, Michael Brown, Peter Baxter, Archibald Gardner, and Levi Herrod.

"*Judgment.*—Prisoner be whipped on his naked back five stripes, pay a fine of $2, be imprisoned one month, pay the owner $5, double the value of the over-alls, pay cost, and stand committed, &c.

"*Fourth Trial.—State of Ohio* vs. *William Hedrick.*—Indictment for stealing one bell and collar, property of William Wallace.

"*Jury.*—Parts of the former.

"*Judgment.*—Prisoner to be whipped five stripes on his naked back, pay a fine of $1, pay the owner $1.50, the value of the bell and collar, pay the costs, and stand committed, &c."

The State pays its first fee.—On motion, a certificate was issued by the Commissioners in favor of Samuel Kratzer, Esq., for his services, for $6, in acting on the part of the State against William Hedrick, who was found guilty of felony.

The sentence of the Court—when, where, by whom and how executed.—The judgment of castigation was executed upon the public square of Mount Vernon, shortly after the adjournment of Court, in the presence of all the people. Silas Brown was the Sheriff, and it fell to his lot as such to serve the "legal process" upon the body of William Hedrick. There was a small leaning hickory tree upon the east side of the public square, between the present Norton building and High street, and a little south of where the jail was afterwards built, and this tree bent in such way that a man could walk around under it. To this delectable spot the culprit was taken, and his hands were stretched up over his head and tied to the tree, and the stripes were applied by said Sheriff to his naked back. He was struck forty times with a heavy raw-hide whip.

A spectator pleads for mercy.—The first few blows with the raw-hide were across the kidney. Mr. Bryant, one of the bystanders, at once called out to the Sheriff to whip him elsewhere—that was no place to whip a man—he should strike higher up; and the rest of the lashes were applied across the shoulders.

How Hedrick acted.—The criminal sobbed and cried piteously, and when released went off weeping and groaning. In many places the skin was cut and broken, and the blood oozed out, making a pitiable spectacle. And yet such was the feeling against him that few seemed to sympathize with the scourged. As he started off he said to the spectators, "You should not blame me for this, for it is not my fault." Bob Walker replied, "No, by G—d, you wouldn't have stood up and been whipped that way, *if* you could have helped it." And at this prompt retort to Hedrick's explanation or apology, the crowd laughed loudly and uproariously.

From Gilman Bryant, Samuel H. Smith, Ben. Butler, Jonathan Hunt and Stephen Chapman of the Grand Jury, and James Loveridge and the Herrods of the Petit Jury, and Richard Roberts, all of whom are yet living, and who witnessed this scene, we have gathered this account of the first and last judicial punishment by whipping in the county of Knox. And scarcely any of the present citizens are aware that such punishment of criminals was ever the law of the land in which they have the good fortune to live.

THE FIRST ELECTION AT MOUNT VERNON.

On the 4th day of April, 1808, the entire people of the county voted at Mount Vernon. The officers of election were Ebenezer Brown, Jabez Beers and Samuel Kratzer, Judges; Wm. Gass and Robert Anderson, Clerks. They were here from the most remote points, as well as from the vicinity of Mount Vernon. The election of the first officers in a new county brings out every body. They elected them by the following votes: John Lewis, for Commissioner, received 56 votes, John Herrod 52, and Joseph Walker 48. Silas Brown was elected Sheriff. Jonathan Craig, for Coroner, had 45, and Francis Hardesty 1 vote. Then for Trustees—for be it remembered, the whole county composed the district—George Downs had 41, Henry Roberts 36, and Joseph Coleman 36. The vote for Overseers of the Poor was, Moses Craig 22, James Walker 2, Alexander Walker 12. The candidates for Supervisor were Sam. Kratzer, who received 35, and Peter Baxter 36. For Fence Viewers, George Zin, Michael Click and Jesse Severe were candidates.

For "House praisers," Archibald Gardner and James Craig each got 12 votes. For Constables, Gabriel Wilkins received 30, Philip Walker 21, Jonathan Hunt, Jr., 15, Dave Miller 3. For Treasurer, Ben. Butler had 12 votes, and James Walker, Jr., 2. None of these parties are now living but Ben. Butler and Jonathan Hunt, who many long years ago dropped the junior and became a senior, and is now one of the oldest of men.

DIVISION OF THE COUNTY INTO FOUR TOWNSHIPS, AND WHAT THEY WERE.

The following entry we find on a piece of paper in James Smith's hand:

"KNOX COUNTY:

"Know ye, that on the 2d day of May, 1808, at a meeting of a Board of Commissioners for said county, to wit: Joseph Walker, John Harrod and John Lewis, Commissioners in and for said county,

"*Ordered*, that the following bounds be laid off into a separate township, to wit: beginning at the west boundary line of said county, between the 6th and 7th township line, and running east to the west of the thirteenth range line, thence north to the center of the 7th township line, thence on the east to the east line of the 13th range, thence north to the county line, which shall be called and known by the name of Wayne township.

"*Ordered*, that the following bounds be laid off into a separate township: beginning at the north-east corner of Wayne township, thence east to the west side of the 11th range, thence south to the center of the 6th township, thence west to the west line of the 12th range, thence south to the south line of the 6th township, thence west on the said line of the side line, which shall be called and known by the name of Clinton township.

"Beginning at the center of the 11th range line where it intersects Licking county line, thence north to the center of the 6th township line, thence west to the west line of the 12th range, thence south to the line between the 5th and 6th townships, thence west to the west line of the county, thence with the county line to Licking county to the place of beginning, which shall be known and called by the name of Morgan township.

"*Ordered*, that the following bounds be laid off into a separate township, laid off as follows: beginning at the north-east corner of Clinton township, thence eastward to the Muskingum county line, thence with the line of said county to the Licking county line, thence west to the middle of the 11th range, thence north to the center of the 6th township, thence west to the west side of the 12th range, thence north to the place of beginning, which shall be called and known by the name of Union township."

Those who are curious to know what these townships comprised, will find that Wayne at that time embraced all of the present townships of Franklin and Chester, in Morrow county, Middlebury, and Berlin, Wayne, and the north half of Morris.

Clinton included Bloomfield, now in Morrow county, Liberty, north half of Pleasant, Monroe and Pike, and the south half of Morris.

Union took in Brown, Jefferson, Union, Howard, Butler, Jackson, three-fourths of Harrison, and the east half of Clay.

Morgan consisted of the west half of Clay, southwest quarter of Harrison, south half of Pleasant, and all of Morgan, Miller, Milford and Hilliar.

THE SECOND, OR FALL TERM KNOX COMMON PLEAS

Was held on Monday, the 5th day of September, 1808. What was then transacted we will briefly state.

A Grand Jury was called and sworn for the body of this county, to wit: Jabez Beers, foreman, Ziba Leonard, John Johnson, James Walker, Jacob

Young, Benjamin Butler, Wm. Nash, John Butler, David Miller, John Merritt, Wm. Douglass, Jas. Walker, Jr., James Craig, who after being sworn, retired out of Court, and after some time returned with the following presentments, to wit:

"*The State of Ohio* vs. *Samuel H. Smith.*—On a presentment for selling goods without license. A true bill, to which the defendant plead guilty. Court on consideration of the offense doth find the defendant in the sum of $2.50, and costs of the prosecution.

"*Ordered*, that the Grand Jury be adjourned till to-morrow morning, nine o'clock, who met according to adjournment.

"*The State of Ohio* vs. *Michael Brown.*—On an indictment. True bill.

"*The State of Ohio* vs. *Aaron Brown.*—On an indictment. True bill.

"*The State of Ohio* vs. *James Click.*—On an indictment. True bill.

"*The State of Ohio* vs. *Sarah Hartley.*—On an indictment. True bill.

"*Samuel Kratzer* vs. *Robert Walker.*—In trespass. Dismissed at plaintiff's cost.

"*Ordered*, that Edward Herrick be appointed a prosecuting attorney for this county.

"James Scott, who is a regular Minister of the Presbyterian Church, is licensed to solemnize marriages.

"*John Armstrong* vs. *John Kerr.*—In trespass. James Bryant came into Court and undertook for the defendant, that in case he should be cast in this suit, that he would pay and satisfy the condemnation of the Court, or render his body to the prison in lieu thereof.

"John Wood is licensed to keep a tavern, on payment of $4.00.

"'On the motion of Samuel H. Smith, it is ordered that license be issued to him to sell and retail goods, wares, and merchandize of foreign growths and manufactories, at his store in the town of Clinton, for one year,' on payment of $10.00.

"Samuel H. Smith is licensed to keep tavern at Clinton, on payment of $5.00.

"*Jacob Young* vs. *Abraham Lyon.*—Plaintiff's attorney ordered to amend writ by adding the words, 'on the case.'

"On motion, Court adjourned till to-morrow at 9 o'clock.

"TUESDAY, September 6th, 1808.

"*James Craig* vs. *Archibald Gardner.*—On an appeal from a judgment rendered by Samuel Kratzer, Esq. This came ye defendant by his attorney, and pleads non-assumpsit, joinder and issue. Whereon came a jury, to wit: Daniel Johnson, Ichabod Nye, Wm. Casper, Stephen D. Menton, John Click, Thomas Bowen, Moses Craig, Wm. Bowen, Robert Anderson, Jesse Proctor, Gilman Bryant, Alexander Walker, who upon their oaths say that they find for the plaintiff, and assess the damages to \$25.26½ cents damages.

"*Joseph Butler* vs. *Elizabeth Vandever.*—On an appeal from Abraham Darling. Judgment awarded for the defendant's cost.

"*The State of Ohio* vs. *Michael Brown.*—Samuel Kratzer, Samuel Baxter and Polly Miller entered into \$100 recognizance to appear and testify on the part of the State.

"*State of Ohio* vs. *Aaron Brown.*—James Walker, Jr., Benjamin Butler and Wm. McBride entered into recognizance of \$100 to appear and give evidence on the part of the State.

"*Jacob Young* vs. *Abraham Lyon.*—Samuel H. Smith came into Court and undertook for the defendant, that in case he should be cast in this cause, that he would pay and satisfy the condemnation of the Court, or render his body to prison in lieu thereof.

"*Thomas B. Patterson, for the use of Moses Bixby,* vs. *Samuel Kratzer.*—In debt. The defendant came into Court and acknowledged the services of the writ; declaration filed and continued.

"The Court proceed to the appointment of a Clerk *pro pem pro,* when James Smith was elected.

"*Ordered,* that Edward Herrick be allowed \$25 as prosecuting attorney for this term.

"Court adjourned till the Court in course.

"WILLIAM WILSON.

"*John Armstrong* vs. *John Kerr.*—The declaration being filed this the 5th day of Nov., 1808, the defendant is ordered to plead to the same within twenty days; otherwise judgment.

"EDWARD HERRICK,

"*Att'y for Plaintiff.*"

THE FIRST SPECIAL TERM OF COURT.

At the request of Michael Brown, John Click and Aaron Brown, a Court of Common Pleas of the Associate Judges was opened at Mount Vernon the 5th of December, 1808. Present, Wm. W. Farquhar, John Mills, and Wm. Gass, Esqrs.

"*The State of Ohio* vs. *M. Brown.*—On an indictment found by the Grand Jury, a true bill, thus appeared the prisoner, and pleads not guilty; the Court then proceed to the evidence of John Williamson, Samuel Kratzer, Samuel Baxter, Polly Miller and Stephen Chapman, on the part of the State, and Thompson Mills and Michael Mills on the part of the prisoner. The Court, upon a full investigation, do order that he do give bail of two persons, which shall be bound in two hundred dollars each, for his personal appearance at the next term, then and there to abide the order of Court; otherwise to be remanded to jail.

"*The State of Ohio* vs. *A. Brown.*—On an indictment for a breach of the peace. The Court order him to enter bail in one surety of fifty dollars.

"*The State of Ohio* vs. *John Click.*—On an indictment for a breach of the peace. The Court order him to give bail in $50.

"William Fuller became surety for Aaron Brown, and Gilman Bryant for John Click.

"*Ordered,* that the Court do adjourn.

"JOHN MILLS."

THE FIRST ELECTION BY TOWNSHIPS—SPECIMEN OF A POLL BOOK—REFLECTIONS.

At the October election the first regular vote was taken for State and county officers, the terms of those elected in April having been, in Clerk Lofland's phrase, only "*pro pempore.*" The following poll-book of one of the most populous townships shows who were voted for:

Poll-book of an Election held in the Township of Wayne, in the County of Knox, and State of Ohio, the 11*th day of October,* 1808, *at the house of Daniel and Abner Ayres, in the town of Frederic. John Kerr, Chairman, Nathaniel M. Young, John Cook, Henry Roberts, Judges, and Jacob Young and Wm. W. Farquhar, Clerks of the Election, were duly sworn as the law directs, previous to their entering on the duties of their respective offices.*

Certified by me, WM. W. FARQUHAR, A. J.

1	Casper Fitting,	13	Henry Markley,
2	Joseph Talmage,	14	Nathaniel M. Young,
3	Amariah Watson,	15	John Walker,
4	Abraham Lyon,	16	William W. Farquhar,
5	Joshua Vennom,	17	Jacob Young,
6	Samuel Wilson,	18	John Cook,
7	Charles McGowen,	19	Richard Hall,
8	Joshua Milligan,	20	Thomas Durbin,
9	Ruben Skinner,	21	Samuel Durbin,
10	Jacob Cook,	22	Jeduthan Dodd,
11	Henry Roberts,	23	Thomas Townsend.
12	John Kerr,		

"Samuel Huntingdon had at the above election, for Governor, a majority of 23 votes (all cast;) Jeremiah Morrow, for Congress, received 21, and Philemon Beecher 2.

"Wm. Trimble and Jacob Burton had a majority of 21 votes each for the Senate.

"Hezekiah Smith had 2 votes for Senator, and Elnathan Scofield 2.

"Alexander Holden, for Representative, had 20 votes, and Jeremiah R. Munson 2.

"For Commissioners—Wm. Douglass had 21, Calvin Shepherd 2, Henry Markley 23, Matthew Merritt 21.

"For Coroner—John Merritt had 21.

"For Sheriff—Silas Brown 13, Ichabod Nye 9.

"John Harrod had 2 votes for commissioner, and Joseph Walker 2.

"Attest: WM. W. FARQUHAR,
"JACOB YOUNG,
Clerks."

Fifty-four years have not yet passed by, and yet earth has closed upon all the above list of voters and voted for: and at this day there are but seven of the above numbered who have any "kith and kin" within our county limits. Of 126 voters at an election in the entire county, in 1808, but seven are now living—the mementos of the past—the connecting link of the living and the dead; soon, alas! the last one of the pioneers will have departed from among us. Is it not, then, of the utmost importance to gather from the lips of the few who stand, as we write, at the very threshhold of death, their recollections, and to treasure up, for future generations, an account of their perils and sufferings, and the incidents connected with the first settlement of this great and glorious land?

DOINGS OF THE COUNTY COMMISSIONERS—THEY ARE DEATH ON WOLVES, AND "DOWN ON" ROADS, BUT DETERMINED TO DO THE FAIR THING FOR THE TAX-PAYER.

"A Board of Commissioners for the county of Knox was seated at Mount Vernon, on Monday, the 24th day of October, 1808.

"Present: Gentlemen Henry Markley, Matthew Merritt and William Douglass, Commissioners, who, at their first meeting, proceeded to the appointment of a Clerk, and James ——— was duly elected Clerk, and qualified accordingly; then, according to law, proceeded to cast lots relative to their ceasing to continue in the office, and it is by them declared that Henry Markley continue in said office three years, Matthew Merritt two years, and William Douglass one year. *Ordered*, that this Board do adjourn until next Friday."

Thus simply and concisely is given the proceedings of the first meeting of the Commissioners of Knox county of which we have any record. On

Friday, the 28th of October, the following business was transacted:

" *Ordered*, that the Clerk issue an order on the County Treasurer of this county for the sum of one dollar and fifty cents for killing one wolf, proven before Wm. Y. Farquhar, Esq., in favor of James Durbin.

" *Ordered*, that an order issue in favor of James Smith for the sum of two dollars, for carrying returns of the annual election to the town of Newark.

"P. S.—The above meeting was intended for the purpose of examining and regulating the papers and books relative to the Commissioners.

" *Ordered*, that this Board do adjourn until the first Monday in December next, unless occasion Require a sooner meeting of this Board."

"Occasion" did "Require" a "sooner meeting," for we find that wolves had been killed, and it was a "case of emergency," justifying an extraordinary meeting of the Board of Commissioners at Mount Vernon, on the very next day, and we give the journal entry in its own words:

" *Ordered*, that an order do Issue to the County Treasurer of this county, in favor of Jesse Morgan, for the sum of three dollars, for killing two Grown Wolves.

" *Ordered*, that an order do Issue to the Treasurer of this County, in favor of Jonathan Morgan,* for the sum of three dollars, for killing two Grown Wolves.

" *Ordered*, that this Board do adjourn until the next meeting in course."

At the December term, 1808, the Board was in session two days. On the 5th an order was granted

* Query.—Was not Morgan township named after the distinguished wolf-killer, to whom we find many orders to have been issued for killing wolves? May not a spirit of regard for such public benefactors have caused the old settlers to perpetuate the name of Morgan?

Philip Walker, constable, of seventy-five cents for one day's attendance on the Grand Jury at the May term; to William W. Farquhar, Esq., $4.50 for one day's attendance on a call court, on an indictment of the Grand Jury, on the case of M. Brown; to John Mills $3 for the same; to William Gass $3 for the same; and the following wolf orders: To John Simpkins $1.50 for killing one grown wolf, proven before Samuel Kratzer, J. P.; to John Butler $3 for killing two grown wolves, proven before Abraham Darling, J. P. On the 6th day of December:

"*Ordered*, that the Treasurer of this County do pay the following sums to the following persons: To James Dunlap $22 for fixing the county seat of this county; to Isaac Kook $22 for the same; to James Armstrong $22 for the same.

"*Ordered*, that 10 cents be erast off the Collector's Duplicate, for an error made by the lister, who personally appeared and confessed the same, in favor of Samuel Lewis.

"*Ordered*, that the Treasurer of this County do pay to James Smith, Clerk, $6.67 for his services in elections until the said term, likewise 75 cents for Blank Books.

"A petition was handed the Board, praying a view of a Road from the town of Clinton Running to intersect the County Line, near the south-west corner of the County; which review they declare Inexpedient and Rejected.

"A petition was handed the Board, praying a view of a Road from the town of Clinton through the Settlement of Skenk's Creek to the Eastern Line of Knox County, and it is declared by the Board that the said petition is rejected.

"A petition was handed the Board, praying a view of a Road from Mulberry street, in the town of Mount Vernon, to Wm. Douglass' mill, and they declared the same Inexpedient.

"*Ordered*, that the Treasurer of this County do pay Archibald Gardner the sum of $1.50 for killing one Grown Wolf, proven before Samuel Kratzer, Esq.

"*Ordered,* that the Treasurer of this County do pay to Henry Markley the sum of $15 for to defray expenses and charges relative to procuring a Duplicate from Fairfield county to enable the collector to collect and pay the taxes on Resident Lands in this county.

"*Ordered,* that the Treasurer do pay to Silas Brown $13.33 for his services eight months in criminal cases; for do. in elections, $4; the above allowances for the year 1808; 3 hasps and 1 lock, $2.50; summoning 2 Grand Juries, $2 each; and fifty cents for the *diet* of Wm. Hedrick, prisoner.

"*Ordered,* that this Board do adjourn until the next meeting in course, unless necessity require an extraordinary meeting."

Such was the action of Markley, Merritt and Douglass, in the year 1808. How economically our affairs were managed in the early days of the Owl Creek Republic! Officers then were simple-minded, and wrote with grey goose-quills; expending but 75 cents for blank-books; gold pens were then unknown, nor *steel*-ing either. The item of "stationery," which has since figured so extensively in county exhibits, was not then in the official dictionary. Blessed days were those, when an "error of 10 cents was ordered erast," and "confession" of the same made by the collector upon the county records in favor of the aggrieved sovereign; when roads through "the settlements on Skenk's Creek" and to "county lines," as well as from "Mount Vernon to Mill," were declared by our pioneer board "Inexpedient," and "the petitions" of interested citizens were "rejected;" when it took only "50 cents" to pay "the Diet" of prisoners, and the "chief end of man" was to kill grown wolves, and of County Commissioners and Clerk to receive certificates of proof thereof and issue orders to pay for their scalps!

CHAPTER IV.

THE COUNTRY AS SEEN IN 1801.—A TRAGEDY IN OWL CREEK IN 1800, AND THE PLACE OF ITS OCCURRENCE.—REMINISCENCES OF EARLY SETTLERS AND THEIR FAMILIES.—THE FIRST TERRIBLE STORM VISITS MOUNT VERNON.—THE FIRST DOCTOR AND HIS RECEPTION.—THE BUTLERS, THE WALKERS.—GILMAN BRYANT, JIM CRAIG, AND THEIR EXPLOITS.—WHO GAVE THE NAME TO MOUNT VERNON.—WHO BUILT THE FIRST CABIN?—EARLY PREACHING.—FIGHTING AND OTHER INCIDENTS OF THE FRONTIER, AND AMUSING EVENTS OF THE ANCIENT TIMES.

THE first of our race known to have been within the limits of this county, as stated heretofore, was John Stilley. The second, of whom we have reliable information, was the reckless frontiersman, Andy Craig. And from all we can learn, we are of the opinion that cotemporaneous with him was the oddest character in all our history, Johnny Chapman, *alias* Appleseed, who was discovered in this country when the Walkers, and Butlers, and Douglass and others landed here, and whose name is found recorded among those voting at the first election ever held in this district.

Ben. and John Butler, in September, 1801, made a trip up Owl Creek as far as to the mouth of Center Run, and camped over night about one hundred yards north of the Owl Creek bank. At that time Andy Craig was living there in a little log hut, with a great raw-boned woman as his wife. She had been married to some man about Wheeling, when Andy took up with her, and they ran off into the Indian country together. She was a trifling, coarse piece, and said Ben: "I'd as soon have slept with a man as her, and why he should have taken her into the wilderness for a sleeping companion I can't see." Not a white person was then living in our route from Lewisville up to where Mount Vernon now is, and not a settlement had been made in Knox, Morrow, Richland, Ashland, Wayne, or any part of the country watered by Owl Creek, the Mohican, and their tributaries. An old Indian Chief with his Tribe was then camped near by, and they had a grand pow-wow there. The Indian Field, in the bend south of the camps, was covered with beautiful grass, and looked charming.

The Butlers were greatly pleased with their exploration, and returned by the mouth of Owl Creek to Lewisville. In 1803, John settled near the mouth of the stream. In the spring of 1805, Ben. takes up his residence in Mount Vernon. During the intermediate time the Indians held undisputed possession. Andy Craig, having fallen into their customs and mode of life, remained with them; and, after settlers began to pour in, he pulled up stakes, and went up to Greentown and continued in their company. There were three beautiful spots of ground without timber, and known from that time as the "Indian Fields." The one we have named was the "Little Indian Field," and contained about twenty acres, known to settlers of many years as on the Ann Carter tract, now owned by Judge Hurd. It is in Clinton township.

Another "Indian Field" contained about forty acres, upon the John Ash tract, now owned by Amen M. Shipley. It is in Howard township.

The ten-mile settlers selected a beautiful level prairie for their commencement of operations.

The beautiful little prairie in Morris township, where Henry Roberts settled, was also a choice spot. And the Me-me-kausen prairie down the creek, now known as the Darling prairie.

These were all favorite places of resort for the Indians as long as they were in this country. Armstrong with his Tribe once every year visited the Indian Fields on Owl Creek, and hunted and fished, and camped by the waters of the stream they loved until the war of 1812, when they had reason to cease their visits in this direction.

This country is described by those who knew it at that early day as the most beautiful region the eye ever rested upon. The work of nature was captivating. Subsequent cultivation by man has added to its interest, though, in some respects, it may have marred the beauty of the original scene.

Beyond the recollection of the oldest inhabitant now living within our borders, a tragedy was enacted on the point of bluff between Centre Run and Owl Creek, of which much has been said by old citizens, but very little is known. The exact time of its occurrence is usually stated at about 1805, but in fact it must have occurred as early as 1800, if not before that. Two slaves had run away from their master, Tumlinson, who lived in Virginia, and had got into this part of the country and taken up with squaws. Their pursuers tracked them through Zanesville and up Owl Creek, and finally came upon them at Andy Craig's. One of the boys was a mulatto; and, recognizing his master's son as he approached with two other men, sprang to the bank and into the Creek, pursued by the men, who overtook him in the middle of the stream, and a deadly struggle took place, in which he killed his young master, but was then overpowered, taken to the hut, tied, and shortly after placed on the horse his young master had rodé, and the company started for Virginia with him. The second night after leaving Craig's, they built a camp-fire. and left the mulatto tied by it, when they went out for game. On their return, he was found to have been shot, but neither could say that he did it. The belief was, that they had become tired of taking him along, and as he was surly and troublesome, he was killed to get rid of him, and out of revenge for the loss of Tumlinson.

Ben. Butler informs us that on his trip to Owl Creek in 1801, Andy Craig told him the particulars of this fight; and that in 1805, when he made a trip out to the Sandusky plains, he saw the negro who escaped, and was then living with a squaw among the Indians, and talked with him about this affair.

Dr. J. N. Burr and J. W. Warden, in hunting over the ground where this scene occurred, came across the bones of Tumlinson, who had been buried there.

Among the early settlers of this part of Ohio, were the Virginia family of Butlers. They were John, Thomas, Benjamin, Joseph, Isaac and James, and all made their settlements upon Owl Creek and Whitewoman at first, and subsequently lived upon these streams or their tributaries, and in the division and formation of counties were found in Knox and Coshocton, in what was about the same neighborhood in those times. John settled in 1803, on land which he bought of Capt. Taylor, at the mouth of the Mohican, near where Cavallo was located. He died on Mohican, in his 85th year. Thomas died in his 84th year. Joseph died about 1837. Isaac was drowned in Whitewoman, about 35 years ago. James died on his farm on Mohican, about 1832. They were hardy, sinewy men, good hunters, and well calculated to endure the hardships and privations of frontier life.

Ben. Butler, in his 84th year, is yet of vigorous physical frame and of strong mind. Few men of forty can be found with more rugged constitution. The Butlers were always fond of fun and frolic, and never occupied a back seat when any sport or fighting went on in early days. Ben. is about five feet nine in height, weighs about 150 pounds, is straight as an arrow, and fleet as an Indian. He is ready to-day to run a foot race with any man of his age in the world, and a few years since gave a public challenge through the press to run for a wager a foot race with any man of his age in the State or nation.

He was born in Monongahela county, Va., April 18th, 1779, and when just turned of twenty years he married, on the 2d of May, 1799, Leah Rogers, of Crab Orchard, Va., then in her sixteenth year, and by her had fourteen children, seven boys and seven girls. Betsey, their oldest child, was born in Monongahela county, Va., February 22d, 1800. She married John Rouse, who died at Racine, Meigs county, leaving five children. Betsey is now living with them at that place. Hiram was born on the Tuscarawas river, about two miles from Coshocton, in October, 1801; he is dead. Ben. was born on Whitewoman, July 31, 1804, and is also dead. Joseph was born in Mount Vernon, the 23d of October, 1806. Matilda in Mount Vernon, October 8th, 1808; she married Charles Critchfield, and is now dead. Huldah was born on his farm down the creek where he has ever since lived, in 1810. Reasin was born August 12th, 1812, and is now dead. Laban R., born March 7th, 1814, married Lucinda Peckham, and lives in Union township. Maria was born October 1st, 1815; married S. W. Sapp, and is now dead. Polina, born August 31st, 1817, married Robert Grimes, and lives in Iowa county, Iowa. Hetty, born July 5th, 1819, wife of John Carpenter, with her two boys and two girls, lives at the old farm with Ben. Squire John, born in 1821, and George Washington, born in 1823. Squire John married Mary Jane, daughter of Joseph Workman, and George W. married Miss Lydick, daughter of another old settler. They live in Union township. Joseph married Polly Biggs, and lives in Newcastle; Huldah married Joseph Jones, and lives in Knox county, Ill. Three of the boys and three girls are dead; the rest living, together with seventy-five grandchildren. "Pretty well done, is it not," said Uncle Ben. to us this 8th of June, 1862, "for old Virginia and a little Quaker gal!"

In 1800, Ben. Butler settled in the neighborhood of Dresden, and raised a crop on land belonging to Major Cass. In 1801, he moved to Lewisville, two miles above Coshocton, and in 1802, he settled on Whitewoman above the mouth of Kilbuck, and from thence to Mount Vernon in April, 1805 where he resided until 1809, when he moved down the creek, where he has ever since resided. Before he moved to Mount Vernon he had bought thirty-six acres of land of Joe Walker, which he had purchased of Matthews and Nigh, and Matthews executed the deed to Butler. Patterson, Walker and himself conceived the plan of laying out a town on their possessions, and accordingly in July, 1805, it was surveyed by Bob. Thompson, and taken to Lancaster, and recorded in Fairfield county records.

Captain Walker's house was the first one within the town plat; the next buildings were two little log stables, built by Ben. Butler, on the corner now owned by Adam Pyle—Gambier and Main streets, north-west corner. In one of these log stables Ben. Butler lived and kept entertainment until he built his log cabin on the corner, which for many years continued the principal tavern of Mount Vernon. He paid for shingles and work on that house $150. This was the building wherein the Commissioners who came to locate the county seat were most hospitably entertained. Ben. moved into it in the fall of 1805, and lived in it until 1809. It continued as the war office under successive administrations.

Ben. bought two hundred acres on Licking, and built a log cabin on it, intending to move his family there in 1809, but having met with a favorable offer he sold it to Hanger, who occupied the place until his death.

The most extraordinary event of those early times was a terrible tornado in the summer of 1806, which played havoc with the early settlers. It came up suddenly, and was very violent. It tore off the roofs of all the houses, killed most of the stock running about, and tore down all the large white oak trees that were on Ben.'s thirty-six acre tract, as also many trees on Walker's land. In its course it took in Andy Craig's old stand on Center Run. Ben. had nine head of horses; as the storm came up they attempted to run out of its way; two of them were killed; one of the horses ran all the way to Craig's, and jumped into his garden patch; its skin was torn and flesh scratched in many places by limbs of trees hurled against it by the storm as it ran to get out of its reach. Walker had some horses killed; also Patterson and Kratzer, and a little fellow from Virginia who lived on the hill, named Zinn.

A little doctor named Henderson was with us when we laid out the town. He was from Baltimore, Maryland, and proposed that we should call it after Washington's home-place, and we all sanctioned. When it came to giving any name that pleased Washington, it pleased all proprietors.

Henderson was a clever young fellow; his father made a regular doctor of him, and started him out with a good horse and outfit, but he was too d——d lazy to practice. The first time Ben. saw him, Patterson came out into the lot where he was plowing, and introduced him to Ben., who was mad at the infernal beech-roots catching the plow so much, and when Patterson said he was a doctor, and Henderson spoke up and said he had just been inoculating a child, and wanted to inoculate Butler's, Ben said, "G—d d——n you, haven't I moved away up here to get rid of the d——d small-pox, and now d——d if you shall inoculate my child. I didn't know exactly what inoculating then meant, but I was mad, and I threatened to put my knife into him, and scared him so that he would not attempt to 'noculate any more in that town. He stayed about for a time, until he ran away with a woman, and no other doctor dared to show his face there during my stay. We had no lawyers either in them days."

The first election Ben. recollects of attending, the neighbors and himself went down to Dresden and voted in 1803 or 1804. Another election he recollects of was held at Bill Douglass'. David Johnson wanted to be a constable, and 'lectioneered hard, and agreed to take on executions and for fees raccoon skins, if he was elected. But when the votes were counted, he was beaten by Dimmick. This was the first time he voted a ticket. In old Virginia it had been always the custom to vote by singing out the name of the candidate voted for. Speaking of raccoon skins: old Amos Leonard preached Presbyterian doctrine, and would often say when he commenced, "Now, you had better pay the preacher a coon skin or so." It was with him "poor preach and poor pay." "Once I passed along where he was preaching, with corn on my back, to feed about one hundred hogs that I had about where Norton's mill is, and seeing Walker listening to him, I hallooed to him to come along with me—that he could learn no good from Amos—that he knew nothing; and Walker came along with me. Another Sunday I was out hunting calves with my brother Tom, and when we had found them and were driving them along the road, preacher Leonard took off his hat and shook it at them, scaring them off, so I told him if he ever did so again, preacher as he was, I would whip the hide off of him; and I would have done it, too, for at that day I could whip anybody; I was little, but never saw the man I couldn't whip.

"Leonard went on to his meeting, and took satisfaction out of me by preaching at me. Captain Walker said to me the next day: 'Oh! you ought to have been at meeting just to hear Leonard abuse you; he laid it on to you severely.' I thought that may be so. Many a man can whip with the tongue that is afraid to try it with the fist."

One of the greatest fights of that early date was between Ben. Butler and Jim Craig, in which Craig was badly whipped. Butler's hand had been tied up from a hurt, but he took off the poultice and gave him a severe thrashing. The next day Jim and Ben. met together and took a drink over it; the quarrel was dropped, as Jim said he deserved the whipping and would not fight it over again.

When Ben. bought his land of Captain Walker he had no thoughts of laying out a town, nor had Walker. He gave $2 an acre for it.

Ben. helped dig the first grave, that of Mrs. Thomas Bell Patterson, the first person that died in Mount Vernon. He says that Col. Patterson was a very smart man, much smarter than any in the town now.

The old school house stood near where the market house stands, and the public well, with a sweep or pole, was north of it, nearly in the centre of High street. He helped wall the old well.

Gilman Bryant said, that he came to the county in 1807, and landed in Mount Vernon from his pirogue in March, and at that time there were only three families living within the then limits of the town, viz; Ben. Butler, who then kept a sort of tavern; James Craig, who kept some sort of refreshments and whisky, on the corner, east side of Mulberry and north of Wood street; and another family, who lived south of Craig's on the opposite side of the street. These buildings were all log. On the west side of Mulberry, opposite to ——, was a little pole shantee, put up by Jo. Walker, a gunsmith, who had a little pair of bellows in one corner, and tinkered gun-locks for the Indians. Further west, on what is now Gambier street, and beyond the town plat, stood the building occupied by —— Walker, also a log. There was also at that time a small log house with a roof, but the gable ends not yet filled, standing on the west side of Main street, between the present market house and where the court house stood in 1849, which would be in High street. There was at the time living in the neighborhood, and recollected by Mr. Bryant Colville, on his farm east of town; Bob. Thompson, where Stilley now lives; Andrew Craig, at or near the old Indian fields (on Centre Run, above Turner's mill); old Mr. Walker, near Banning's mill, on the left hand side of the road; and old Mr. Hains, south of town. Mr. Bryant brought eight barrels of whisky by water to Shrimplin's mill on Owl Creek, and from thence had it hauled by Nathaniel Critchfield's team, Joe driving, to Mount Vernon. Tradition says that the first log shelter occupied by old man Walker was made of little round poles by Casper Fitting in 1802, but we can find nothing to sustain a claim to its erection at so early a period. Fitting, doubtless, was the builder, we should think about 1804, though it may have been in 1803; however, as our own recollection does not extend *quite* that far back, we give it as it has been told to us.

Joseph Walker, Sr., of whom we have been speaking, emigrated to this county from Pennsylvania about 1804, and settled near where we now write. Philip, Joe, Alexander, James, Robert and John were his sons, and two daughters—Sally, who married Stephen Chapman, and lives three miles south of this town, and Polly, who married Solomon Geller, a Pennsylvania Dutchman, who was one of the early settlers of Mount Vernon, and subsequently moved into what is now Morrow county. Joseph Walker, Sr., and his wife, both died many years ago, and their bodies were buried in the Clinton graveyard, with no stone to mark the spot where they lie, and this record, it is hoped, may serve to perpetuate their memory. From all accounts, they were very worthy pioneers.

James Craig, one of the three men living in Mount Vernon in the spring of 1807, was grit to the back bone, and was constantly harrassed by peace officers. It became almost an every-day occurrence with him to have a fight; and, if no new comer appeared to give his fighting life variety, he would, "just to keep his hand in," scrape up a fight with his neighbors or have a quarrel with his wife—all for the love of the thing, for "Jamie was the broth of a boy." He had as high as four fights in one day with Joe Walker, who was also a game chicken! When arraigned before court for assault, etc., he would always put on his most pleasing smile, and say to the judge: "Now, will yer honor jist please be good to the boy, for he can't help it."

We have been told by an early settler of a little incident, illustrating the sports of the pioneers in 1807, at James Craig's house, after he had moved out to the log cabin, erected, and yet leaning, not standing, on D. S. Norton's farm, south of High street extension, on the Delaware road. Craig had tended a few acres in corn, and had the only corn for sale in that part of the county. Mrs. Rachel Richardson sent her son Isaac to buy some for bread, and, after spending a short time in the village, he went out to Craig's, got his corn, and stayed all night. The family had just got to sleep, laying down on the floor, when the wild fellows of the town came in to the doors and fired a volley over their heads. Craig at once sprang out of bed in his shirt-tail, grappled with one of them, and in a short time all present were engaged in a lively little fight, just for the fun of the thing. "Knuck Harris," a "colored gemmen," the first one ever in Mount Vernon, and Joe Walker, are recollected as having been among the parties.

One of the most noted fights that ever came off in this county was between James Craig and his son-in-law, Jack Strain, and two of the Georges of Chester township. It occurred in this way: Old Jim was, as he said, in a fighting humor, when, in company with Jack, coming along the road home on foot they met the Georges near Clinton riding sprucely on horse-back, and required that they should get off their horses and fight them. Parson George explained that they were in a hurry to go home, and had neither time nor disposition for a fight. But Jim swore that they must get off and fight; and, there being no way of getting past them, as they held possession of the road, they reluctantly got off their horses and "pitched in." Jack soon whipped his man, but it puzzled Jim to make his fight out, and the conclusion arrived at was, that they had taken too large a contract when they undertook to whip the Georges. Jim, in after years, would revert to this one fight with regret, as it was entirely uncalled for and only provoked by his own determination for a trial of strength.

After the marriage of Jack Strain into his family, old Jim counted himself almost invincible. Jack was a very powerful and active man, unsurpassed for thews and sinews, bone and muscle.

The great fight of the county might, with propriety, be called that of Strain with Roof. The county pretty much *en masse* witnessed it. It was a regular set-to—a prize fight not inferior, in the public estimation, to that of Heenan and Sayers.

Jack fought with great spirit; he fought, if not for his life, for his wife; for old Jim swore that he (Strain) should never sleep again with his daughter if he didn't whip him.

When Craig was indicted the last time for fighting he told Judge Wilson "not to forget to be easy with him, as he was one of the best customers the court had."

In wrestling with Tucker, Jim had his leg broken, which he often regretted, as he couldn't stand on his forks right. He was not a big, stout man, but struck an awful blow, and was well skilled in parrying off blows. He called his striking a man giving him a "blizzard." He was a backwoodsman from Western Virginia, but of Irish extraction—fond of grog, fond of company, fond of fighting, fun and frolic—kind-hearted, except when aroused by passion, and then a very devil. He fought usually as a pastime, and not from great malice. His wife was an excellent, hospitable and clever woman. We have heard very many anecdotes of Craig, but have space for only one more. One of the last kind acts of the old settler was his endeavoring to treat Bishop Chase when he first visited our town. Jim having heard much said of him as a preacher and a distinguished man, met him on the street, and, desiring to do the clever thing by the Bishop, accosted him with an invitation to treat. The Bishop was somewhat nettled at the offer, but declined going to a grocery with him, whereupon Jim pulled a flask from his pocket and insisted upon his taking a drink there. The Bishop indignantly refused, and Jim apologised, *if* the Bishop considered it an

E. B. & E. C. Kellogg.
Hartford Conn.
Philanr. Chase

insult. "Bless your soul, Bishop, I think well of you, and have no other way to show that I am glad you have come to our county but by inviting you to drink. Don't think hard of me."

Craig's family consisted of eight girls, and he often regretted that he had no boys to learn how to fight. If the girls did not fight, they did run, and run well too. One of them, we recollect, was very fleet; many a time did she run races in the old lane, between Norton's and Bevans', and beat William Pettigrew and other of the early boys, notwithstanding the scantiness of her dresses, which then were made of about one-third the stuff it takes for a pattern in these fashionable days of 1862.

At one time old Jim was singing to a crowd, when a smart young man, in sport, winked to those present and kicked his shins. The wink having been observed by him, he instantly drew back his fist and drove it plum between his eyes, felling him to the ground, at the same time exclaiming: "There, take that, d——n you, and don't *you* ever attempt again to impose on 'old stiffer!'"

5

CHAPTER V.

RESUME OF THE COUNTY SEAT QUESTION.—THE GRAPES WERE SOUR, AND MOUNT VERNON IS DISCOVERED BY THE CLINTONIANS TO BE "INELIGIBLE AND UNHEALTHY."—THE LEGISLATURE OF 1808–9 WERE IN SOME DOUBT.—THE ANTI-VERNONITES THINK THE COUNTY SHOULD BE ENLARGED.—THE GENERAL ASSEMBLY OF OHIO THINK NOT.—AGITATION CONTINUES 1810–11 AND 1811–12.—THE DREAM IS OVER—THE INHABITANTS BEG FOR ROADS—THE GREAT CLINTON LIBRARY STRUGGLES FOR LEGISLATIVE RECOGNITION, AND THE LIGHT EXPIRES!

THE indomitable will of Samuel H. Smith and his associates from New England, among whom we may mention the Nyes, Ichabod, captain of the troop of horse, and his brother Samuel, Henry Smith, Samuel's nephew, Dr. Timothy Burr, the Barneys, Alexander Enos and others, kept the country in commotion about the seat of justice. No stone was left unturned, no effort untried, to bring about its transfer to Clinton. Petitions were drawn up and runners traversed the country for signers. From the official record we give the following exhibit of the disposition made of them:

December 26th, 1808, Mr. Holden presented to the House sundry petitions from a number of the inhabitants of Knox county, setting forth that they feel much aggrieved in consequence of the ineligible and very unhealthy situation of the present seat of justice of said county, and for various other reasons therein stated, praying that commissioners may be appointed to fix the seat of justice for the said county of Knox in some more eligible and healthy situation; which said petitions were read and referred to a committee of Mr. Holden, Mr. Owings, of Fairfield, and Mr. Blair, of Franklin and Delaware, to report their opinion thereupon by bill or otherwise.

Mr. Merwin, (Elijah B.) of Fairfield, presented, on the next day, a remonstrance from sundry citizens of Knox county against action as prayed for in above named petitions.

The cunning old fox managing the Clinton claim devised an additional scheme whereby to bring about such increase of territory northward as would throw Mount Vernon farther from the centre than Clinton, and accordingly we find that—

Mr. Holden presented to the House petitions signed by sundry inhabitants of Knox county, setting forth that it will be greatly to their advantage, and to the advantage of the public in general, to have the county extended so far north as to take in one tier of townships, as it will be perceived, by the map of the State, that the county lying north of them, known by the name of Richland, is much larger than Knox, and by attaching one tier of townships to said county of Knox it will be giving a more equal number of square miles to each county than there is at present; which was received and read, and referred to the same committee to whom was committed, on the 20th inst., the petitions, remonstrances, &c., on the subject of the seat of justice of Knox county.—*House Journal, page* 93, *Dec.* 30*th*, 1808.

On the 30th of December, on motion of Mr. Thomas Morris, of Clermont, and seconded, *Ordered*, that Mr. George Clark, of Columbiana and Stark, be added to the committee appointed on the 26th inst., on the subject of the seat of justice of Knox county, and the matters from time to time to them referred.

On the 12th of January, 1809, on motion, and leave being granted, Mr. Holden presented at the clerk's table two remonstrances, of the same purport, from sundry inhabitants of Knox county, remonstrating against petitions presented to this House, praying for a review of the seat of justice of said county, and a removal of it from Mount Vernon to some more eligible and healthy situation. The remonstrants therein set forth that they are fully of opinion that, unless a fraud or neglect be made to appear against the first viewers appointed by the Legislature at the last session for the purpose of permanently fixing the seat of justice of said county, that your honorable body will not grant a view barely for the purpose of gratifying self-interest; that, in consequence of the seat of justice being established at Mount Vernon, a number of lots have been purchased and improved, and also that upwards of $400 have been appropriated for the building of a jail, and for other reasons, by the aforesaid remonstrants set forth more particularly, praying that the said petition praying for the removal of the seat of justice aforesaid may be rejected; and the same being received and read, were referred to the committee upon that subject appointed on the 26th ult.

On page 145, House Journal, January 14th, 1809,

the following entry stands: "On motion, and by leave of the House, Mr. Holden, from the committee appointed on the 26th ult., presented at the clerk's table a report, as follows: 'The committee to whom was referred the petition of sundry inhabitants of the county of Knox, praying that one tier of townships lying south of Richland county be attached to the said county of Knox; also sundry petitions from the inhabitants of said county, praying that commissioners be appointed to review and fix the seat of justice of said county in some more healthy and eligible situation than Mount Vernon; have, according to order, had under their consideration the said petitions, and are of opinion that the prayer of the said petitions is unreasonable, and ought not to be granted.'"

Monday, January 16th, said report came up, and it was *Ordered*, that it be committed to a committee of the whole House, and made the order of the day for Saturday next.

On the 25th of January, House Journal, page 181, Mr. Merwin moved for the order of the day, whereupon the House, according to order, resolved itself into committee of the whole House, and, after some time spent therein, Mr. Speaker resumed the chair, and Mr. Jewett reported that the committee, according to order, had under their consideration a report of the select committee, made on the 14th inst., on the petitions from sundry inhabitants of Knox county, and had agreed to the said report; and the same being read was agreed to by the House, viz: that the petitions aforesaid are unreasonable, and ought *not* to be granted.

At the 9th session of the General Assembly, held at Zanesville, December 3d, 1810, the subject of removal of the county seat from Mount Vernon was again agitated. By the Senate Journal, page 163, we find that Mr. Trimble presented a batch of petitions, praying a review, which was referred to a committee. On page 166, we find Mr. Trimble, from committee, reported that, in their opinion, commissioners ought to be appointed to examine and make report to the next Legislature the place they think proper for the seat of justice of Knox county. The said report was read. A motion was made that said report be committed to a committee of the whole Senate, and made the order of this day; and on the question thereon it was decided in the negative. On motion, *Ordered*, that the further consideration of said report be postponed till the first Monday in December next.

At the next session it received its final quietus. Mount Vernon had improved in the intermediate time very much, and thenceforth its star has been in the ascendant. Clinton continues but a few years longer as a business place, and after the departure of its chief worker to other parts, its people moved to Mount Vernon, Fredericktown, and elsewhere, and not one of the old inhabitants there remains to tell that Clinton has been an important town in the history of Knox county.

On the 23d of January, 1809, Mr. Holden presented at the clerk's table a petition from sundry inhabitants of the county of Licking, also a petition from sundry inhabitants of the counties of Licking, Knox and Richland, setting forth their remote situation from water carriage, and the necessity of having good roads; that they have *no road whereby they can receive letters, or any kind of intelligence, or any property from any part of the United States, or this State*, except by chance or private conveyance, nearer than Newark or Zanesville, and praying for the establishment of a road from Newark, in Licking county; thence to Mount Vernon, in Knox county; thence to Mansfield, in Richland county; and thence to the mouth of the river Huron, Lake Erie, &c.; which were read.

On motion, and on leave being granted by the House, Mr. Merwin presented at the clerk's table a petition from sundry inhabitants of Fairfield county, of a similar nature to the before mentioned petitions, praying for the establishment of a road from Lancaster, in said county, through Mount Vernon, in Knox county, to the Portage, in Cuyahoga.—*House Journal, page* 177.

Among the questions of great moment at this time to the people of the State was, whether the Clinton Library Society should be incorporated or not. It appears that Samuel H. Smith and other live Yankees of Clinton had conceived the idea of founding a vast and comprehensive library at that point, and at the session of the General Assembly of 1807, Mr. Dillon laid before the Senate a petition of Samuel H. Smith and others of the town of Clinton and its vicinity, in Fairfield county, for the incorporation of the "Clinton Library and School or Academy Society." After its reference to a committee, and about two months travail, it finally got through the Senate on the 6th of February, 1808.

In the House it had a perilous trip, was attacked upon several sides, discussed elaborately, and at length went down before the storm.—*House Journal, page* 171.

At the next session our literary friends at Clinton again pressed their favorite measure; they petitioned, implored, entreated, supplicated and prayed, they had lobbies on the ground to leg for it, and triumphantly they carried it through the House into the Senate, with an amendment to it, that was not *very* acceptable; but this time the grave and reverend Senators were obdurate and flint-hearted, and page 114 of the Senate Journal of the Seventh General Assembly shows how they "killed it."

"Once more unto the breach, dear friends, once more!"

With a pluck worthy of a noble cause, the Clintonians beseeched and beset and besieged the next General Assembly for an act that would enable them to preserve their fine library from destruction by those literary Goths and Vandals—the moths and vampires; but all their efforts were unavailing, and posterity have been thus deprived of an accumulation of books that might in time have eclipsed the far-famed library of Alexandria. One of the oldest inhabitants has kindly placed in our hands one of the books, bearing the Clintonian mark, which he bought at the winding up of the concern for the just sum of 18¾ cents lawful money.

Indignant at the conduct of the illiterate General Assembly, the stock-holders withdrew from the enterprise, and sold at auction the library for $7.50 and the book-case for $10; and thus terminated a great measure which agitated three sessions of the General Assembly of our State, costing the people in time consumed upon it by their Representatives, Senators, etc., from eight to ten thousand dollars, and illustrating fully the character of the greater part of special and local legislation which, like much of a general character, may be termed all "cry and no wool," and show no substance, all ending in smoke. At the time, however, the natives of Mount Vernon regarded it as a seven horned monster that would drive them out of existence, and they looked with holy horror at having such an incorporated body at Clinton, which might accomplish their overthrow and cause them to lose the county seat. The sons of some who shook in their breeches with dread, may now shake in their boots, convulsed by laughter at this reminiscence.

CHAPTER VI.

TRANSACTIONS OF THE YEAR 1809.

THE COMMISSIONERS IN TROUBLE ABOUT TAXES.—THE HEAVY DRAIN ON THE TREASURY FOR WOLF SCALPS.—THE CLERK'S BRAIN BECOMES CONFUSED BY REPEATED DEMANDS.—THE WOLVES INVADE THE TOWN.—DOINGS OF THE COURT AND COMMISSIONERS.—THE COUNTY JAIL COMPLETED.—THE FIRST SETTLEMENT WITH THE TREASURER, AND SKETCH OF THAT OFFICER.

IN the beginning of this year the people of the county were in sore distress at prospects of heavy taxation, the money in the treasury having been exhausted in paying the commissioners who had located the county seat, the heavy demands for killing wolves, and such like expenses.

On Monday, the 23d of January, 1809, the commissioners met at Mount Vernon, and were in a "peck of trouble," if we may judge from the following entry:

"The board, taking into consideration the situation of the taxes on resident and non-resident lands, the board, on an investigation of the business, do order Every paper and document thereunto belonging to be forwarded to the Auditor of State.

"*Ordered,* that the board do adjourn until next Monday."

Among the orders issued this year, we find the following for killing wolves:

"To George Cooper $1.50 for killing one grown wolf, proven before John Green.

"To John Cook $4.50 for killing three grown wolves, proven before Wm. W. Farquhar.

"To James Black $3 for killing two grown wolves, proven before Wm. Y. Farquhar.

"To John Jennings $1.50 for killing one grown wolf, proven before John Green.

"To Ephraim McMillen $3 for killing two grown wolves, proven before Abraham Darling.

"To Levi Herrod for killing two grown wolves, proven before John Green.

"To Francis Hardista $3 for killing two grown wolves, proven before Matthew Merritt.

"To John Lash $1.50 for killing one grown wolf, proven before John Green.

"To George Sap $3 for killing two grown wolves, proven before Abraham Darling.

"To Joseph Harriss $1.50 for killing one grown wolf, proven before John Green.

"To Francis Hardista $3 for killing two grown wolves, proven before M. Merritt.

"To George Sap $1.50 for killing one grown wolf, proven before Abraham Darling.

"To Joseph Bryant $1.50 for killing one grown wolf.

"To Ephraim McMillen $4.50 for killing three grown wolves."

So much in the habit of issuing wolf orders had James Smith, clerk, gotten by this time, that we find on the journals an order issued for commissioner's services reading thus:

"*Ordered*, that the treasurer pay to Henry Markley the sum of $3.50 for killing two wolves as services as commissioner of this county."

The day's services being confounded in the clerk's mind with wolf scalps.

Notwithstanding the abundance of game of this kind, and the facility with which the old sportsmen could take the scalps, the howling varmints seemed to be on the increase, and, like grey hairs, for every one plucked two took their place, and hence our commissioners grew more determined to extirpate them, and made the following order on the 7th of June, 1809:

"*Ordered,* that all persons who shall kill and procure the scalps of grown wolves and panthers within our Balawick, and produce a certificate thereof, according to law, after this date, shall be allowed $2, and all those who shall kill and procure the same of wolves and panthers and scalps of six months and under shall be allowed $1."

The first demands made upon the treasury under this act were by John Mitchell and Francis Hardista, each of whom had killed a grown wolf. For a time these inhuman devils disputed the mastery with the white man, and it seemed somewhat doubtful which would come off victor in the contest and retain possession of the lands upon Owl Creek. They neither had fear of the church ecclesiastic or the military power; they frightened the women and children, and hung about the heels of men, setting all laws and threats at defiance. One old settler has told us of his having on a Sabbath day killed a large wolf near God's barn at Clinton which was making off with one of Sam. Smith's geese, while the people were serving the Lord; another of his friends having been present with the whole military of the county parading on general muster day, when a fierce black wolf attacked one of George Zin's pigs within a stone's throw north-east of the public square, when the army gave pursuit, and it was finally killed by Captain Joe Walker; whereupon a grand spree was taken by the whole military and citizens of the town, glorifying over the great engagement till whisky was drank to more than the value of the wolf scalp.

Grand events those in the hardy pioneer's life! And yet, at this day not a spot bears the name of Wolf, nor does a creek or branch commemorate such achievements. And posterity, were it not for these pages, we fear, would be in blissful ignorance of the fact that there were any other inhabitants of these classic lands than owls and Indians when the men of the hunting shirt and rifle first navigated this famous river in scallops and pirogues.

THE THIRD TERM OF DISTRICT COURT, AND WHAT WAS DONE THEN.

"Court of Common Pleas was opened at Mount Vernon the 2d day of January, 1809. Present: Jentlemen the Honorable William Wilson, President, John Mills and Wm. Gass, Associate Judges. A Grand Jury was called and qualified for the body of this county, to wit: Jas. Walker, Sen'r, foreman, Eleazer Biggs, John Baxter, John Beam, Joseph Walker, Levi Herrod, Nathaniel Scritchfield, Wm. Herrod, David Johnson, Jas. Strange, Jas. Walker, Jr., Wm. Cooper and Jonathan Craig, who, after receiving their charge, Returned out of Court.

"On the 2d day of the Term the Grand Jury returned, but found *no* Indictments.

"*Ordered*, that the Court adjourn until 2 o'clock this evening.

"The Court opened according to adjournment. Present: as before.

"*John Armstrong* vs. *John Kerr*.—On Trespass. Continued by consent of parties.

"*Jacob Young* vs. *Abraham Lyon*.—On an action of Trespass on the case. Continued by consent of parties.

"*The State of Ohio* vs. *Aaron Brown*.—On an Indictment. The defendant plead guilty, and is fined $1.00 and the costs of prosecution, and stands convicted until the whole be complied with.

"License is granted to William Perrine to retail goods for three months, on payment of $2.50.

"John Green is admitted Administrator of Isaac McClary. Bond, $1000. Abner Brown and John Herrod securities.

"License is granted to Benjamin Tupper to sell goods three months, on payment of $2.50.

"*The State of Ohio* vs. *John Click.*—Nolle is entered by Herrick, att'y.

"*Thomas Parr* vs. *John Craig.*—William Walker undertook for the defendant in case he should be cast he would satisfy the condemnation of the Court, or render his body a prisoner in lieu thereof.

"Court adjourned till to-morrow morning, 9 o'clock.

"The Court opened according to adjournment, and present, as yesterday.

"*Thomas B. Patterson, for the use of Moses Rigly*, vs. *Samuel Kratzer.*—Parties agreed to reference to the Court, who adjudged $2.55 debt and costs for the plaintiff.

"Court adjourned till 2 o'clock.

"2 o'clock P. M.

"William Wallace is authorized to keep a publick house of entertainment for one year, on payment of $5.00

"William Fuller is licensed to keep a publick house of entertainment on the road leading from Mount Vernon to Newark, on payment of $4.00.

"*Ordered*, that the Court adjourn until the Court in course.

"WILLIAM WILSON."

THE COUNTY JAIL BUILT, AND ITS FIRST OCCUPANT—ACCOUNT OF ITS SUBSEQUENT CAREER, AND THAT OF ITS SUCCESSOR.

On the 6th of June, 1808, the commissioners of this county, finding the great want of a jail in said town, and by virtue of the powers vested in them by law,

"*Ordered*, a jail to be built, 24 feet long, 16 feet wide, 9 feet high, with square timber of one foot square, including the upper and lower floor, and a petition of like timber, with a good shingle roof, and stone or brick chimney, three windows, with iron grates, of 6 lights each, and 2 sufficient doors, one on the outside and one in the petition in the inside, and the walls, petition, and lower floor lined with 3 inch plank, spiked on with spikes 7 inches. The front door marked A and petition door B to be of 1½ inch stuff; C chimney. The jail to be built on the public square of said town, on a corner."

On the 31st of January the following entry is made upon the journal:

"This day the board has proceeded to the Ex'n of the jail, and finding the same unfinished they do allow the undertakers thereof until the first day of May next to finish the same, agreeable to the article of agreement in that case made and provided."

On the 2d of May, 1809,

"*Ordered*, that the commissioners do receive the jail from the hands of John Mills, Alexander Walker, and James Walker, Sr., provided that the said Mills and others do saw down the corners of said jail, and then our Clerk shall have authority to issue orders on the treasury for the sum of 433 dollars and 50 cents, as shall appear by a reference to the agreement, and that the Clerk issue orders of such sizes as the Claimants may desire, with their proper numbers to the above amount."

The jail being then declared completed, the commissioners ordered 50 cents to be expended by Joseph Walker for two steeples and hasp for the jail.

The calaboose having been duly prepared, the officers of the law became exceedingly self-important, consequential and overbearing. Michael Click, an old Dutchman, who was fond of grog, was taken up, "tight as a musket," and locked up in the quarters. The constable had gone down street and was boasting of his exploit in taking up Mike, when the voice of the old fellow was heard just behind them, shouting at the top of his lungs: "By tam, they can't keep me in their tammed shail—I am trumps, by G—d." He had crawled up the chimney till he got near the top and stuck fast, when, as he said, he "swelled and bursted" it open, and then jumped to the ground, a free man once again.

The chimney was repaired at the expense of the county, and Click, several weeks after, when confined "broke out," and, meeting Judge Wilson on the street, narrated his several jail exploits in great glee, vowing that they never could keep old Mike in that jail any longer than it suited him to stay, for he had lent a hand when it was built and knew all its weak points. For several years, however, this little log concern served as a nominal terror to evil doers. At length so many escapes were made from it, that its fate was sealed, and it was sold to Wm. Y. Farquhar, who moved it to the outskirts of town and constructed out of it a sort of a tobacco house.

The commissioners, on the 4th of December, 1823, determined to erect another jail and jailor's house, on the square, of brick, which remained an eye-sore to the people of the town until about 1850, when John Armstrong, Street Commissioner, and A. Banning Norton, Councilman of the Third Ward, in grading and excavating the north-east part of the public square, with "malice aforethought" undermined it, and caused the removal of that pile of rubbish.

FOURTH TERM COURT OF COMMON PLEAS—1ST DAY OF MAY, 1809.

"*Grand Jury.*—David Demmick, foreman, Moses Craig, Wm. Downs, Jas. Craig, David Johnson, Jeremiah Brown, Charles Cooper, Ziba Leonard, Nathaniel M. Young, John Kerr, John Cook, James Loveridge, James Walker, Jr., who returned *out* of Court, and after some time returned *in* Court, with the following indictments, to wit:

"*The State of Ohio* vs. *Wm. Wallace.*—For salt and battery, a true bill, and pleads guilty, the Court do say, that the defendant do pay a fine of $1 and costs of this prosecution.

"*The State of Ohio* vs. *Wm. Cooper.*—For same offense, the same fine is assessed.

"*The State of Ohio* vs. *Wm. Cooper.*—Same, and same fine.

"*The State of Ohio* vs. *Wm. Scritchfield.*—For same offense.

"*The State of Ohio* vs. *Peter Baxter.*—For same offense.

"*Luke Walpole* vs. *Wm. Wallace.*—James Craig becomes security.

"*Thomas Parr* vs. *James Craig.*—Judgment by confession for $91.81 and costs of suit.

"*Wm. A. Enui* vs. *Samuel Kratzer.*—Judgment by confession, $66.92 and costs.

"*John Beesy* vs. *Samuel Kratzer.*—Michael Click becomes security.

"*Wm. Douglass* vs. *John Young.*—Nathaniel M. Young becomes security.

"One o'clock P. M.

"*John Armstrong* vs. *John Kerr.*—Tried by Jury, and defendant not found guilty of Trespass. The plaintiff, by E. Herrick, his attorney, gives notice of an appeal.

"*Wm. Biggs, who sues as well for himself as for the State of Ohio,* vs. *William Darling.*—*Ordered,* that the plaintiff appear in Court to-morrow morning and enter security for costs, or he become *non plus.*

"License issued to Benj. Tupper to retail goods 4 months for $3.33⅓.

"James Smith is appointed clerk for seven years.

"Court adjourns till to-morrow morning at 9 o'clock.

"May 2—9 o'clock A. M.

"The Biggs case is disposed of by the following entry: *Ordered*, that the plaintiff be non-suit for not entering security for costs.

"Edward Herrick is allowed $25 for each term as prosecuting attorney.

"*Ordered*, that the clerk have authority to issue license to John Baxter and Michael Click each to keep a public house of entertainment until next term, on their paying the proper sum.

"Adjourned till the next Court in course."

IMPORTANT ACTS OF COMMISSIONERS IN REGARD TO RATES OF TAXATION AND OTHER MATTERS—PECULIARITY OF THE OLD CLERK IN SPELLING—HIGH AUTHORITY QUOTED.

On the 5th of March "a petition was forwarded to the board of Commissioners of this county, praying for a Road Leading from the town of Mansfield on a South East direction, to intersect with the State road near the fifty-four mile tree, to run on a straight direction as the ground will admit, to intersect the State road, and the board do declare that the same is *inexpedient*."

"The tax on William Douglass' mill is ordered to be taken off, as it is a public benefit.

"James Morgan is ordered to be taxed fourfold for refusing to give in five horses to the lister of Union Township."

On the 7th of June the Commissioners "*Ordered*, that the rates of licens* of Taverns hereafter obtained for one year in this county shall be as follows: In the town of Mount Vernon, on the Public Square, and on Market Street, shall be rated at six dollars; all Taverns in the Town of Frederick and in the Town of Clinton, and on the road leading from the Town of Mount Vernon to Newark, within the county of Knox, at Five dollars; all Taverns in any other part of the Town of Mount Vernon, at five dollars; all taverns on roads leading through any part of the county, or Richland county, at four dollars."

The rates of taxation on the county levy were established as follows:

* The first clerk was a very good pensman, a gentleman and scholar; but like General Jackson, he had his peculiarities of spelling and pronunciation, as, for instance, license without the E final, and gentlemen with a J.

"On each stud horse and jack at the rate of what he stands at the season."

"On each other horse, mare, mule and ass, 30 cents.

"On each head of neat cattle, 10 cents; on houses, and other property made subject to taxation by law, one-half per cent. on its appraised value."

At this time horses were valued for taxation at $30 per head, and cattle at $10. The trouble about the tax duplicate and matters connected therewith was satisfactorily adjusted, as appears by the following entry on the 27th of June:

"This day we have prepared our duplicate for Collection, and prepared our Returns for the Auditor of the State of Ohio."

Great was the relief of the board at having arranged matters which had troubled them from January till June 27th!

"James Smith is appointed collector of the Taxes for the year 1809, and gave bond.

In September, 1809, we find: "On return of a Road laid out from Mount Vernon to a point on Mohicking, the viewers return the same unprofitable, and the same is Rejected."

KNOX COMMON PLEAS—FIFTH TERM—SEPTEMBER 4, 1809.

"*Grand Jury.*—Jabez Beers, Joe Walker, George Downs, Gilman Bryant, John Baxter, George Lybarger, Henry Roberts, Thomas Townsend, Jonathan Hunt, Sen'r, John Green, James Craig, Samuel Wilson, Benj. Thompson, and Wm. Johnson, returned into Court and brought in the following Indictments:

"*The State of Ohio vs. Henry Smith.*—For retailing liquors contrary to the statute of this State; a true bill; who appears and pleads guilty. The attorney for the State of Ohio will no further prosecute this Indictment.

"ED. HERRICK, *Pro. Att'y.*

"*Same* vs. *Benjamin Butler.*—For retailing S. liquors contrary to the statute of this State; who comes forward and puts in his plea—Guilty. The Court, in consideration of his offense, do assess his fine to $3.

"*Same* vs. *Samuel Martin.*—For same. Henry Roberts, John Harod and James Bryant enter into recognizance of $50 each to give evidence in this case.

"*Same* vs. *Wm. McDougal.*—For retailing goods without license. Pleads guilty, &c.

"*Luke Walpole* vs. *Wm. Wallace.*—Trespass on the case. Judgment by confession, $91.88, and Interest from 11th Jan'y, and costs.

"*The State of Ohio* vs. *Peter Baxter.*—For assault and battery.

"*Jury.*—James Walker, Jr., Peter Kyle, Sr., James Bryant, Abraham Sperry, Alexander Walker, John Hown, Daniel Demmick, Isaac Bonnett, Charles Cooper, James Walker, Sr., John Click, David Pettigrew, who do say the defendant is guilty.

"*The State of Ohio* vs. *Wm. Scritchfield.*—Assault and battery. Defendant pleads guilty, and is fined fifty cents and costs.

"*John Barry* vs. *Samuel Kratzer.*—On the case. Judgment confessed by defendant for $200, with interest from 26th April, 1806.

"*The State of Ohio* vs. *Peter Baxter.*—John Merritt becomes his security in $50 for his appearance next Court.

"*The State of Ohio* vs. *John Morryson.*—For assault and battery. Jury's verdict—Not guilty.

"*John J. Bruce* vs. *Thomas B. Patterson, Joseph Walker, Gilman Bryant.*—This cause is to be continued until 1st of October for answer to bill of plaintiff.

"*Wm. Douglass* vs. *John Young.*—On the case. The parties appeared and settled.

"*Christian Shoolts* vs. *James Walker, Jr.*—On the case. Settled.

"*John Byard* vs. *Wm. Walker.*—On the case. Settled.

"*Sylvanius Lawrence, for the use of Benjamin Rush,* vs. *George Davison.*—Nathaniel Spurgeon and Wm. Scritchfield appeared and undertook for the defendant's appearance, &c.

"License is granted to Henry Smith to keep public house for one year.

"*The State of Ohio* vs. *Peter Baxter.*—On Indictment. Defendant pleads guilty, and is fined 50 cents and cost.

"*Robert Dalrymple* vs. *Joseph Talmage.*—On the case. Continued till next term.

"5th September.

"Michael Click, John Baxter, Samuel Lewis and Abner Ayres obtain licenses for houses of public entertainment.

"Wm. McDonald and Benjamin Tupper are each licensed to sell goods.

"Samuel H. Smith is also licensed to retail goods one year, on payment of $10.00.

"Letters of administration on Michael Shinabery's estate are issued to Catharine Shinabery. Gilman Bryant and George Downes, securities; John Mills, Matthew Mant and James Smith, appraisers.

"Court adjourned till the next Court in course."

THE FIRST SETTLEMENT OF THE COUNTY TREASURER.

The first fiscal year of Knox county made the following showing on settlement of the Treasurer with the Commissioners, and "from a full investigation of all the accounts and monies paid into his hands as Treasurer, that the said Treasurer has paid and accounted with us for above, the same twenty-three dollars seventy cents and four mills, which is as follows:

Dr. Treasurer to am't of monies Due to the county....		$906.60.4
Cr. By monies paid and accounted for from June last until this day, June 6th, 1809........................		930.30.8
To order in your favour on settlement........	23.70.4	
Balance..............................	906.60.4	
	930.30.8	

"*Ordered*, that Henry Hains be allowed the sum of $23.70.4, which is a balance due him on settlement as Treasurer of Knox county, and the Treasurer is ordered to pay the same."

THE TREASURER OF KNOX COUNTY FOR SEVEN YEARS—HIS MELANCHOLY EXIT.

Henry Haines, first Treasurer of Knox county, was one of the best men in the county at its organization. He was a native of ——, and settled on the tract of land, since owned by Beams and others, next to the Merritts.

He had been a man of education and property, and was in easy circumstances. He was a very ingenious, handy man, had a turning lathe, made chairs, farmed, etc. He became deranged on the subject of religion, was an active and leading member of the Disciple or Christian denomination, at that time called "New Lights." He officiated with James Smith in the first conference held in the county, of which David Young, of Zanesville, was Presiding Elder.

Haines became a loud exhorter, and, becoming deranged, got a tin horn and rode around the town and county, day and night, notifying the people to prepare for judgment, as the world was coming to an end. He proclaimed the same doctrine in his derangement that Millerites subsequently did.

When he became ungovernable he was taken to Dr. R. D. Moore, who confined him in a mad shirt, or straight jacket, and treated him for several weeks until he was restored to reason; but he said if he ever became insane again he would kill Dr. Moore. Shortly after this the doctor removed to Fayette county, Pa., and Haines again became deranged, and was missing for some time. Search was made for him, but the first information that his family received of his whereabouts was in a letter from Dr. Moore. He had made his way into Connellsville for the purpose of killing the doctor, and had stolen the family silver spoons to pay his way in. Upon arriving there he had become rational again, and he told what his purpose had been, and stayed several weeks with the doctor, and was treated very kindly by him. Not long after this he took a rope and hung himself to a tree on his own farm.

CHAPTER VII.

THE SEAT OF JUSTICE FOR THE LAST TIME.

BEN. BUTLER'S VERSION OF THE WAY MOUNT VERNON WAS MADE THE PERMANENT COUNTY SEAT, SHOWING THAT OLD VIRGINIA WAS UP TO TRICKS.

THE only one of the proprietors now living related to us the following interesting story:—

"When I moved my family to the thirty-six acres of land which I had bought, I had no thought of ever laying out any portion of it in town lots, or of any town ever being laid out there, nor at that time had Walker or Patterson. The idea, when suggested, was pleasing, and we at once took up with it. Clinton had been laid out by Sam. Smith, and had never been paid out, I believe. It was started chiefly on the donation principle. Those who would put up buildings had their own time to pay for their lots, if ever they could.

"When we got word that the Commissioners were coming on to locate the county site, we were greatly stirred up about how we should manage. Kratzer and Williamson and Walker came to see me about it, and we all had a general consultation. I thought we had no chance of getting it, for I told them that they had, at Clinton, Bill Douglass' mill and a lot of good houses, and Sam. Smith's big brick house, and a plenty of smart Yankees to manage, and they had at Frederick Johnny Kerr's mill and a lot of rich Quakers around it, and both those places looked better then than our d——d little scrubby place; and Sam. Kratzer asked me

Bengamen Butler J.P.

what I would do about it? And I said to them that I had studied out a pretty d——d bad trick that I could manage if they would only go into it, and if they wouldn't there wasn't a d——d bit of chance for us; and they said, let's hear it; and I told them I would give $10 myself, and each of them must give $10, to make up a purse and get liquor for the devils we had, and engage them to go up to Clinton and Frederick, and get drunk, and fiddle and fight and play hell generally when the Commissioners came up there to look, and that we would get two good yoke of oxen to work on the streets, and the rest of the men must take hold and spade and shovel and pick and roll logs and dig up stumps, and be fixing up the streets right, while all the women and girls must get out into their gardens, hoeing and weeding and working like good fellows, and I would have the best victuals cooked and the best cheer the little old tavern could afford, so as to please the bellies of the Commissioners, and we might then come out first for the county site selection.

"My plan struck their fancy, and Sam. Kratzer, although he was a great Methodist, didn't say a d——d word about its being a sin to cheat them that game, but at it he went, and they all fell into the plan. And we had a clever fellow named Munson, from Granville, and a big fellow named Bixbee, from over about Big-belly, and they agreed to go along and each to captain a gang of the rowdies, and see that it was played out right.

"It was Thursday afternoon when the Commissioners first came to our town, and they rode up and asked me if they could get to stay all night, and I told them that it was hard fare we had, but if they would put up with it they could, and they stopped. I guessed who they were at once, and passed the word around, and everything went on as we had planned it, and the next morning about daylight the busiest set of bees ever collected about a hive were at work, hammering, pounding, digging, hoeing, scraping and working on the streets and in the lots. Leah had breakfast bright and early; I had their horses all cleaned up and well fed, and ready after they eat to start. They wondered at the work they saw going on, and if it was kept up always as they had seen it in town, and I told them we were all poor and hard working, and we never lost any time in our little town. They said they were going up to Clinton and Frederick to see those places, and were going to fix the county seat, and wanted me to go along, but I tried to beg off—that I was poor and must work, and couldn't lose the time, as it would take them two or three days to determine it. They said no, it wouldn't take them that long, and I knew d——d well if the trick was played out well by the rowdies that they would soon be back, so I sort of hesitated as though I would and I wouldn't go, and finally told Kratzer if he would go too, I would, as I would like to see them fix the county seat up there, and then Jim Dunlap, who was a jovial fellow about 35, spoke up and said to come ahead; the other two were sort of gruff, it seemed to me, and didn't say much, but looked solemn. They asked if we didn't expect to get the county seat at Mount Vernon, and I told them no, that we were too poor to try for it; that I felt too poor really to go up with them, for some fellow might come along and stop with me, who would want me to go with him and look at land, and every fellow that I showed land to, gave me $2, which helped right smart. There were three sorts of poor—God's poor, the devil's poor, and poor devils, and that we were all poor devils; but Sam. Smith was long headed, and Johnny Kerr had lots of rich Quakers to back him, so us poor devils were left out of the question.

"We then rode together up to Clinton, and there the rowdies were cutting up, and the fiddle going, and shouting and cursing being done of the tallest kind, and when we went to go into the tavern there was a rush to the door way, and two men scuffling and fighting, and before the Commissioners could get in they were jammed and scuffed about, and in the din and confusion, and yells of 'pull them off,' 'part them,' 'don't do it,' 'fair play, by G—d,' 'hit him again, d——n him,' 'let 'em fight it out,' and all such calls, the Commissioners backed out from the tavern, and proposed to go and look at Fredericktown. About that time old Sam. Smith came up, and when he found out they were the Commissioners, and going, he tried the hardest kind to get them to stop, but it was no go; they had seen enough of that place then, but promised him to call again to-morrow. On the way to Fredericktown I talked much with them, and apologized for the way our people up there had acted, and they asked me if they cut up like Indians all the time, and I told them that about Clinton and Frederick there were a great many rich men's sons, and they had no trades, and would frolic a little just to put in their time, but they were a mighty clever set of people, &c. And I pointed out to them the pretty scenery, and bragged on the land around, but said not a word for Mount Vernon. When we got to

Frederick, they stopped at Ayres' tavern, and found a good deal such quarreling going on as at Clinton, and I got afraid then that they might see through it, and suspect that we had a hand in getting it up, and so I got down about the mill, and sat on the logs awhile with Kratzer and Patterson, and left them up at the tavern to see the fighting in the yard, and just before going in to dinner I called one of the rowdies to me and told him it was all working well, and gave him more money, and told him to swear the others not to revulge on them ever, and we would make it right with 'em. After dinner the Commissioners sauntered around, and I proposed going back and leaving them, as they would want to stay all night there, and I had some work to do and chores to attend to at home before night; but they would have me wait a while longer for them, and I did it. While there sitting on a log, we bet two gallons of wine with Johnny Kerr, as to which place would get the county seat. When they were ready they started, and we rode back to Mount Vernon, where Mrs. Butler had the best kind of a supper cooked up, and it put them in right good humor. She knew how to fix things up right on such an occasion.

"The men about Mount Vernon were all quiet, and kept so, and when Dunlap asked Coyle's two boys to take a dram with him, they hung back and hesitated, until I told them to come up and take a drink with the gentleman—that there was no harm in it; and they poured out the least bit of drams they ever took in their lives. The next morning the Commissioners got ready to start, and I had got Knuck Harris, the only nigger in the country then, to sleek their horses off, and they came out looking first rate. Dunlap was a funny fellow, and he thought he could hop, and bantered some of the boys to hop, but they were afraid they would be beat by him, and said it warn't no use to try, as they knew he could beat them. But I told him to make his hop, and he went out in the road and gave a sample; I went over it just a little, and we hopped several times, until I concluded to show him what Ben. could do, and I hopped so far over his furtherest mark that they all laughed him right out, and he gave it up, saying I could hop some. In those days I never found the man that could beat me. When they were about starting I asked them if they were not going back to Clinton and give it another look, but they said no, and the Clintonites never saw them any more. They wanted to go to Delaware, and asked me to pilot them a part of the way, which I did, and when I got out with them back of George Lewis' place, I tried to find something out of them as to what they had determined on, but they evaded my questions, and gave me little satisfaction. On bidding them good-by, I hoped they were not put out with our place on account of the hard fare I had given them—that I had nothing nice to give them, as I kept only a little log tavern, and supplied my table by hunting and butchering. One of them remarked that if they ever came this way again, they were well enough suited to call on me. I then said that I was poor, and felt discouraged, and thought that I would quit off and go some where else and make a better living for myself and family. Dunlap then said I was doing well enough, and must not get out of heart. And so we parted. When we got back to town all the men gathered around me to find out what was our chance. I told them what had passed between us, and that I was satisfied it would be found that our side was ahead, and I called them all up to take a good drink at my expense on Mount Vernon being made the permanent county seat. That little trick of ours, I am sure, made the scales turn in our favor, and when we knew that it was established at Mount Vernon, you can imagine that we had loud rejoicing over it."

In this time of war, when the public mind is educated to believe that it is fair in any way to gain an advantage over an enemy, there will be but few who will not consider this little county seat contest to have been properly conducted upon the part of the Vernonites. The rule that "all is fair in politics" having of late years gained general acceptation and credence, those who have dabbled in govern mental affairs will say that this was rightly done, and all who have won in matters of love, and who has not, will concede that "the end justifies the means," and all who believe that "whatever is is right," will determine that Mount Vernon honorably, justly and legitimately became the permanent seat of jus tice of Knox county.

JONATHAN HUNT'S RYDER.

Jonathan Hunt informs us that he was one of the volunteer workers on the streets at the time the Commissioners came on, and that Gilman Bryant sort of bossed the work, and, being a cripple, he tended on them and gave out the whisky and water, cheering them up as he came around, saying: "Work like men in harvest, but keep sober, boys." Mike Click, and John Click, his brother, drove the oxen." Mike was a bully hand with a team, and made them tear up stumps, haul logs, plow and scrape, as necessary. Men never worked better on a road than that force then did. They chopped down trees, cut off logs, grubbed, dug down rough places, filled up gulleys, burned log heaps, and made a wonderful change in the appearance of things. It was the first work ever done on the streets of Mount Vernon.

CHAPTER VIII.

SIXTH TERM OF COURT—JANUARY 1st, 1810.

THE LAW AND THE TESTIMONY.—COURTS, FINANCE, AND ELECTION, 1810.

"*Grand Jury.*—Isaac Bonnett, foreman, David Miller, Peter Bricker, Abner Brown, Jr., John Johnson, Casper Fitting, Francis Hardesty, Josiah Talmage, Willis Speakman, Wm. Darling, Robert Dalrymple, Joseph Coleman, David Johnson, John Merritt, James Walker, Jr.

"Indictments were found vs. Henry Smith, Eli Freeman, John Click, Thomas McBride.

"*Robert Dalrymple* vs. *Joseph Talmage.*—This case was tried by a jury, who do find for the plaintiff and do assess his damage $1.

"Wm. Sapp was appointed guardian for John Melton, and gave bond in $50.

"John Green, administrator of Isaac McClary, was allowed till next September Term to settle.

"William Wallace was licensed to keep public house on paying the proper sum.

January 2d.

"*Isaac Applegate, by his Agent, Israel Ross,* vs. *Thomas B. Patterson.*—On Saassarara. *Ordered,* that a Declaration be filed vs. two o'clock.

"*The Case of John J. Brice* vs. *Thomas B. Patterson, Gilman Bryant, and Joseph Walker.*—In Chancery—is disposed of by ordering defendants to pay $50, in nine months, or make a deed and to pay costs.

"*Robert Dalrymple* vs. *Joseph Talmage.*—By consent of parties this action is to lie open for a new trial, and continued on the Issue Docket.

"Plumb and Murray are Licensed to retail goods three months.

"Notice is given of an appeal in the cases of Dalrymple vs. Talmage, and John J. Brice vs. Patterson, et als.

"Letters of administration are granted to ——— Simpkins on the Estate of John Simpkins. Joseph Coleman and Sele Simpkins securities for $400.

"And the Court adjourned till Court in Course."

SEVENTH TERM—COURT OF COMMON PLEAS—30TH APRIL, 1810.

"James Colville appears as an Associate Judge in place of Wm. Gass.

"*Grand Jury.*—Joseph Walker, foreman, Nicholas Riley, Jas. Walker, Jr., Daniel Demmick, George Davis, Jonathan Craig, C. Loffland, Wm. Fuller, Jacob Lybarger, C. Cooper, Peter Majors, Henry Haines, John Ervin, Nathaniel Critchfield.

"Bills of Indictment were found vs. Ichabod Nye, Samuel Nye, Alexander Enos, Richard Alspaugh.

"But one case was tried by Jury—that one vs. John Click, for assault and battery.

"Another State case for assault and battery vs. Thomas McBride was disposed of by the Court assessing a fine of $1 and costs, and two cases were dismissed at defendant's cost, and one at the plaintiff's cost.

"*Ordered*, that an additional Justice of the Peace be added to the township of Morgan.

"Benjamin Barrey was Licensed to keep public tavern at Clinton, on payment of $5.

"This term continued two days, and the above is the business transacted."

THE JAIL BOUNDS DEFINED.

Special Term—2d day of June, 1810.

"*Ordered*, that the jail bounds of this county be as follows, to wit: Front street, thence to include all the balance of the town of Mt. Vernon lying North said street, which does include the Jail of said county."

"LO! THE POOR AFRICAN" DEMANDS ATTENTION.

"The Court convenes at 2 o'clock P. M. to determine the negroe's case.

"*The State of Ohio* vs. *Ned Jackson, a negro.*—For Larceny. The criminal comes forward and pleads not guilty, and the Court, from the testimony given, do consider and order that the said criminal be confined in jail until the Court in course."

HAVING A QUAKER JUDGE CAUSES A QUAKER MEETING—4TH DAY, 6TH MONTH.

"Court met. Present: John Mills, Wm. W. Farquhar, and James Colville."

The record is silent as to the cause of their meeting—only sheweth that the three gentlemen met and adjourned until the Court in Course.

EIGHTH TERM—COURT OF COMMON PLEAS—3D SEPTEMBER, 1810.

"*Grand Jury.*—Robert McMillen, foreman, John Wood, Wm. Wallace, John Herrod, John Shrimplin, John Merrit, Silas Brown, John Hown, John Wheeler, David Johnson, Nathaniel Critchfield, Ziba Leonard, Jas. Wallace, Jr.

"Bills of Indictment were presented against Robert Davidson and James Butler, each of whom were on plea of guilty of assault and battery, fined $2 and costs."

The cases must have been exceedingly aggravated, or the Court become more severe upon the offenders, and doubled the fine.

Three causes were tried by jury, to wit: Robert Dalrymple vs. Joseph Talmage; Lawrence, for use of Rush, vs. George Davidson; and Martha Zenick, by her guardian and father, vs. David Miller and Mary Miller. This time Dalrymple was awarded $5 damages, but neither party, as usual in law, was satisfied with the decision; hence, on the next page we find, side by side with each other, the following entries:

"*Robert Dalrymple* vs. *Joseph Talmage.*—Notice is hereby given by the plaintiff of an appeal.

"*Robert Dalrymple* vs. *Joseph Talmage.*—Notice is hereby given by the defendant of an appeal.

"The Jury in the second case gave judgment for the defendant, George Davidson, for costs, and the plaintiff gives notice of appeal."

In the Zenick case, the Jury, "upon their oaths, do find the defendants guilty, and assess the damages of the plaintiff to $30." This was the *first slander suit* ever tried in Knox county. The defendants moved, in arrest of judgment, "that the words contained in the third count in the plaintiff's declaration are not actionable," but, having been overruled in this effort, then gave notice of an appeal. This was a case of unusual interest, and William Guardian, for failing to appear as evidence in it, was fined $1.

Three cases were dismissed at plaintiff's cost. Three judgments were entered by default, and one by confession. The highest amount of any judgment was that of Josiah Morriss vs. David Debel, alias Debolt, for $70 and costs. A case of David Miller vs. Martha Zenick, on the case, was dismissed with judgment for costs vs. plaintiffs. Such was the business of two days of the 7th regular term.

"On the 5th of September George Coffinbery was Licensed to keep a publick house of entertainment in the town of Mansfield for one year on his payment of $4.

"John Green, Esq., was still further allowed 3 years to settle the Isaac McClary estate.

"Catharine Shinabery, Ex. of M. Shinabery, dec'd, settled with the Court.

"Daniel Demmick was Licensed to keep a publick House of entertainment for one year, and Michael Click also.

"Henry Markley was allowed for 12½ days services as Commissioner.

"Matthew Merritt was allowed for 9 days services as Commissioner.

"William Douglas was allowed for 10 days services as Commissioner.

"Edward Herrick was allowed $25 as Prosecuting Attorney for the Supreme Court for 1810."

COUNTY SETTLEMENT—5TH SEPTEMBER, 1810.

"The Court met with the Commissioners for the purpose of settling with the Court in County Charges, &c., which is as follows, (to wit):

"County of Knox, Dr., for, including from the June, 1809, to Sept. 6th, 1810:

Commissioners of Knox County	$137	27
Associate Judges	109	44
Elections	48	75
Roads	130	82
"	3	10
Treasurer	40	46
Boarding & Imprisoning Negro	2	75
" " "	1	83
Coroner	3	50
Iron—Negro	5	25
Wolf Scalps	67	50
Collector's fees	102	59.8
Clerk's fees	41	00
Clerk to Commissioners from Jan'y, 1808	87	17
Sheriff's fees	28	6½
Prosecuting Attorney	100	00
Repairs of Jail	9	47
Jury Boxes	1	00

Delinquents in Tax	$24 20
Listing Townships	73 00
Petit Jurors	15 15
Postage of Letters	95
Witnesses	4 00
Grand Jurors	60 00
	$1,194 16½

Cr. By County Levy for 1809	$265 98
By Land Tax, 1809	252 52
By Draft on District Collection	118 30
By fines, &c	48 55
By stores and taverns	73 32
	$759 67

" *Ordered*, that the Court do adjourn until the next meeting in course."

VOTE FOR GOVERNOR IN 1810.

The vote of Knox county in 1810 stood: For Return J. Meigs, 97; Thomas Worthington, 90. All the votes cast in our county at that election were 187. Our county was then on the winning side, as Meigs carried the State by 2,193 majority.

CHAPTER IX.

SKETCH OF THE FIRST WHITE MAN KNOWN TO HAVE BEEN UPON THE KO-KO-SING.—THE INDIAN CAPTIVE IN 1779.—THE ADJUTANT IN 1812—AND COMMISSIONER IN 1824.

THE first of the citizens of Knox county to tread upon its soil, was John Stilley. In the month of June, A. D. 1779, he was a captive among the Indians upon the banks of Ko-ko-sing. We have thoroughly investigated the early history of this country and can learn of no white person who penetrated the wilderness prior to that time. His father was one of the pioneers of Allegheny county, Pennsylvania, who was killed by the savages when John was but a small child. Immediately after his father was massacred, John (about the year 1774) was taken, with one of his little sisters, by his brother-in-law, Kennedy, to his home in the back part of Washington county, where he was living exposed to the privations, toils and sufferings incident to border life. At that time the people of the new country were in constant dread of the savages, and sleeping or waking they were alike in danger of becoming their prey. In the spring of 1779, when the corn was just sprouting out of the ground, a band of Indians of the Wyandot tribe one night attacked the house of Kennedy, took Kennedy, his wife and one child, John Stilley and his little prattling sister, plundered the house of such things as they fancied, set fire to the house, and burned it to the ground. While they were witnessing the destruction of the house and its contents, they became alarmed by the approach of some of the whites living nearest to Kennedy, and hastily seized his horses, and took to flight. One of the neighbors, called Captain Jack, an old Indian hunter, living about two miles from Kennedy's, thought on the evening of that day that there were Indians about, and being unable to get to sleep on account of this presentiment, kept his family awake until about midnight, when he swore that he "smelt Indians," and seizing his rifle, powder-horn and bullet-pouch went out to his nearest neighbor, and while there discovered the fire in the direction of Kennedy's, and with such of the settlement as could be hastily gathered together came up to the ruins of the house, hurrying the Indians away with their captives and plunder. They followed close in pursuit, and came so nearly up to them when crossing the river that Captain Jack shot the Indian having young Stilley in charge across the right hand, cutting off his thumb. They heard the crack of rifles, and the balls whistled by them as they crossed the river. The Indian held young John in his left hand, and swam his horse over the river and rode some distance with the reins in his mouth. The band of Indians—sixteen in number—hastened rapidly across the country with their prisoners, crossing the White Woman near its mouth, and following on up the Ko-ko-sing, as Stilley distinctly recollects, until above where Fredericktown has since been built, and thence on out to the Sandusky plains. They camped one night at the Little Indian Fields, near the present site of Mount Vernon.

This country was then an unbroken wilderness. They did not see a single white man, or the trace of one, this side of the Ohio river; nor could John Stilley recollect of seeing one of his own race for five years, except a few prisoners who were at times brought through the country where he was, and occasionally his sisters and brother-in-law. They were parceled out by the captors as suited their fancy, and were sometimes for months without seeing each other. John was a stout, hearty boy, fond of rough exercise, and having not a particle of fear he soon became a great favorite with the tribe, and was often taken by the warriors in their hunting and fighting expeditions. He was several times brought with a portion of the tribe down to the Ko-ko-sing and White Woman country, and remembers that this was considered the most beautiful part of their hunting grounds. It then looked to him far handsomer than it ever has since, and because of its prepossessing appearance he determined, when he started in the world with thoughts of settling down permanently in one place, to make this his home and final resting place.

After the Revolutionary War was over and peace established, Kennedy and his wife and the two children were delivered up at Detroit. The Indians had taken a great liking to John, and determined to keep him. He was adopted into the tribe, had learned their language, and almost lost his own.

Trained up as their little Indians were, he had fallen into their ways, and fell in love with their mode of life, so that he had no desire to return to the white settlements. He bore no marks of ill treatment, unless we except that the end of his nose had been bitten off by one of the Indians in a fight. In all their sports and games he took part, and was a worthy "boba-sheeby." Our old settlers, who recollect the "whoop" that Uncle John could give when so disposed, say that he surpassed the real Indian in that line. He has often spoken to us of the events of his captivity, and how he was for a time fascinated with their wild and roving life. He subsisted for days upon a little corn parched and pounded up, and used to affirm to us that he never relished any thing so well in his life as that simple food.

But he was not doomed to live always a savage life. His family determined to rescue him from their wiles and allurements. His brother-in-law, with several others, undertook this mission, and at length succeeded in getting him away from them while they were camped down on Detroit, not far from where Malden has since been built. He remained with Kennedy and his friends at Detroit some months. There was then a British Fort there, and the village was the smallest kind of a four-cornered place.

It is a satisfaction to know that several of the gang who captured Stilley and Kennedy's family were afterwards in one of their marauding expeditions overtaken by justice. The Poes met and killed them near the mouth of Yellow Creek. Stilley and his sister became conversant with this fact shortly after the occurrence from Indians concerned in that dreadful fight.

John Stilley with other prisoners retaken from the Indians, to the number of about ninety, embarked in a vessel at Detroit, and landed in Sandusky Bay, and hired two Indian pilots to guide them back to the settlements. When they got pretty near the Ohio river, they began to talk over their position, where they were from, and with sadness parted with each other, scattering in different directions, never more to meet. Some were from Kentucky, others from Virginia and Pennsylvania. But few of them crossed the river with Stilley into the edge of Allegheny county. Stilley says that he then passed through the Ko-ko-sing and White Woman country, and not a particle of improvement was discernible from the time he was first taken through it by the Indians.

After remaining in his native country a short time he became restless, and longed for a newer condition of things. His desire for adventure took him to the "dark and bloody ground." He went alone—a poor boy, but strong of heart, and with resolution indomitable. Alone, and in a light canoe of his own make, he navigated the rivers, and landed at the Limestone, about three miles from where the city of Maysville now stands. The only settlements then commenced on the Ohio river in his way were at Wheeling, Gallipolis, Marietta, and at the mouth of the Kanawha. These were all very small. He pushed his way into the interior of Kentucky, and voyaged along the waters of the Elkhorn, and was struck with the surprising beauty of the country, and the nobleness and generosity of the people with whom he fell in company, and there he sojourned for some time. "There was," he said, "a considerable settlement along the waters of the Elkhorn, and above and between Paris and Lexington more white people than I had ever seen before. Lexington I thought a mighty clever town. We could raise along the old Elk's horn quite a number of men to take a fight every now and then, and I felt that I was man enough for any of them in any way they were a mind to take me. I knew Simon Kenton personally and right intimately, and a mighty true man he was too. He then lived down, I think, sort of northwest of Paris. He did not live as high up as I did. He kept four minute men down there always ready. We kept watch fifty miles along the river for a while, and went back and forth twenty-five miles; I was one of them. I also knew Neal Washburn well, and I tell you he was a real brotherly feeling man. The Kentucky hunters were as good men as God ever made. They were the clear noblemen spit—all soul—all bravery—all generosity. Would to God there were more such in the world." * * * "I remained upon Elkhorn enjoying myself finely, farming a little, and hunting more, and wrestling and fighting, and all that, till the pesky Indians up in the Maumee country, and in the Miami, got to cutting up so intolerable bad that we couldn't stand it any longer—they were depredating and thieving, and murdering and scalping, and I got my blood up and concluded to try my aim on them, so I 'listed among the first in the country, and there was no better shot with a rifle among the crowd."

John Stilley served for four months as one of the Kentucky volunteers, and upon discharge of the company, by General Wayne, returned to the Elkhorn country. But he did not long remain quiet. Repeated acts of cruelty and inhumanity on the part of the savages and their worse than savage allies, again rendered it necessary for the Kentucky boys to shoulder their rifles and march into the enemy's country to avenge the wrongs of their countrymen. Stilley then served five months, and said he would like to have continued with old Mad Anthony the rest of his days, but the old hero said he did not require his services any longer. He returned to Kentucky and remained farming, hunting, and shooting at a mark, until the country, where he was, became too thickly settled for him to enjoy life there, and then he concluded to look up again the fine country which he had admired so much, when a boy, on the Ko-ko-sing.

He is found living in this county in 1806, making his location, building his log cabin, and settling down for the remainder of his term on earth. His wife, Rebecca, daughter of old Robert Thompson, the surveyor and pioneer, rests by his side beneath the soil of Knox county. The Stilley farm, west of Mount Vernon one mile, where their sons Morgan F. and Gilman B. and daughter Dorcas now live, was cleared off and first cultivated by Thompson and Stilley from 1805. Of John Stilley's twelve children—Sarah E., wife of Jacob Maxteller, is in this township; Julia Ann, wife of Col. Benjamin F. Smith, in Minnesota; Joel F. in this county, Rebecca Kimbal in Morrow county; Nancy, wife of Wm. McFarland, deceased, in Oquawka, Ill., and the others, not above named, are dead.

In our chapter upon the military of Knox county it will be seen that the bellicose spirit of John Stilley is made manifest. In the war with Great Britain he served as Adjutant of Col. Kratzer's Regiment, Ohio volunteers, until honorably discharged. He again entered the service when Fort Meigs was attacked by the British and Indians, and received another honorable discharge. We became conversant with the events in the life of this worthy old settler several years ago, when forwarding an application for a land warrant, which he desired mainly as evidencing an evidence of appreciation of his services and sufferings by his government, but the lamentable delays of officials in the great circumlocution departments at Washington prevented his receiving this just acknowledgment of his country's gratitude. On the 10th of March, 1852, he died of palsy, at his home, in Clinton township. His widow, after his death, received the tribute of a land warrant for 160 acres.

John Stilley was a true hearted, a brave man—ready, whenever occasion offered, to assert his rights and evidence his courage. He performed four tours of service, and under the most trying circumstances acquitted himself handsomely. He was a great admirer of General Wayne and General Harrison, and never grew tired of praising them. We might give many anecdotes and incidents connected with the life of this worthy old pioneer—who first walked upon the banks of Owl Creek, (Koo-koo-san he said it was pronounced by the tribe who captured him.) We have thought a chapter in the History of the county to be justly due to John Stilley—the old Adjutant—the old Commissioner—the old citizen who was proverbial for his honesty and integrity—and who possessed, at four score years, as good a memory, as sound judgment and irreproachable character as any man ever within the limits of Knox county.

CHAPTER X.

WHAT WAS DONE BY COURTS AND COMMISSIONERS IN THE YEARS 1811–12–13 AND 1814 THAT MAY BE OF INTEREST TO CITIZENS OF THE COUNTY.—COUNTY ROADS.—COUNTY BUILDINGS.—COUNTY REVENUE.—WHAT IT COST TO GUARD A PRISONER AND TO BURY A NEGRO IN 1812–14.—PRICES OF BARK AND RABBIT SKINS.—THE GLORIOUS FOURTH COMMEMORATED BY STRONG'S SETTLEMENT.

NINTH TERM OF COMMON PLEAS—JANUARY 1, 1811.

"*Grand Jury*—Charles Lofland, foreman, Thomas Beaty, Abraham Lyon, James Craig, Geo. Lybarger, Nathl. M. Young, J. Dunlap, John Morrison, Samuel Wilson, John Herrod, John Cook, James Herrod and James Cunningham.

"Indictments presented vs. Wm. Wallace, James Smith, Solomon Geller, John Stilley, John Barney, Francis Spratt, John Foglesong, Benj. Barney, Andrew Clark and Samuel Arbuckle.

"This term continued three days. The minutes show but one Jury Trial: The State of Ohio vs. Henry Smith for passing counterfeit money, and the Jury found him not guilty.

"Gilman Bryant was granted Licens to retail goods for 8 months, and Abner Ayres to keep a public house one year.

"An additional Justice of the Peace was added to the township of Clinton.

"The Indictments vs. Francis Spratt and Wm. Wallace were disposed of, each being fined $3 and costs."

TENTH TERM—29TH APRIL, 1811.

"*Grand Jury*—Isaac Bonnet, foreman, Charles Cooper, Robert Wright, John Hawn, Peter Bricker, Timothy Burr, Isaac Dial, Bartholomew Bartlet, Evan Holt, John Trimble, John Wheeler, James Miller, Oliver Strong.

"Indictments were presented vs. David Demmick, Sele Simpkins.

"John Stilley appears and pleads guilty to Indictment for assault and battery found vs. him at last Term, and is fined $4 and costs." The dignity of fighting is increased, and those who indulge in that luxury have to pay higher.

"Benjn. Barney, arraigned on charge of assault and battery, pleads not guilty, and on trial Jury so find.

"Andrew Clark, on indictment for same offence, is fined $4 and costs.

"John Barney stands a jury trial on his indictment, and is found not guilty.

"So also Samuel Arbuckle is acquitted.

"Licens is granted Benjn. Barney to keep publick house one year at Clinton.

"The case of Joseph Foos vs. Archibald Gardner is tried by a Jury, who find 'that Gardner was only to pay for the improvements done by Foos on the House.'

"Two suits were dismissed, two settled by the parties, and two judgments entered for small sums.

"John Sawyer is fined $2 and costs for not attending as a witness. This being the second fine of this character in the Common Pleas Court, the penalty is increased 100 per cent.

"Licenses to retail goods are granted to Wm. H. Selby & Isaac Vore, and Tavern license to Jno. Baxter & Amoriah Watson.

"George Sapp is appointed admr. of George Sapp, decd.; Danl. Sapp & John Greer, Securities."

ELEVENTH TERM—9TH OF SEPT., 1811.

"*Grand Jury.*—William Gass, Jabez Beers, Joseph Coleman, Casper Fitting, Abraham Darling, Jacob Young, John Green, Henry Ankeny, James Bryant, Charles Lofland, John Wheeler, David Johnson, Jonathan Hunt, Jr.

"Indictments found vs. Sele Simpkins, Thos. McBride, Benj. Rush, Francis Wilkins, John Davis, James Walker, Jr. and James Smith.

Four Jury causes came off, to wit; Andrew Craig vs. Henry McCurb & James Cunningham, Trespass on the case; Wm. W.

Farquhar vs. James Craig, for debt; The State of Ohio vs. Sele Simpkins, for felony; and James Smith vs. Samuel H. Smith, assumpsit.

"The Prosecuting Attorney entered 'nolle' on Indictment vs. James Smith for not making Election returns to Fairfield C.

"The State vs. Francis Wilkins. Defendant was fined $1 for assault and battery.

"Eleven other causes were disposed of—mainly dismissed at costs of Pltff.

"John Green, Esq., of the Methodist Church, is licensed to marry people so disposed.

"Henry Markley was allowed $53.37½ for sevices as Commissioner.

"Matthew Merrit was allowed $1.75 for services as Commissioner.

"Robert McMillen was allowed $36.75 for sevices as Commissioner.

"License to keep public house was granted for one year to Michael Click, John Jones, Jesse Procter, Daniel Ayers, Daniel Demmick.

"Store License was granted to Gilman Bryant, Benjn. Rush, Saml. H. Smith.

"On the return of John Heckewelder, John McConnel and Moses Koss, Esquires, who were appointed by a Joint Ballot of both Houses of the Legislature of the State of Ohio to fix the seats of Justice in the Counties of Wayne and Richland in the State aforesaid, which passed the 28th of March, 1803, who did report for the seat of Justice in Richland county aforesaid to be affixed at the town of Mansfield. Signed the 20th day of April, 1809."

Settlement with the Commissioners of Knox County, to wit: Expenditures from Sept. Term, 1810:

Paid out to different collectors	$62 17.5
" for wolf scalps	12 00
" for Grand Juries	52 75
" for Pettit Judges in State prosecutions	20 20
" for Witnesses fees in same	88 15
" Sheriff for his services	65 50
" Coroner " "	4 00

Paid Jas. Smith, as Clerk to Com. Pleas and Comr......	$89	95½
" Public Buildings..............................	111	87.5
" accommodation of Courts.......................	5	50
" Edwd. Herrick, Esq., as Prosecuting Attorney ...	100	00
" expences of Roads, &c.........................	49	27.5
" Treasurer	20	59
" Associate Judges..............................	60	00
" locating County and Townships.................	63	50
" out for elections	35	50
" James Smith 25 dollars for books.		
	$840	97

Amount received by Treasurer to same date:

Received by fines and license...............	$123	38½	
" County levy for year 1810, C T'nship	113	32	
" " " " Union "	79	30	
" " " " Morgan "	54	30	
" " " " Wayne "	62	88½	
" " " " Madison "	15	92½	
" State Tax for Morgan.............	80	89¾	
" " Wayne............	90	33¾	
" " Union	30	25	
" " Clinton............	161	44	1 mill.
" " State Treasurer	117	66	
" " Walker & Slater's land	4	25	
" State Tax for 1809	117	00	
	$1050	95	1 mill.

TWELFTH TERM—JANY. 6TH, 1812.

"*Grand Jury.*—Charles Lofland, foreman, Joseph Walker, Alexander Enos, Saml. H. Smith, John Stilley, Ziba Leonard, John Baxter, Moses Craig, John Spratt, Benj. Currin, James Craig, Andrew Craig, Solomon Geller."

This vacation had proven fruitful of knock-downs, as we may judge from bills for assault and battery being found vs. George Lybarger, Henry Ankeny, Samuel W. Culberson, Joseph Dunlap, John Strain, Benjamin Rush, John Foglesong.

Culberson was fined 6 cents and costs; Lybarger, $3; Ankeny, $5; John Foglesong, the unprecedented sum of $50 and costs. A jury in the State vs. John Davis found him guilty to the tune of $20 and costs.

Daniel Demmick is fined $1 and costs for retailing spirituous liquors without license.

The solitary civil jury trial resulted in Henry Smith obtaining a judgment of $8.12½ against Oliver Strong.

There is an increasing demand for marrying officers, and we find License issued to Elisha Bowman and James Smith of the Methodist Church.

George Coffinberry renews his Tavern License for Mansfield, and James McClure is also Licensed to entertain the publick.

Jos. Talmage is allowed $2.25 for taking the enumeration, &c.

THIRTEENTH TERM—4TH MAY, 1812.

"*Grand Jury.*—Isaac Bonnet, foreman, Wm. Marquis, Solomon Geller, Benj. Corwin, Thos. McKee, John Stilley, Matthew Merritt, John Hawn, Ziba Leonard, Chas. Cooper, H. Ankeny, Chas. Lofland and Joseph Berry.

"Bills were found vs. Joseph Walker and James Craig, William Walker, Elizabeth Walker.

"Two causes were tried by jury—Hiram Ball vs. Alexander Enos; verdict for defendant for costs; and The State vs. Elizabeth Walker; verdict not guilty.

"On Indictment for an affray, Joseph Walker is fined $1 and costs; and William Walker is fined for an assault and battery $3 and costs.

The following order appears upon the court minutes which "old settlers" may understand:

"*Ordered,* that James Walker, jr., deliver up to Benoni Gardner his daughter, Nancy, with her clothing.

"Store license issued to Isaac Vore, and tavern license to Azariah Davis, John Baxter and N. C. Boles.

"Eight judgments are entered up for sums varying from $2.07½ to $18.66

"*Luke Walpole* vs. *Ichabod Nye, Sheriff.*—The Sheriff is

amerced for $6, received from Wm. Wallace and not paid over. This is the *first amercement case on record in Knox county.*

FOURTEENTH TERM—14TH SEPTEMBER, 1812.

"License to retail goods was granted to John Garrison, and tavern license to Daniel Ayres.

"Court remained in session but a few hours. The following entry shows the cause: No venire for Grand or Petit jury returned in consequence of a *National calamity.* Ordered that the court do adjourn until the next court in course.

WILLIAM WILSON."

FIFTEENTH TERM—11TH JANUARY, 1813.

"*Grand Jury.*—Wm. Mitchel, foreman, Wm. Davis, Jacob Young, Henry Markley, Wm. Knight, Peter Kinry, Henry Haines, John Murphy, Cornelius Vanosdolle, John Shrinplin, John Harrod, James Craig, Oliver Strong.

"Indictments found vs. John Jackson and Michael Click, Jos. Middleton, Wm. Stansbery, Leonard H. Coales.

"There were three trials by jury—Henry Smith vs. Allison Strong; verdict for pltff. $12 and costs; Eleazer Morely vs. Alex. Enos, for pltff. $56.37 and costs; Platt & Harrison vs. Enos, for pltff. $40.80.

"Store license issued to Enoch Harriss, Richard Fishback, Gilman Bryant.

"Tavern license issued to John Davidson on payment of $6 for one year, Richard Fishback, Amos H. Royce, Stephen Stilwell.

Not a single State case was tried. The presumption is that the fighting men had gone to the war!

SIXTEENTH TERM—5TH SEPTEMBER, 1813.

"*Grand Jury.*—Isaac Bonnet, foreman, James Loveridge, Solomon Geller, John Kerr, Philip Melker, Benj. Corwin, Thos. McKee, Jacob Hauger, John Dunlap, Wm. Marquis, Joseph Walker, Isaac Bean, W. H. Selby.

"Four bills were found for usual offenses. These and several other Indictments quashed for want of form. This Court continued in session three days. There were three jury trials, and many old cases on the docket were disposed of.

"Wm. C. Enos is appointed Master Commissioner in Chancery.

" Robt. McMillen allowed 8 days, $14, for Commissioner services.

Daniel Cooper	" 5 "	8.75,	"	"
John Harrod	"	5.25,	"	"

" Store license was granted to Anthony Banning, Stephen Butler, S. H. Smith.

" License to marry was granted to John Green and James Smith, regular ordained ministers in the Religious United Societies or Christian Church.

SEVENTEENTH TERM—10TH JANUARY, 1814.

" *Grand Jurors.*—Isaac Vore, foreman, John Davis, Abraham Caimes, John Grear, Nathaniel M. Young, Moses Merrit, Evan Holt, John Stilley, John Johnson, Jabez Beers, Philip Melker, James Low, A. H. Royce, John Spratt.

" Five jury causes are tried.

" License to marry is issued to Amos Mix of the Baptist persuasion.

" License to retail goods is issued to Eli Miller, Richard Fishback, L. S. Silliman.

" C. K. Sherman is appointed Prosecuting Atto. for this co.

" Letters of administration are issued on estates of Isaac Jackson, Benj. Simpkins, Joseph Sieberson, Joseph King and Anny Woodruff.

Our old townsman, Gilman Bryant, seems to figure about these times as general appraiser.

" James Smith, Clerk of the Court of Common Pleas and Clerk of the Supreme Court for the county of Knox, appoints Alexander Ellioitt Deputy in either Court, Feb. 24, 1814.

EIGHTEENTH TERM—9TH OF MAY, 1814.

" *Grand Jury.*—Isaac Vore, jr., foreman, John Wilson, Joseph Walker, John Bean, George Low, Matthew Merrit, Isaac Bonnet, John Bricker, David Ash, Joseph Higgins, Jesse Severe and Anthony Banning.

" Four trials by jury.

" Samuel Kratzer, Esq., appointed Master Commissioner in Chancery.

" License issued to James Smith, John Green, to retail goods, and to N. C. Bowles to keep tavern.

NINETEENTH TERM—11TH AUGUST, 1814.

"*Grand Jurors.*—Azariah Davis, Benj. Brown, Bartholomew Bartlet, Ebenezer Brown, Wm. Downs, Thomas Ireland, Wm. Henry, Jacob Rabb, David Johnson, Jonathan Hunt, jr., John Garrison, Isaac Coen, James Harrod, John Kerr, John Mills, foreman.

"Upon bills of Indictment for assault and battery, James Adams and Wm. Mefford were fined $3, each, and costs; James Martin $10 and costs, Charles Lofland was also fined $5 and costs, and Samuel Baxter $10 and costs, and Thos. Prather $3 and costs.

"Four trials by jury.

"John Harrod as Commissioner allowed $22.75, Robt. McMillen $29.75, Daniel Cooper $26.25, Wm. Mitchell $5.25.

"License issued to John Fuller, of Christian Church, to marry. L. H. Smith, Benj. Barney and Ichabod Marshal, Ex'rs. of Richard Fishback, deceased; and Gilman Bryant, Daniel Cooper and Timothy Burr, appraisers.

TWENTIETH TERM—22ND DECEMBER, 1814.

"*Grand Jury.*—John Trimble, foreman, Thomas Axtell, Henry Markley, Jas. McCracken, Samuel Newell, Sam'l Johnson, Cornelius Vanosdall, John Adams, John Irvine, Nath. M. Young, David Johnson, Jacob Cooper, L. H. Smith.

"License to vend goods issued to Anthony Banning, Gilman Bryant, John Garrison, Eli Miller, L. S. Silliman.

"License to keep tavern issued to Jacob Nixon, Amos H. Royce, Abner Ayres, Wm. Van Horne.

We have given the Court transactions for twenty terms as much for the purpose of letting the present generation know who, in those early days, performed service as Jurors and otherwise, as with the view of giving an account of what was done. By reading over these pages the names of many settlers will be known whom otherwise we could not find had lived upon our soil.

THE FINANCES IN 1812-13-14, AND THE FIRST SALE OF LAND FOR TAXES—1812, 3D JUNE.

" At settlement with the Treasurer.

Dr. Treasurer—

Amount of Land Tax 1811	$523 76.7
do —	20 36.2
Duplicate for Wayne 1811	73 22
do Madison "	35 5
do Union	91 50
do Morgan	60 80
do Clinton	204 62.5
Wolf scalps	32 00
Gilman Bryant, license	6 66.5
Am't of license, permits and fines received	81 09.5
	1129 8.6

By amount of County orders received...	$10 79.7½
do do do ...	1079 73
do do do ...	59 42 ½
	1149 95
	1129 8.6
At settlement balance due Treasurer.	$20 86.4

" Treasurer pay Henry Haines $45 19.4, for his commission on revenue Taxes 1811; for traveling trip to Zanesville $5.

" At settlement with the Treasurer June 8th, 1813.

Treasurer Dr. for—

Tavern license	$91 32
do do	12 49½
Richland duplicate	64 25
Duplicate for Clinton	135 53½
do Morgan	79 80
do Wayne	74 32
do Chester	20 30
do Union	90 60
do Morris	47 36
do on duplicate now due	502 54.6
Daniel Demmich	4
Butler's license	30
	1122 82.6

Cr. by	orders produced and delivered	$1076 45
"	your com. per centum	44 39
"	traveling fees	5
		1125 84

Cr. the Treasurer on settlement $3.01.

James Berry, Collector 4th District. Collector's office, Zanesville, 17th Dec., 1813, received $359 23, the full amount of the Resident Land Tax of Knox county, of John Green, Collector.

9th June, 1814—At settlement with Treasurer of Knox co.

Treasurer Dr.—

For license taverns and stores	$103 58⅛
Cash rec'd of collector of non-residents on land for 1813	451 70
County, as paid by collector, for C. Levy for 1813	405 16
	960 44⅛

Cr. by	orders paid in	$923 00.7.5
"	treasurer's fees	38 41
"	traveling fees to Zanesville	5
		966 41.7.5

Balance due to Treasurer on settlements the sum of $5 97.5, as per order number 1251."

"July 5, 1814. The Board this day examine the duplicates for County Levy for the Township agreeable to the return of the listers of Townships as follows:

Morgan Township		$83 10
Union	do	104 07.5
Morris	do	73 40
Chester	do	31 50
Wayne	do	93 61
Clinton	do	140 96
		526 64.5

"Collector Green collected all on these lists and $2.58 more in Clinton township, than listed

"The first lands sold for Taxes were in January 12th, 1815, when collector John Green sold for Abram Emmett 2-8 of lot 120 north side taxes and costs—75; and ¾ of lot 34 south side—75. Isaac Vore, jr., ¼ of lot 19 south side, and ¼ of 20 north side—for 75 each.

"Parts of lots belonging to John Hawn, jr., James Smith, (Skenk's creek) Nathan Majors, Ichabod Nye, John Marquis and Wm. Marquis, jr., for which he charged for deeds and acknowledgments $1.25."

ITEMS SUGGESTIVE FROM COMMISSIONERS' JOURNALS OF 1811–12–13–14.

Among the bills audited by the Commissioners in 1811, we find one to John Butler $4, for extra services in summoning jurors and witnesses for May Term; Nicholas Kyle $3, for use of their house for third Court, Sept. 1811; Ichabod Nye, sheriff's fees in criminal cases, 1811, $25; Associate Judges James Colville $18, W. W. Farquhar $21, John Mills $21; Edward Herrick for Prosecuting Attorney two terms, and at Supreme Court also, $9.75. A pretty cheap attorney's fee!

Order No. 626 issues to Ichabod Marshal 75 cts. for gaging a half bushel for the County standard, and 627 to James Walker for making seal for standard for Knox county.

Timothy Burr appeared and gave bond as Coroner, with Gilman Bryant and Robert Jones as sureties. Ichabod Nye gave bond as Sheriff, with John Hawn and Richard Fishback as sureties.

1812, January. Wm. Roberts, deputy coroner, is paid $4.45 "for viewing a dead body, for drawing the necessary writing in the same, for traveling, venire," &c. James Bryant for taking care of the dead body $5.

"Ordered that one acre of land be taken off Morgan township and added to Clinton, which acre was purchased of Martin Cosner by Silas Brown, in range 12, township 6."

"The Overseers of the Poor is directed to seize and sell the property of a *negro* called Wm. Jackson."

The Commissioners held their meetings at different places as the following orders show:

"To John Jones 50 cents for house rent last meeting." "To —— Ash 75 cents for same this meeting."

A *new court house* is being erected, and the Journals state that

"Solomon Geller and George Downs did receive by subscriptions $745."

On the 10th of April, 1812, the following entry is made:

"The Commissioners this day did examine the court house built by George Downs and Geller, and do receive the same."

No sooner is the new court house ready for use than the Commissioners become involved in trouble about its occupancy, by different sects, as will be explained by the following entries on the Journal:

"Whereas, a number of the inhabitants of this county has made application for the use of the court house in Mount Vernon, for the purpose of occupying the same for preaching and holding public worship therein; it is, therefore, ordered that the different denominations of christians are allowed to occupy the same for the aforesaid purpose provided that each denomination shall have the use of the same for one meeting once in four weeks; provided also, that the different denominations aforesaid shall meet and mutually agree upon the time or times they shall hold the same, which shall be in force for one year unless they do not agree on the times they shall hold their meetings aforesaid, and each denomination failing to clean up the house and have the same in as good repair as they found it within three days, it shall forfeit their privilege aforesaid, and shall at all times be liable to make good all damages done by such denomination at their meetings aforesaid; and James Smith shall keep the key of the house aforesaid; it is further provided, that each denomination aforesaid shall furnish the said house with at least fifty feet of good strong Benches for the use of the house aforesaid, which shall be left there for the use of all publick business which shall be necessary previous to such denomination occupying the said house for the purpose aforesaid."

Eminently catholic and practical—especially the Bench part!

The brethren could not occupy together in unity, and accordingly the Commissioners on the 8th of June, 1813, pass this resolution:

"*Resolved,* That the court house, from this date, be closed and kept lockt from all denominations except courts."

This brought about a cessation of hostilities, and again petitions poured in for use of the court house agreeing to agree as to time of using it, &c. Thereupon Commissioners Herrod, Cooper and McMillen, on the 22d of June, meet for the special purpose of ordering

"That the court house be opened as formerly by and under the same rules as formerly."

One great difficulty was that the Methodists were unwilling to let the "New Lights," who had split off from them, come in under the order as first made. These were times fraught with great peril to the churches, as elsewhere recorded.

The following order appears: "Treasurer pay to George Davis 75 cents for being accommodating with load of wood for the court."

John Lee is paid $2 for riding with returns of Senatorial election of 1812 to Newark. John Shrimplin endeavors to get a road from his mill, which Wm. Darling, James Rightwire and John Green report as not of public utility, and the petition is rejected. Stephen Stilwell is taxed fourfold for refusing to give in four horses to the lister for taxation, and Amos Yarnard is also taxed fourfold upon one horse. Samuel Kratzer is allowed $1.62½ for iron for the jail, and Archibald Crofford $4.75 for iron and labor done on the jail. The rate of taxation on taverns in 1812 is $8 for all located on Market st., Mount Vernon, all others on other streets of Mount Vernon and on road from Mount Vernon to Newark and in Fredericktown $7, and all others in the county $6.

In 1814, July, Francis Hardista is taxed fourfold for refusing to return seven head of cattle to the lister. G. Downs and J. Martin are allowed $80 for shutters for court house. And the court house, but recently erected, is found to need alteration and repairs, so Solomon Geller purchased the job of making certain repairs for $799.70. The county, at this time, seems to have had a troublesome prisoner, as the following payments were made for standing guard over the prisoner, Beldon:

"Calvin Hill 3 nights, $1.50; Wm. Dehart 10 nights and one day, $5.50; Henry Burge for 9 nights and one day, $5; James Irvine 19 nights and one day, $10; John Cramer 13 nights and one day, $7; Thomas Sprague one night, $1; Samuel Kratzer for guarding, $7.50; Jacob Woodruff, $14.75; Samuel Breese, constable, .95; Michael Click for trailing after prisoner Beldon, $1; Eli Gregg $1 for aiding in committing A. Beldon to jail, and Wm. Dehart for trailing after Beldon, $3."

Thus the snug little sum of $58.20 was expended in guarding, because Mike Click had convinced the people that, as he said, the "jail is not worth one tam!"

VARIOUS NOVEL ITEMS AND ADVERTISEMENTS OF THESE TIMES.

"FRIENDLY ADVICE !!

"The person who made so free as to *borrow* my AXE without my liberty, is *respectfully solicited* to return it immediately—otherwise, he will find his *Axe*, like the Indian's GUN, *to cost more than it comes to*. He can either leave it himself or by *proxy* at my wood-pile. T. BURR.

March 1, 1813."

Oak bark for tanning was worth in April 1813, at Clinton, $2.50 per cord. Samuel H. Smith was then carrying on a tanyard there.

A concert was held at Mt. Vernon, in the court house, May 6th, at 10 o'clock, P. M., under direction of M. D. Lewis, of different singing societies in the county. "All those who feel willing to participate with us are earnestly solicited to attend."

May 3d. James Smith's Vindication is now published, and offered for sale at Clinton and Mount Vernon—"for resisting the ecclesiastical power and authority of their Episcopal dignity, *Michael Ellis* and *David Young*."

"TO WHOM IT MAY CONCERN.

"This may certify that I was present when Mr. *Isaac Beam* examined a trunk and bundle belonging to POLLY McCRACKEN, for table cloths, but found nothing resembling such in either trunk or bundle. T. BURR.

May 3, 1814."

George Paul, Col. 27th Infantry, was appointed, by Maj. General Harrison, to take command of the recruiting service for the 27th Reg't., and established his office at Zanesville, March, 1814.

"Samuel H. Smith having added a large stock of goods to his former assortment, will trade for butter, sugar, country linen, rye, corn, hides, deer skins and furs. Doct. T. Burr is duly authorized to attend to his business, and will prescribe GRATIS to purchasers of drugs and medicines, &c.

December, 1813."

John H. Piatt, of Cincinnati, advertises, April 4th, 1814, for 5,000 barrels flour, and 200 barrels whisky delivered at Fort Meigs, "or at any convenient place on the Lake shore to save transportation by land."

Samuel H. Smith gave 75 cents per dozen or 96 cents in fine hats, for Rabbit skins.

GRAND CELEBRATION OF FREEDOM'S BIRTH-DAY, 1814.

On the morning of the 4th of July the flag of the United States was hoisted near Mr. Zebulon Ashley's dwelling house, on a liberty pole 68 feet in length, and the day was celebrated by a respectable number of the citizens of *Strong's* settlement and its vicinity. After an elegant dinner 18 *toasts* were drank, accompanied with the discharge of musketry. From the number we extract the following:

"*The President of the United States,* prefers republican principles to British tyranny—May the Constitution be his life guard.

"*The American Sword,* which is drawn in defense of our country—May it never be returned till it has pierced the heart of our enemy.

"*Perry and his brave crew on Lake Erie*—May they ever be victorious while their swords are drawn in defense of America.

"*The United States of America*—May they ever be too independent to be governed by any other nation.

"Success to the American Eagle, not forgetting Great Britain, hoping its kingdom may be brought down."

The others alike partake of the warlike spirit engendered by the war, and breathe hate and defiance to the foe.

CHAPTER XI.

THE ECCENTRIC CHAPTER IN OUR EARLY HISTORY—BEING ALL THAT IS KNOWN OF THE HISTORY OF JOHNNY APPLESEED.

AN original character flourished in this part of the country at an early day, who was always conspicuous in times of excitement and danger, and his vigilant care of the early settlers entitles him to a tribute at our hands. The *sobriquet* of Johnny Appleseed attached to him, though his real name was Chapman, in consequence of his being ever engaged in gathering and planting appleseed and cultivating nurseries of apple trees. Many of the earliest settlers recognized in him an old acquaintance, who had wandered about for years along the streams of western Pennsylvania, engaged in the same pursuit and preparing the way for those who might follow upon his trail to have their own orchards.

He would find suitable spots of ground along the banks of creeks and rivers, in which to make small clearings, and there he would plant the seed he had gathered, fence in the ground, and then leave it to germinate and grow in coming years into fine nurseries, which he would have in readiness for the coming settlements. He would make just as many nurseries as he could get seed to plant, and he never lost any time in gathering and preparing for the future. He did not restrict his operations to the settled portions of the country, but went into the wilderness regions and among the Indians and wild beasts, having his trust in God and fearing no harm.

In personal appearance he was prepossessing, when one could get sight of his eyes and well formed head; about medium height, quick and restless and uneasy in his motions, and exceedingly uncouth in dress. In truth he cared not what he wore, nor who before him might have worn the garment upon his back—whether it was too large or too small for his person. The greater part of his traffic with the world was in exchanging his trees, at a nominal price, for old worn out clothes. He incased his person, at all times, in what might be called thrown away garments. For covering to the head he was not particular whether he wore an animal's skin, a cloth, or tin case. He has been seen with head gear of each kind, and without foot apparel of any description. For a time, after the war, he wore an old military chapeau, which some officer had given him, and thus accoutred he came suddenly upon a dutchman, who had just moved into the country, and scared him most to death as he stood in his bare feet with "one tam muscle shell cocked on his head." The sides were ripped, and as it flopped in the wind—on a head covered with long black hair, a face with a long beard and dark black eyes peering out from the vast undergrowth, and a body enveloped in a coffee sack with

9

a hole through which he had run his head, it was enough to frighten any honest dutchman almost out of his wits.

He lived the roughest kind of a life—slept the greater part of the time in the woods—by the side of logs—and on the bare ground. He was harmless and inoffensive—always striving to save the feelings of mankind and of the brute creation. Very many anecdotes are remembered characteristic of Johnny Appleseed. The following show the native goodness of his heart: One night he built his camp fire at the end of a hollow log, in which he intended to pass the night, but as a bear and her cubs had a pre-emption claim to the hole in the tree, he moved his fire to another spot and slept all night on the snow, exposed to the storm, rather than disturb the varmints. Another time, when he had a camp-fire near the creek where the musquitoes were very bad and flew into the blaze and were consumed, he took off his tin head gear, filled it with water, and put out the fire, saying, "God forbid, that I should build a fire for my own comfort that should be the cause of destroying any of his other created works." And still another is that one morning he was bitten by a rattlesnake, and some time after he related the circumstances with tears in his eyes as he said "poor fellow! he only just touched me, when in an ungodly passion I put the heel of my scythe on him and killed him."

He had the following told at the expense of his bare feet, which had become hardened beyond belief by long usage "out of doors" and exposure to the cold. At one time he crossed Lake Erie on the ice barefooted, and when night overtook him—the man traveling in company with him was frozen to death—but old Johnny, by rolling about on the ice, kept warm, and in aftertimes was none the worse for it.

An old citizen of Mansfield vouches for the following: A traveling preacher was at one time holding forth on the scriptures in the public square, to a miscellaneous audience, when he exclaimed, "where is the barefooted christian traveling to heaven?" Johnny Appleseed was among the auditors, laying flat on his back on a piece of timber, and he stuck his bare feet high in the air and cried out "*here he is!*"

This artless child of nature was a man of much intelligence, and in his day and generation, much as he was hooted at and derided by the scoffers and jibers of the country, yet did he in his life time perform far more of good than they all did. If it is true, as claimed, that he who causeth a single blade of grass to grow, or plants a single shade tree, is a public benefactor, how much greater is the meed of praise due to poor old Johnny Appleseed, who caused thousands of fruit bearing trees to grow, and hundreds of orchards to blossom and bear fruit for the people. What lasting obligations are we not under to him here in Knox county—in all central Ohio—in western Pennsylvania—in northern Indiana—and of a verity in all the "Great West," for our present most excellent fruits. God preserve his memory! To help perpetuate it we have devoted this Chapter in our History—to be read by many whose parents and relatives would have fallen victims to the relentless hate of the savage had Johnny Appleseed not have traveled from settlement to settlement along the Mohican, Owl Creek, the White Woman, the Muskingum, the Tuscarawas, and other water courses, notifying the families of the pioneers of the approach of danger. Much, very much, may also be due this man of peace, this child of nature, for his kind offices among the children of nature in turning their hearts from wrath and averting their purposes of destruction. Reader—think of these things. Native Owl Creeker ponder over them and cherish the memory of good old *Johnny Appleseed.*

The promises he made he faithfully redeemed. Among other evidences of his keeping his word, we have the following:

In 1819, Isaiah Roberts, then on his way to Missouri, finding no boat at Zanesville ready to start on the trip down the river, footed it to Marietta, and on the road met with Johnny Appleseed, who promised to call at his fathers in Knox county, and tell him where he parted with him, etc. Shortly after, Johnny made his appearance one night about dark, and was cheerfully received. He then had an old tattered coat and slouched hat, with hair and beard uncut and uncombed, and barefooted. After eating some supper, he espied a copy of "Ballou on Atonement," which he took and read for some time by candle-light, thinking at first it was good Swedenborg doctrine, and desired to take it with him; but after he read further, and found the kind of doctrine it inculcated, he threw it down indignantly, expressing his disappointment, and in a few moments after stretched himself out, and went to sleep.

Johnny Appleseed sometimes clipped his beard with scissors, but never used a razor. His nurseries, near Mount Vernon, were located at the following places: One in the then called Indian Fields, on the north bank of Owl Creek, directly west of Center Run, and another on the ground where James W. Forrest established his pottery, and known more recently as Rich's pottery.

The last time he was in this country, he took Joseph Mahaffey and pointed out to him two lots of land, at the lower end of Main street, west side, about where Morey's soap factory was carried on, which he said belonged to him, and sometime he might come back to them. The tail-race of the Clinton Mill Company passed along there, and some of the ground has since been washed away by the water, and upon another portion stands the Mount Vernon Woolen Factory building. He has not been seen about here since 1829; but many a stray apple-tree that has been found upon the borders of our streams, marked the spots where the barefooted pilgrim had marked his way.

In 1837, the Rev. John Mitchell, when traveling on the Plymouth Circuit, met him traveling along the road on foot and in his shirt sleeves, as contentedly as a prince. He told him then that he lived "out west."

Johnny Appleseed in religious belief was called a Swedenborgian; in truth, he was of the primitive Christian style, taking little thought for the morrow, satisfied that God would provide for his people, living in meekness and humility, and walking uprightly. He had his peculiarities—who have them not? He had his frailties—who is clear of them? No wonder the Indians liked him. They could read his character at a glance. All was revealed by his eye, clear as the sunlight of God. He was without selfishness; he sought not to intrigue with or cheat them—he would do them no wrong. He put confidence in their honor, and they never would do him wrong. Many and many a time has that faithful old hermit traveled through the settlements on foot and alone, putting his countrymen on their guard. Often have we been told of these trips by those who have passed and now are passing away. Of him it was strictly and literally true, as sung by the poet:

> "Man wants but little here below,
> Nor wants that little long."

A few apple-seeds—a few sprouts—a few old books to read, and life to him was full of happiness. He had been favored with education, men knew from his knowledge of books, and his desire to read and have others read induced him at times to distribute Swedenborg's books, and when he had not enough to go around the company he would tear them in pieces, and give a part to each. Nothing more was known of his early days. It was said that he was from Connecticut—a stray Yankee—who wandered off from the fold into these wilds, but no one knew for certain as to who he was, where he came from, or what became of him. We will give, however, to such as feel an interest in his history all that we have been able to gather of his later years.

Having disposed of many of his nurseries, and having others destroyed in part, which had began to grow from fourteen bushels of apple-seed last planted by him on Owl Creek, the Black Fork of Mohican, and the Whetstone, he concluded to migrate farther west, and managing to get an old mare or two loaded with seeds, he left this part of the country for Sandusky prairie; and from thence made his way west,* planting nurseries, and living after the manner he did here, till finally the old fruit ripened, and was gathered near Fort Wayne, Indiana, leaving nothing save the fragrance of good deeds and charitable acts to teach the future that such a being as Johnny Appleseed had ever been and passed like an exhalation—the moisture of the morning's dew dried up by the heat of the sun at meridian!

---

* NOTE. Silas Mitchell informs us since the above was written that in the fall of 1843, when living in Whiteside's county, Illinois, Johnny Appleseed passed through that county on foot, and stopped all night with Aaron Jackson, son of Ziba, and left in the morning, stating that he was then from the Iowa prairies on his way to a Swendenborg Convention in Philadelphia.

CHAPTER XII.

KNOX COUNTY DURING THE WAR.—POPULATION PRETTY MUCH AT A STAND STILL.—EVENTS.—VOLUNTEERS, &C.—SOME INCIDENTS OF A MORE STIRRING CHARACTER.—A TOUCH OF INDIAN WARFARE.—FORTS AND BLOCKHOUSES ERECTED TO SAVE LIVES AND SCALPS.

THE settlements in Knox county being upon the borders, it may be presumed that the news of the declaration of war in 1812, and the threatening aspect of affairs kept our citizens wide awake and active. The Indians at that time were far more numerous upon Owl Creek, Mohican and in all parts of this country than the whites, and they required the closest kind of watching to keep them from depredating, killing and scalping the people. North of our present county line, the settlers were few and far between, and the county of Richland at that time made its returns to, and for judicial and other purposes was a part of, Knox. Hence within our borders, we may say, were enacted some of the deadliest scenes of slaughter. The killing of the Seymours and Rufner, and the massacre at Copuses are within the recollection of many of our oldest citizens. From several of those who were at the time familiar with these horrid murders we have obtained full statements, but as from the termination of the war, and the organization of Richland to the present, the scenes where the tragedies were enacted have belonged to our sister county, we will not go into detail in regard to them.

The people clustered together more closely than formerly, and at once made calculations for succor and plans for defence from the savage foe. A block-house was constructed at Frederick, and surrounded with pickets. After the war the building was converted into a school house. It was a frame, built on the square under direction of Captain Ayers, and moved on wheels to a point near where the railroad now runs. It was used for church and educational purposes for many years. Many families went to the fort at Frederick for safety. William Mitchell prepared his house for a siege—made heavy batten doors with iron bars, port holes for guns, etc. One of his boys rode express, another kept out with scouting parties, and the old man with two workmen, who staid with him, were constantly on the look out for attack. The girls practiced shooting with rifles, so as to be ready for a large force of Indians at any time, and with his two dogs, "Gunner" and "Rover," that two story log house was prepared for one fight at least.

At John Lewis' was erected a blockhouse, where that neighborhood could defend themselves.

Upon the tax duplicate of Madison township, for the year 1811, is found the names of "James Copus, 4 cattle, 40 cents;" "Philip Zeamore, 1 horse, 30 cents," and "Frederick Zeamore, 2 horses and 2 cattle, 80 cents," as returned to the commissioners of our county.

These men were among the victims of Indian barbarity in the commencement of this war. The

Seymour's lived on the Rocky or crooked fork of the Mohican, a little stream which headed above Mansfield. They were plain, simple minded people, who had been cultivating a small patch of ground and making slow but sure improvements on their location. Their nearest neighbor was a dutchman named Martin Rufner, who lived in a little cabin with only a small dutch boy. The Seymour family consisted of Frederick and his wife, and their children Philip and Catharine. One night four Indians were seen about dark prowling around the neighborhood of Seymour's house, and Rufner went to their house and urged Philip to go over to Mr. Copus and get help from there to capture them. No sooner had he started than the Indians entered the front door, when they were received in a friendly manner, and Catharine at once prepared supper for them, but the Indians instead of eating at once set upon the household and proceeded to kill and scalp them. Rufner was a very strong man and fought like a tiger, but he was soon overpowered, killed by two balls through his body, and left scalped in the yard and with several of his fingers cut off by a tomahawk. The father, mother and daughter were killed and scalped. In a few days after this an attack was made by a party of Indians upon the cabins of Mr. Copus, who lived at the Black fort. Some men belonging to a scouting party were at the time stopping at his house, and four of them had gone to a spring a few rods off to wash, when they were fired upon by the Indians who were hidden from view. Three of the men were killed and the fourth escaped into the house with a bullet in his thigh. Mr. Copus, when in the act of looking out the door to see what was the affray, was shot in the breast, and the door was at once closed, and a vigorous resistance made to the attack of the savages, who came on with terrific yells and a volley of balls. The daughter of Mr. Copus was shot in the thigh, and herself and mother for safety stowed away in the cabin loft. One of the men had his arm broken by a ball, and the house was completely riddled by bullets. Several of the Indians were killed, and at length, after an hour's hard fighting, they withdrew from the field.

The particulars of the Seymour massacre, we have got from a Knox county man who was near the scene, and saw the place where the hellish deed was committed the next day. William and Richard Roberts had been for some time engaged building a mill for Andrew Newman, within one mile and a half of Seymour's. The night they were killed the dog kept up such a disturbance that Newman aroused those in the house, telling them "by shure Indians about, I know py my tog"—the Indians were then always uppermost in the thoughts. The guns were got in readiness—a man named Shere helped load them as Newman cried out "by shure I shall spill all my powder, I can't load the gun"—and the score axes were also laid hold of, expecting an attack. There was no sleep for that night, and early in the morning word was got from Mr. Hill's, a neighbor, that Seymour's family was killed. Upon examination about where the forebay had just been raised, several moccasin tracks were discovered, and the evidence was clear that the Indians had meditated an attack there, but feared they were too strong for them to succeed. During the night howling as of wolves had been heard about where the race and dam had been dug. There were but the four men at Newman's. Within an hour from the time of hearing of the massacre, Newman got up his team and took all of his tricks to Mansfield. William Roberts at once rode around to Seymour's and viewed the scene.

After this a trader in Mansfield, by name of Jones, was killed and scalped by the Indians on an out lot north of the houses near where the depot of the railroad now is. He had a wife and two children. The Roberts' had at that time a job of work about one of the blockhouses. The news of this was carried by Johnny Appleseed, on horseback, to the Richardson neighborhood, and thence on to Frederick. The greatest excitement prevailed throughout the country, and many amusing things were said and done in this general panic. Among the most ludicrous was that of Samuel Wilson, who lived near the Quaker meeting house, and was so badly scared that he rushed from his house with his overcoat on and his pantaloons under his arm, and in that condition ran all the way to Frederick.

Application was made to Gov. Meigs for Rangers, and he sent an order for a company of twelve to be raised by Abner Ayers, whose beat was assigned them on the frontier, and this, with other bodies out, kept quiet in the settlements.

The friendly Indians of the Delaware tribe in this portion of country were mainly of the Greentown gang. That place, so much talked about by early settlers, was about eight miles northeast from the Richardson settlement, in Knox county, and within twelve miles of the Mansfield blockhouses. It was situated in the township of Green, laid out by our commissioners the 7th of January, 1812. The Indian village contained about sixty huts, and a council house built of posts and clapboards, sixty feet by twenty-five feet was its size. From 300 to 500 Indians congregated about it. During the summer various acts of hostility were attributed to this band, and many of the whites, whose friends and relatives had been killed by the Indians, were disposed to make no distinction between tribes, but to kill an Indian whenever it could safely be done. Collisions between parties of settlers and Greentown Indians became frequent, and it was at length determined to drive them from the soil. Two distinct races of people never have or can long live together in peace—one or the other must remain as subjects, or seek homes and freedom elsewhere. This little band of Indians became impressed with this historical truth and made ready to leave—some few, however, were loth to depart from the hunting grounds of their youth—the graves of their fathers—the homes of their race.

This was no time for sympathy with the race, and no tears were shed or regrets expressed by the settlers when the order come from the government for their removal. Under direction of the United States authorities they were removed via. Mansfield to Urbana, and thence to other western lands. From three of our old citizens, then young soldiers of Major Kratzer's command, we have gathered the particulars of their transfer, and have been told of a most brutal act committed by some white men, which shows more fully than language can express, the feelings of the greater part, if not all of this christian people. At the Mansfield station, our good old pastor, then of the Methodist, but subsequently of the New Light persuasion, James Smith, was officiating as Chaplain to the Regiment—for even in those early times soldiers thought such an officer necessary to their welfare. While there an Indian and his plighted squaw came up to the Reverend Smith to have him marry them in the most approved manner of whites. While the guard were looking at the performance of the ceremony, an old Indian and his daughter made their escape, but before they got a mile off they were discovered by two men from Coshocton, named McCulloch and Morrison. Morrison shot the old Indian, who ran a short distance and fell to the ground. The young girl fled to the woods. The men having shot the Indian ran back to the blockhouse greatly excited and told their exploit, and under Kratzer's orders Sergeant Gilkison, with a squad of twelve, followed up the Indian to the spot where he lay bleeding from the wound of a bullet in his chest, and to Gilkison's inquiry as to who he was, he replied "a friend." Morrison and McCulloch having joined the band at this answer, the latter exclaimed "d—m you! I'll make a friend of you!" and struck at his head with his tomahawk. And then stamped his foot on the neck of the dying Indian and sunk his tomahawk in his head. Sergeant Gilkison tried to prevent this fiendish act but could not accomplish it. Many of the old settlers tell of this feat of McCulloch's with great gusto, and add that he subsequently roved about among the western wilds taking revenge for two of his brothers who had been killed by Indians, by waylaying and shooting down and scalping every friendly or hostile Indian he met.

Such are some of the traditions of frontier life. The early settlers underwent many hardships and privations; but their sufferings from the savage foe were greater than the imagination of their descendants who occupy beds of down at night and cushoins of quilted ease by day—who dress in silks, satins, and fine velvets with furbelows—who clothe themselves in purple and fine linen—can realize or comprehend.

MUSTER ROLL OF CAPT. JOSEPH WALKER'S COMPANY, UNDER THE COMMAND OF COLONEL LEWIS CASS, MUSTERED TO THE FIRST OF NOVEMBER, 1812.

Joseph Walker, Captain, engaged 8th June for 12 months.

R. M. Brown, Lieutenant.
John Elliott, 1st Sergeant.
John Barney, 2d "
Archd. Crawford, 3d "
Peter Kyle, 4th "

Saml. Everett, 1st Corporal.
George Dickinson, 2d "
Josiah Trimbly, 3d "
Lewis Grindstaff, 4th "

PRIVATES:

Abram Emmett,
Saml. Yoman,
Michael Barton,
Jacob Wolf,
John Smith,
Harley Strong,
Alex. Enos,
John Wefford,
James Wood,
John Sunderland,
David Elwell,

Alexr. Walker,
Philip Walker,
Robert Davidson,
Andrew Welker,
Powel Welker,
Paris Sprague,
Isaac Rogers,
Joseph King,
John Ryan,
John McConnell,
Benjn. Simpkins,

Rivenus Newel,
Daniel Swagert,
Emanuel Hawn,
Adam Lynn,
Michael Davis,
Nicholas Kyle,
Wm. Wallace.
Rawley Clark, fifer.
Henry Clemmens, drummer.

Among the number of volunteers was JOHN H. MEFFORD, a native of Connelsville, Fayette co., Pa., who at the time of the breaking out of the war was teaching school in Hawkins' neighborhood, about five miles from Shrimplen's mill. He served under Capt. Walker and also in Capt. John Spencer's company, of which last he was a Lieutenant and had command after Hull's surrender.

After his return to Mount Vernon he married Abigail Mitchell, and worked at his trade, as a saddler, in partnership with his brother. He served the people as Justice of the Peace and as Associate Judge, and was a man of much popularity. He was possessed of some poetical talent, and it is said, by some, was the author of a noted song about "Hull's surrender." He was a good singer, which, in early times, in a country, is considered a great accomplishment. He died at Findlay about 1845, leaving two boys and three girls. His widow survives, and with the family now resides at Norwalk.

Another was Richard Montgomery Brown, whose name will be found as Lieutenant in Capt. Walker's company. He was born in Massachusetts, of revolutionary stock. His father, Samuel Brown, was under Montgomery at Quebec, was taken and imprisoned 9 months, and was subsequently a pensioner of the U. S. His father emigrated to Brooke county, Virginia, and from thence to the neighborhood of St. Clairsville, Ohio, in 1805; from there, in Oct., 1811, Richard M. moved to Mount Vernon, and engaged at his trade as a chairmaker and house painter. He has been in three new countries where the Indians yet were inhabitants. When he lived in Brooke county, Va., no roads were then cleared out, nor streets in Wellsville or St. Clairsville. Indians then and there were plenty and savage. He volunteered at Mount Vernon, June 8th, 1812, and was mainly instrumental in getting up the company to which he belonged. One company was then raised at Newark and another at Granville. Enos was then Col. and Kratzer Major of the militia. Major Munson, the recruiting officer, came to Mount Vernon when the Regiment was out on parade, and on call for volunteers the whole company of Joseph Walker, with Brown as Lieutenant, turned out. There were 42 in the company. Emanuel Hawn was to have been Ensign, but no election was gone into for that office on account of a quarrel with the Clintonites. They volunteered for one year, and served until surrendered by Gen. Hull, in August. This company mustered in a Regiment, of which Lewis Casswas Col., and the other officers, my informant believes, were Munson, Major, and Norton, Adjutant.

The company rendezvoused at Urbana with regiments of Col. McArthur and Col. Findlay, of Hull's brigade, and from thence marched to Detroit. They were piloted on an Indian trail to Detroit, by roads which were cut out from the Scioto to the Maumee, and from there to French Creek and River Raisin, etc., following trails. A band, part Indians and part white blood—the Zanes and McCullochs, of Zanesfield near Bellefontaine, who had intermarried with Indians, and they had half breed children, acted as principal pilots. When Hull surrendered, Walker's company returned by

Greentown, Black Fork of Mohican and Wooster. The militia of the county was then called out *en masse* by Major Kratzer, and every man in Mount Vernon went out to guard the frontier but old George Lybarger, who was left in charge of the women and children. When Fort Meigs was beseiged Lieut. Brown, now Captain by brevet, says that two thirds of the men in the county went on to the Fort, and after the siege was raised he returned, having in his company Swigert from Fairfield, a man from Coshocton and some from other counties. All men who could go—impelled by the sense of danger went without delay—singly and not waiting for battalions.

Capt. Brown in 1816 married Mary Hawn, and settled down to his trade, at which he succeeded in making a competency, and now in his 73d year, with his wife and a portion of his children yet lives in Mount Vernon. Two of his children, James F. and Mrs. Elizabeth Updegraff, now reside in Wisconsin; two, Samuel R. and George W. in Colorado Territory, and one Mrs. Mary Sapp in Nebraska.

Colonel Alex. Enos, was one of the number surrendered up by General Hull, and on his return he attempted to take command of the men raised in Knox county, but Major Kratzer contended, that as he was a prisoner of war, he had no longer a right to the command.

Another active man in these times was Captain John Greer, who raised a company in the eastern part of the county, of which Daniel Sapp was Lieutenant, and George Sapp, Ensign.

The regimental adjutant was John Stilley; surgeon, Dr. Timothy Burr; chaplain, Rev. Jas. Smith.

CHAPTER XIII.

NOTABLE EVENTS OF 1815.

NINETEEN INDICTMENTS FOR FIGHTS AND 'FRAYS.—NEW ROADS ESTABLISHED. —THE JAIL A COSTLY THING.—LICENSES TO PREACH, TO SELL AND TO ENTERTAIN.—THE SUPREME COURT FOR SEVEN TERMS.—THE OLD FOLKS SING.—WHAT PAY SOLDIERS RECEIVED IN OLDEN TIME.—THE LAWYERS GET INTO THE COUNTY.—ELECTION OF 1815 FOR STATE AND COUNTY OFFICERS.

THE Grand Jury at the spring term of Common Pleas Court consisted of Anthony Banning, foreman, John Merritt, Peter Bricker, John Hawn, David Hawn, John Green, Wm. Marquis, George Davis, Moses Craig, James Strange, Azariah Davis, Jacob Martin, Benjamin Bell and Gilman Bryant. They returned 19 indictments for "assault and battery" and "affrays." Quite a number of the parties plead guilty, and were fined $2 and costs. Of this Grand Jury but one man is now living. Adnal Hersey, of the Christian Church, was licensed to marry. John Cook, of the Baptist, was also licensed to do the same. Samuel Mott was appointed Master Commissioner in chancery. Tavern licenses were granted this year to Jonathan Hunt, Elisha Cornwall, Abner Ayres, John Baxter and A. H. Royce; and store license to Nicholas McCarty, George Girty, Eli Miller, Anthony Banning, L. S. Silliman, Gilman Bryant, John Wilson and

James N. Ayres. Two important roads are opened this year, namely: from Mount Vernon towards Sandusky, under the supervision of John Lewis, as commissioner, for which he is granted by the county commissioners orders for $100, and is paid $15 for his services; another, a road opened by Benjamin Rush, as commissioner, to Mansfield, for which services he is paid $9, and $200 is expended by the county in work upon the same. Among the bills paid in November, 1818, by the commissioners, are: to Anthony Banning, for 182½ lbs. iron, and brick for jail, $26.55, and Archibald Crofferd, for the following work for the county: 1 pr. hand-cuffs, $3; 1 hasp, 50 cents; shackles and hasp, $1.50; 2 grates, $13.80; eight spikes, 50 cents—$19.50. The job of making further improvements to the jail and jailor's house is given to Wm. Douglass at $125. The commissioners were determined, if possible, to make the jail burglar proof. That little log thing was a great institution truly—a first rate concern to sink money in, without any prospect of ever getting it back.

SUPREME COURT—1810-16.

The *first* session of the Supreme Court of the State of Ohio held in Knox county was on the 3d day of August, 1810, by Honorables William W. Irwin and Ethan Allen Brown.

James Smith was appointed clerk for seven years.

The only cases were those of the State vs. Ichabod Nye and Samuel Nye. Upon oath by the defendants that they did not believe an impartial trial could be had, the venue was changed to Licking county.

E. Herrick, Esq., attended as prosecuting attorney.

The *second* session was held May 1st, 1811, but two causes were on the docket. Sylvenias Lawrence, for the use of Benjamin Rush, vs. George Davidson, and James Peuthres vs. Samuel Kratzer; both of which were dismissed. No other business was to be transacted, and the court adjourned until the next court in course.

The *third* term was held April 9th, 1812. In addition to the former cases the docket shows the following: Joseph Butler vs. Elizabeth Vendrew; Wm. W. Farquhar vs. James Craig; Andrew Craig vs. Henry McCart and James Cunningham; James Smith vs. Samuel H. Smith; Henry Smith vs. Benjamin Barney; Henry Smith vs. Samuel H. Smith and Benjamin Barney; and Thomas Slater vs. Lovina Slater. Attachments were issued vs. Amos Yarnold and Alexander Enos for refusing to attend as witnesses.

The case of Slater vs. Slater is the *first divorce question* ever presented in Knox county.

The *fourth* term was held on the 2d of August, 1813, by Thomas Scott and Ethan A. Brown.

Wm. C. Enos was qualified as attorney and counsellor at law as the law requires.

The case of Lawrence for use of Rush is dismissed for want of bond to prosecute the appeal.

In Craig vs. McCart and Cunningham, judgment of non-suit is entered, because of non-appearance of plaintiff. Farquhar vs. Craig is continued, and the defendant is to pay all costs of this term within six months, or judgment, &c. John Jones vs. Joseph Cherry Holmes and George Lybarger—the complainant being thrice called did not appear, nor any person to prosecute this suit for him, therefore the injunction is dissolved and bill dismissed. The injunction case of Benjamin Barney vs. Henry Smith is heard by counsel, and the injunction is made perpetual, plaintiff to pay all costs. James Smith vs. Samuel H. Smith is argued by counsel, and the court decide that the defendant go hence, without day, and recover of plaintiff costs, &c. David Davis vs. John Cambridge, removed from Licking county, is continued. Slater's divorce petition is dismissed at cost of plaintiff. Lewis Dent and Co. vs. John Wheeler—judgment for plaintiff for $493.80 and costs. Another divorce case, Isaac Bonnet vs. Elizabeth Bonnet, is continued at cost of plaintiff, to be paid in six months, and upon condition that he give personal notice to the defendant of the pending of this suit in six months.

On the evening of the 3d of August, having spent two days, court adjourned.

The fifth term was held August 15, 1814—*Judges*, William W. Irwin and Ethan A. Brown.

John Williamson vs. Samuel Farquhar is continued at defendant's cost.

Isaac Bonnet vs. Mary Bonnet, divorce. "After argument the court continued the cause under advisement until the Coshocton Supreme Court, their decision to be certified from that or some other Court to this Court." The *first jury cause* ever tried in the Supreme Court for this county is that of Wm. W. Farquhar vs. James Craig.

Jury—Wm. Harriss, John Harriss, John Sawyer, Jacob Cooper, John Kerr, Bartholomew Bartlett, John Davidson, John Wilson, Thomas White, Francis Mitchell, Isaac Bonnet and Benjamin Martin. Verdict for plaintiff, $103.60. A motion is made by defendant for a new trial, argued by counsel, and overruled by Court.

The State of Ohio vs. Martin D. Lewis. On indictment by Grand Jury of Licking county for larceny. On motion, and affidavit of defendant, the Court ordered venue to be changed to this county, on defendant giving bond for $500 and security in $200 to appear first day of next term. Henry Markley becomes his security. After two days' session, Court adjourned.

The *sixth* term was held August 7th, 1815. *Judges*—Ethan A. Brown and John A. Couch, who produced his commission in room of Hon. Thomas Scott, resigned, &c.

The only jury trial was that of Samuel Mott vs. Gilman Bryant. *Jury*—Isaac Vore, Sr., John Vennoms, Samuel Durbin, James McGibeny, Joseph Hunt, John Arbuckle, Thomas Williams, Moses Merrit, George Dial, Wm. Sapp and John Stilley. Verdict for plaintiff, $5 and costs. Josiah Hedges vs. Samuel Kratzer, Andrew Craig and George Davis. Default against defendants, and cause continued for inquiry. Anthony Banning vs. Samuel Kratzer and John Williamson. On motion of plaintiff's counsel for dismission of appeal, on hearing the arguments of the parties by their counsel, it is therefore ordered that the motion be overruled.

August 8th, 1815. John Williamson vs. Samuel Farquhar. Continued till next term, on motion and affidavit of plaintiff, and at his costs. Wm. W. Alexander vs. John Wilson. Suit dismissed at costs of defendant, except docket fee in court below, which is not to be taxed to either party. Anthony Banning vs. Samuel Kratzer and John Williamson. Decree by court for plaintiff, "as per decree on file, signed by Chief Judge."

The above is a faithful abstract of all the business of this, the sixth, term of the Supreme Court.

The *seventh* term was held August 15th, 1816, by Judges Brown and Couch, the latter having produced his commission for seven years from the 14th of February, 1816. But one cause was tried by jury—Moses Robison vs. Isaac Dial. Verdict for plaintiff, $104.80 and costs. Williamson vs. Farquhar is again continued, with leave to amend, and at costs of plaintiff. Stephen H. McDougal, assignee of Wm. Taylor, vs. Enoch Harris. Judgment by default, for $88.80 and costs. There are four other cases upon the docket, in all of which our old friend Samuel H. Smith figures as plaintiff or defendant. The other parties are Robert Fulton, Erasmus Beaty, Levi Davis, Joseph Walker, administrator of Philip Walker, and John Walker. On the 16th court adjourned till next court in course.

The entire business of seven terms of the Supreme Court for Knox County we have given, that our readers may form an idea of the amount and kind of business dispatched, as also of the old settlers then participating in the luxury of law!

OTHER MATTERS OF SOME DEGREE OF INTEREST.

In February, 1815, George Girty opened a store in Mount Vernon, and also one at Fredericktown. There was but little increase in the number of business men or in other respects this year.

On the 8th of April a "Singing Assembly" of ladies and gentlemen, comprising different singing societies in the county, gave a grand concert at the court-house in Mount Vernon, at 1 o'clock P. M. All persons feeling willing to unite and participate in the exercises came. It was one of the olden kind of gatherings, like the "Old Folks' Concert" given in Mount Vernon this spring of 1862, as we have been assured by one of the vocalists who participated in both "singing assemblies."

In these war times, while some are disposed to grumble at the low rates soldiers receive, it may be well to remind them of the pay in 1815. In March the pay of non-commissioned officers and privates in the army of the United States was reduced to the following prices: To each sergeant-major and quartermaster-sergeant, 9 dollars; sergeants, 8 dollars; corporals, 7 dollars; teachers of music, 8 dollars; musicians, 6 dollars; artificers, 10 dollars; and privates, 5 dollars.

Samuel Mott had come all the way from Vermont to practice law in the wilderness, and was the first lawyer resident in the county. Enos was the second, who, one of the old settlers says, had just been made at home, and "wasn't lawyer enough to hurt."

May 9th, H. Curtis takes this way of informing his friends and the public that he has changed his place of residence from Newark to Mount Vernon, and, in the vacations of the courts, clients will find him in the town of Mount Vernon. In 1817 he became a fixture of the county, and here remained until 1858, as elsewhere told.

At the October election this whole county polled 345 votes. Alexander Enos was chosen Representative; John Shaw, Sheriff; Commissioner, Jonathan Miller; Coroner, Dr. W. Hastings.

Richland county, at this election, gave for Representative—Winn Winship, 156; A. Enos, 22; Robert McMillen, 10.

CHAPTER XIV.

MASONIC INSTITUTIONS.

HISTORICAL SKETCH OF MASONRY IN KNOX COUNTY.—ITS ORIGIN.—CHRONOLOGICAL STATEMENT OF ITS EARLY EVENTS AND PUBLIC TRANSACTIONS—AND THE PRESENT CONDITION OF THE VARIOUS ORDERS.

To the members of the craft the early history of Masonry is of deep and abiding interest. It dates back in the history of our county, as in that of the world, to a very remote period; and its ancient transactions will in the future be regarded with greater concern. The space allotted to this branch of our work will allow but brief mention of the origin and action of Mount Zion Lodge, as established at Clinton, and subsequently removed to Mount Vernon, and a chronological statement of public occurrences, celebrations, funerals, etc.

The first meeting of delegates from all the Lodges in the State of Ohio was held at Chillicothe, on the first Monday of January, A. D. 1808, A. L. 5808, whereat, on motion of Brother *Lewis Cass*, it was resolved "that it is expedient to form a GRAND LODGE in the State of Ohio." General Rufus Putnam was elected on the 7th of January Rt. W. Grand Master, and other business pertinent to permanent organization was transacted. At the Grand

Communication held at Chillicothe the 2d day of January, A. L. 5809, A. D. 1809, a petition was presented, signed by Brothers Samuel H. Smith, Nathaniel W. Little, Richard Fishback, William Little, Alexander Enos, Jr., Ichabod Nye and Thomas Brown, praying this Grand Lodge to grant them a charter, to form a Lodge, by the name of "Mount Zion Lodge, No. —," which was read, and on motion seconded,

> "*Ordered*, that until a charter can be made and granted to said brethren, for the aforesaid purpose, they shall be entitled to receive a dispensation therefor."

By reference to the proceedings of the Grand Lodge of Ohio, held in Chillicothe, A. L. 5810, A. D. 1810, we find "Samuel H. Smith, representative of Mount Zion Lodge, No. —."

In the same year that Knox county was organized the initiatory steps were taken for the organization of a Masonic Lodge; the petition drawn up for this purpose, as above recited, was presented in the first month of the following year, 1809, and the original dispensation was numbered "7," though subsequently changed to "9."

The first Master of the Lodge was Samuel H. Smith. The first public installation of officers was: Samuel H. Smith, W. M.; Alfred Manning, S. W.; Ichabod Nye, J. W.; Samuel Nye, Treasurer; Oliver Strong, Secretary; Wm. F. Roberts, S. D.; James Miller, J. D.; Wm. Bartlett, Peter Wolf, Stewards; Richard Fishback, Tyler.

Among the members of the Lodge in 1811 and 1812 were: Amoriah Watson, George Downs, Peter

Kinney, John Barney, Abner Ayres, John Wheeler, Charles Barney, R. N. Powers, Charles Lofland, Jesse Proctor, Winn Winship, Rufus Crosby, Nicholas C. Boalse, P. M.

Among the visiting brethren were: Wm. Erwin, Wm. Andrews, John Clark, Robert Glass, Lemuel Chapman, Samuel Choate, P. M., Riverius Newell, P. M., from Vermont.

The standing committee for 1811 consisted of Nicholas C. Boalse, Oliver Strong, Alfred Manning.

The Representative to the Grand Lodge in Chillicothe, January, 1812, was Alfred Manning.

Royal N. Powers succeeded Samuel H. Smith as W. M., and he was also elected Representative to the Grand Lodge. Alfred Manning was W. M. after Powers.

Daniel Dimmick was made a W. M. June 20th, 1812, and Lewis Jones, Richard Crooks, Thomas Rowland, Garret E. Pendergrass, Major Phineas Reed, among others, were also raised.

Amoriah and Samuel Watson, at their request, were permitted to pay their dues as quarterly members.

In October it was voted to remove this Lodge to the brick house in Clinton belonging to Bro. Samuel H. Smith.

Samuel Everett and Valentine Giesy were among the visiting members.

John Greer, John Garrison, John Haldeman and Thomas McClure were initiated in January, 1813.

Winn Winship and Levi Jones are considered quarterly members. Their residence, like the Watson's, was in Richland county, a considerable distance off.

June 24th, 1813, St. John the Baptist's day, was duly commemorated. An able oration was delivered by Bro. Winn Winship, and in procession the brethren marched to Bro. Boalse, and partook of a sumptuous dinner. Among the items of the Steward's bill, appears—"this, with the musician's bill, $—." Our venerable friend and brother, Judge Ezra Griswold, of Delaware, this spring gave us an interesting account of this celebration. He was present as one of the musicians, belonging to the first band organized in this part of the State; he at an early day went far as well as near to celebrations, etc.

The Judge formerly lived at Worthington, and is one of the pioneers of the press in this State.

Among the brethren of the mystic tie present were Gilman Bryant, George Downs, James Low, Lothrop Shirtliff, from New York, Wm. Anderson.

In 1814, at the meeting of the Grand Lodge in Chillicothe, Samuel H. Smith was the Representative. The returns at this time show 27 members, 3 fellow-crafts and 3 apprentices, one suspended and one expelled.

John Shaw, Ichabod Marshal, Robert Buchanan, Samuel Yeoman, James L. Priest, Edward Wheeler, George Dickinson, Daniel Ayres, John P. McArdle, Cyrus Langworthy and G. B. Maxfield are among the number initiated and receiving the Master's Degree this year.

The Rev. Bro. Fuller delivered a discourse to

the Masonic Society of Mount Zion Lodge, in Clinton, on Wednesday, May 8th, 1814.

Mount Zion Lodge, No. 7, celebrated the festival of St. John the Baptist at Clinton, on the 24th of June, at 10 o'clock A.M., by public procession and a sermon at the meeting-house by Rev. Bro. Josephus S. Hughes.

On the 27th of December, Bros. John Shaw, J. P. McArdle and Ichabod Marshal, the Standing Committee, agreed with Bro. Ichabod Nye for Lodge-room and refreshments the ensuing year.

Among the visiting brethren were Samuel Chapman, Samuel Choate, P. M., Thomas Munson, Joseph Brown, Wm. Bartlett and John Hawn.

The first funeral attended by the fraternity in this county was that of Richard Fishback, merchant, of Clinton, who died in his 36th year, and was buried with Masonic honors on the 23d of May.

1815.—The anniversary of St. John the Baptist was celebrated in Clinton by procession and the delivery of addresses by Bros. Vandeman and Curtis. Among the brethren present were Martin M. Kellogg, Wm. Wallace, —— Hallerman, —— Forbes, Benj. Helman and Daniel Dimmick.

The Lodge proposed to contract for the new Lodge-room, and the committee reported the amount of money in the coffers for said purpose, $134.80. In November a resolution passed, requesting the Grand Lodge to grant authority to change sessions to Mount Vernon.

The second Masonic funeral was that of Bro. Robert Glass, December 3d, 1815.

In 1816, Winn Winship was Representative to the Grand Lodge.

Among the visiting brethren of this year were Wm. Webster, Robert D. Moore, of Youghiogheny Lodge, No. 10, Pa., and John Warden, of Pa.

The Standing Committee of this year consisted of John Shaw, Timothy Burr and Joseph Brown.

There are very many items of deep interest connected with the history of the Lodge at Clinton. The action of the pioneers of Masonry in Knox will in the distant future be regarded with much curiosity by those whose privilege it is to lift the vail and tread within its sacred precincts. For the present we rest.

MOUNT ZION LODGE, NO. 9, AT MOUNT VERNON.

By virtue of a dispensation of the Grand Lodge of Ohio, predicated upon a petition included in a resolution of De Witt Clinton Lodge, No. 9, introduced May 8th, 1816, and passed by a vote of the brethren on the 5th of June thereafter, and taking into consideration also the reasonable request of said prayer that said Lodge may be removed from Clinton in Knox county to Mount Vernon in said county, and authorized to hold their meetings at said town of Mount Vernon, by virtue of the present charter, Henry Brush, Grand Master, and by resolution of Grand Lodge at their last Grand Annual Communication, did grant full power and lawful authority to hold their regular and special meetings at Mount Vernon.

Done at Masons' Hall, Chillicothe, this 7th day of March, in the year of our redemption 1817, and of Masonry 5817.

By the Grand Master, HENRY BRUSH.

R. KERCHEVAL, *Grand Secretary.*

A meeting was accordingly held by the Free and Accepted Masons, inhabitants of Mount Vernon, on the 5th day of April, 1817, A. L. 5817, at the court-house. Bro. Joseph Brown, Chairman, and Bro. Robert D. Moore, Secretary. The communication from the Grand Lodge was read and accepted, and a committee to draft a system of By-Laws for the government of the Lodge was appointed, consisting of John Shaw, John P. McArdle and Joseph Brown.

Ordered, that the next meeting be held at the court-house, on the 11th inst., for the purpose of organizing a Lodge. On motion made and seconded, that we must meet at 3 o'clock P. M. of the 11th inst.; decided in the affirmative, and adjourned in harmony.

MOUNT VERNON, 11th April, A. D. 1817, A. L. 5817.

At said communication of Mount Zion Lodge, No. 9, the organization of the Lodge was effected, and the By-Laws reported and adopted. Bro. Alfred Manning, W. M.; John P. McArdle, S. W. p. t.; Robert Buchanan, J. W. p. t.; Joseph Brown, Se. p. t.; Jonathan Miller, T. p. t.; Robt. D. Moore, S. D. p. t.; Hosmer Curtis, J. D. p. t.; Gilman Bryant, T. p. t.; John Shaw, John Roberts, John Warden and Orange Granger, Visiting Brethren.

On the 6th day of June the following officers were regularly elected, viz: Alfred Manning, W. M.; John P. McArdle, S. W.; John Shaw, J. W.; Joseph Brown, S.; Gilman Bryant, T.; Royal D. Simons, S. D.; Robert Buchanan, J. D.; John Roberts, S.; James Miller, T. On the 24th day of June they were installed at 9 o'clock A. M., and the anniversary of St. John the Baptist was duly commemorated. A procession was formed, under direction of Bro. Robert D. Moore, as Marshal, and, after marching to the court-house, a sermon was delivered by the Rev. James Smith, and the Lodge walked in procession to Mr. Zimmerman's tavern and partook of a sumptuous dinner. Those present and participating were: Past Masters Royal D. Simons, Robert D. Moore, Samuel H. Smith, and Riverius Newell; Master Masons, G. B. Maxfield, William Bartlett, John Warden, Reeve Chapman; and visiting brethren, Hosmer Curtis, Wm. Guyan, —— Shipman, Ichabod Nye, Lemuel Potter, A. P. Ashley, Samuel Nye; Fellow Crafts, Andrew C. Johnson and Wm. McCartney.

The members of Mount Zion Lodge, No. 9, of F. and A. Masons, met at Masonic Hall, in Mount Vernon, at the hour of 9 o'clock A. M., June 24th, 1817, for the purpose of celebrating the anniversary of Saint John the Baptist. The Rev. James Smith delivered the address.

Alfred Manning was the Representative to the Grand Lodge in 1817.

This year Henry Brush, of Chillicothe, was R.W.G.M., at Grand Lodge July 5th. Philemon Beecher, of Lancaster, Deputy.

From the Minutes of the Grand Lodge at Chillicothe we extract the following, relating to one who, for many years, resided in our county—a public benefactor, distinguished as well for his masonic zeal and faithfulness as for his piety and learning:

"August 4th. The Reverend Philander Chase delivered the address to the Grand Lodge.

"*Ordered,* that the sum of $50 be paid out of the funds of the Grand Lodge to the Rev. Bro. Chase, as a testimony of respect for the discourse delivered by him yesterday."—*Minutes, August 5th,* 1817.

Since we undertook this work, we have met with an aged brother who often sat by the side of Bro. Chase in the Lodge room, and gave us several interesting incidents in the masonic life of the Bishop.

August 1st, 1817, Alexander Elliott and Emanuel Hawn were duly initiated E. A.; on the 5th of September they became F. C.; and, on the 3d of October, Master's degree conferred on the former, and Nov. 2d, on the latter.

Andrew C. Johnson was the first Master raised in this Lodge, September 5th, 1817.

Andrew Clark and Samuel Pyle received the first degree September 5th, 1817; the second, October 3d; the third, November 2d.

Samuel Hawn, E. A., Oct. 3d; F. C., Nov. 2d; M. M., Dec. 5th.

1819, January 12th.—Fee of Bro. Joseph Moody to become F. C., paid in chartered paper $4, and of Bro. Nicholas McCarty, in Owl Creek paper, $5.

The Festival of St. John the Baptist was commemorated, in 1818, by a public procession, address at the court-house, and dinner at Joseph Brown's. Rev. Bro. Nathan B. Johnson delivered the address.

The first masonic funeral by this Lodge, after its removal to Mount Vernon, was that of Andrew M. Roberts, who departed this life April 17th, aged 27 years. He was consigned to mother earth April 18th. Bro. Thomas Rigdon preached the funeral discourse at the court-house from these words—"Be ye also ready."

Bro. Royal D. Simons, W.M.; Nicholas McCarty, Secretary.

The Lodge had the satisfaction of commemorating St. John the Baptist's anniversary in their new hall in the second story of the new brick school house on the hill.

Royal D. Simons was the Representative to the Grand Lodge in 1819, and also in 1820. Among the officers of the Grand Lodge elected at the latter communication was M. Rev. Philander Chase, Grand Chaplain.

December 27th, 1820, a public installation of officers of the Lodge took place in lower room of the Lodge building, where a sermon was delivered by the Rev. Joseph Carper. Alexander Elliott, W.M.

April 27th, 1821, M.W. John Snow, G.M., visited the Lodge.

The second masonic funeral was that of Bro. N. C. Boalse, August 10th, 1821.

1822. The Festival of St. John the Baptist commemorated. A procession was formed by John Shaw, Marshal, and marched to the court-house, where the oration delivered by Brother Cook, at Sandusky, in 1819, was read by Bro. Jo. Brown, after which the brethren partook of an elegant dinner at Mr. Eli Miller's tavern, and then returned to the Lodge room. Among the visiting brethren in attendance were—Samuel Wolf, John W. Harter and James Mumford from Mansfield; Wm. Allison and John Allison from Lodge No. 123, Waynesburg, Pa.; Wm. Coonrod, John F. Adams, Alvin Corbin, Abner Ayres, and others.

The Representative to the Grand Lodge at Columbus, in 1823, was Bro. Royal D. Simons.

In 1824, H. Curtis and Joseph Brown were the Representatives.

The anniversary of St. John the Evangelist was

commemorated by the Lodge, December 27th, 1824. Bro. Joseph Brown, as Marshal, formed the brethren in procession, and after marching to the Presbyterian Church, and hearing an address by Rev. James Scott, the officers elect were duly installed according to ancient usages, and the Lodge and brethren present then returned in solemn procession to the Lodge room. H. Curtis, W.M.

The funeral of Bro. John Warden was attended by the Lodge, May 25th, 1825; Thomas Rigdon acting as Chaplain. The ceremonies were performed according to ancient usage.

The Rev. Bro. Badger, Elder of the Christian Church, delivered a masonic address in Mount Vernon, January 31st, 1826.

1826. The anniversary of St. John the Baptist was duly commemorated. The Masonic Address was delivered by Bro. Ahab Jenks, of Granville.

August 26th. Bro. Royal D. Simons was, by the Lodge, buried according to ancient usages. Bro. Benj. H. Taylor superintending Marshal; Wm. Bevans Marshal for the Fraternity. Elder James Smith delivered the funeral discourse.

1827. Bro. H. Curtis was the Representative to the Grand Lodge.

1828, June 24th. The brethren in procession, under direction of Bros. Day and Tracy, marched to the Presbyterian Church, where an excellent discourse was delivered by Bro. James McMahon; after which a very good dinner was served up at the house of Bro. W. E. Davidson.

1828. H. B. Curtis was the Representative to the Grand Lodge.

1829. H. Curtis and J. N. Burr were Representatives.

1830, January 26th. Bro. John Shaw's funeral attended by the Fraternity.

1833, January 29th. John Roberts was buried by the brethren of this Lodge. He was in his 73d year.

1835, March 30th. Bro. Riverius Newell was buried by the craft. In the fall of 1837, Mount Zion Lodge moved to the present Lodge room, in Bro. Huntsbery's block.

1839, June 24th. This anniversary was duly celebrated by the Lodge. The oration by Bro. Adam Randolph, in the court-house, was listened to by a very large concourse of Masons and citizens. A most excellent dinner, provided by Bro. T. Burr, was disposed of in proper manner, and every thing passed off harmoniously.

1840, February 16th. Bro. Dr. Lyman Wright was buried, at Fredericktown, by the members of Mount Zion Lodge.

1841, June 24th. This anniversary was becomingly commemorated. Bro. David Spangler, of Coshocton, delivered the address, and Bro. T. Burr prepared the dinner. Address delivered in the Methodist Episcopal Church. The Mt. Vernon Choir and Mt. Vernon Band discoursed appropriate music.

At 2 o'clock P.M., June 25th, a procession was formed, under direction of Bro. Johnston Elliott, to attend the funeral of Bro. John Sherman, who was buried according to ancient usages.

August 27th. Funeral of Bro. T. G. Plummer.

September 7th. The funeral of Bro. John E. Davidson.

1843, December 13th. The funeral of Bro. Hill Runyan.

1844, June 24th. A public celebration of this anniversary occurred. Bro. T. G. Drinker, of Cincinnati, delivered the address. Many brethren from Newark, Zanesville, Columbus, West Carlisle, Loudenville and Mansfield participated in the ceremonies of the day. Isaac Davis was Marshal, and John A. Holland, of Wooster, Assistant Marshal. An excellent dinner was provided by Bro. Mackey, and the day passed off harmoniously.

On the 27th of December, the anniversary of St. John the Evangelist was commemorated by a social party in the Hall, whereat the officers elect were publicly installed, and an appropriate address delivered by Bro. C. Delano.

December 15th, 1846, Bro. James Hayes, of Miller township, buried by the Lodge in due form.

1847, February 8th. An act to incorporate the Master, Wardens and Brethren of Mt. Zion Lodge No. 9, was passed by the Legislature, and accepted.

1848, August 3d. Masonic funeral of Bro. Crandal Rosecrans, near Homer.

1849, February 8th. Masonic funeral of Bro. Jonathan Miller.

June 24th. St. John the Baptist anniversary duly commemorated. The address delivered by Bro. Rolla H. Chubb.

1852, May 7th, Masonic funeral of Bro. T. Winne.

" August 28th, Masonic funeral of Bro. Marvin Tracy.

1853, December 11th, Masonic funeral of Bro. Sylvester Pond.

1854, September 1st, Masonic funeral of Bro. Jacob B. Brown.
1855, October 1st, Masonic funeral of Bro. John A. Holland, of Rockford, Ill.
1856, December 7th, Masonic funeral of Bro. William Bevans.
1857, March 13th, Masonic funeral of Bro. John Butler, of Rosco Lodge, No. 190.
1857, December 16th, Masonic funeral of Bro. William Copeland.
1858, April 29th, Masonic funeral of Bro. J. Phifer.
1859, May 12th, Masonic funeral of Bro. George White.
1861, September 22d, Masonic funeral of Bro. Lorin Andrews.
1862, January 20th, Masonic funeral of Bro. W. R. Greer.
" April 6th, Masonic funeral of Bro. James Huntsbery.
" " 30th, Masonic funeral of Bro. Robert Lurkins.

The following brothers have been in attendance on the Grand Lodge:

1830, J. N. Burr, James Huntsbery, Jonas Ward.
1831, Jonas Ward.
1832, P. Sprague, W. Bevans, L. Lake.
1833, J. Ward.
1836, W. Bevans, Alexander Elliott.
1839, W. Bevans, A. Randolph, at Lancaster.
1840, B. F. Smith.
1841, J. N. Burr, B. F. Smith, James Huntsbery.
1842, B. F. Smith, T. Winne.
1843, " J. N. Burr, Isaac Davis.
1844, " M. Tracy.
1845, " J. N. Burr, J. B. Brown.
1846, " " M. Tracy.
1847, J. B. Brown, S. P. Axtell, M. Tracy.
1848, " "
1849, " G. W. Williams.
1850, " J. N. Burr, W. Dunbar.
1851, " " G. W. True.
1852, " "
1853, " G. W. True, James Smith, Jr.
1854, G. W. True, G. W. Stahl, B. F. Smith.
1855, " " F. B. Plimpton.

1856, Dennis Smith, G. W. Stahl, S. P. Axtell.

1857, G. W. True, J. N. Burr, S. P. Axtell.

1858, J. N. Burr, J. C. Devin, "

1859, John Adams, S. P. Axtell, J. B. Beardslee, Dr. J. N. Burr, D. G. M.

1860, C. S. Pyle, S. P. Axtell, J. B. Beardslee.

1861, " "

Present Officers.—C. S. Pyle, W. M.; W. B. Brown, S. W.; J. B. Beardslee, J. W.; James Huntsbery, Treasurer; S. P. Warden, Secretary; H. W. Owen, S. D.; L. B. Curtis, J. D.; J. R. Wallace, Tyler.

Standing Committee, 1862.—J. N. Burr, S. P. Axtell, N. E. Lewis.

Relief Committee.—L. B. Curtis, Thomas Harvey, John Ringwalt.

Among the members of this Lodge of long standing we may mention the venerable William Beardslee, who was made a Master Mason at Stephentown, N. Y., in 1804, who in 1817 represented Center Star Lodge, No. 11, in the Grand Lodge of Ohio, at Chillicothe, and whose three sons—Job H. G., Wm. B., and John B.—are also of the craft.

Adam Pyle, our much-respected townsman, was made a Master in 1821; and Dr. Jonathan N. Burr is the oldest Past Master in this part of the country. In 1825 he was raised in this Lodge, in 1829 became its W. M., and since then has served in that position longer than perhaps any Master in the State. For his zeal and fidelity he was presented by the brethren of Mt. Zion Lodge with a beautiful Past Master's Jewel in 1852; and the Sir Knights for like cause in 1859 presented him with a Templar's sword. Long may this bright light be permitted to illustrate the virtues of Masonry.

Thrall Lodge No. 170, Fredericktown, was chartered October 18th, 1849.

First Officers.—Chancy Hill, W.M.; T. V. Parke, S.W.; A. Keller, J.W.; J. Wages, Treasurer; O. W. Rigby, Sec'y; D. C. Beach, S.D.; D. P. Coffinbury, J.D.; N. S. Reed, Tyler.

Number of members, 32.

Ohio Lodge No. 199, Bladensburg; Chartered October 28th, 1851.

Eli Farnum, W.M.; A. C. Scott, S.W.; G. M. Hill, J.W.; E. Bebout, Treasurer; J. H. Miller, Sec'y; G. Upfold, S.D.; J. N. Hurry, J.D.; Johnson Hill, Tyler.

Number of members, 26.

Antioch Lodge No. 286, located in Danville, was chartered Oct. 26th, 1856.

First Officers Under Charter.—John White, W. M.; Wait Whitney, S. W.; U. B. Kinsie, J. W.; S. W. Sapp, Secretary; M. Hildreth, Treasurer; Z. Hibbetts, S. D.; —— ——, J. D.; A. S. Church, Tyler.

Chartered Members.—John White, Wait Whitney, U. B. Kinsie, Samuel Kinsie, Isaiah Hieth, S. W. Conner, Z. Hibbetts, John Biggs, Daniel Hess, B. S. Church, A. S. Church, Miner Hildreth, S. W. Sapp, B. Casteel, C. W. Page.

First Initiation in Lodge.—Henry Hibbetts.

Present Officers.—M. Hildreth, W. M.; S. W. Sapp, S. W.; A. S. Church, J. W.; Calvin Simmons, Secretary; Alonzo Gardner, Treasurer; John C. Gaines, S. D.; Henry Hibbetts, J. D.; Mark Greer, Tyler.

Present number of members, 45.

Clinton Royal Arch Chapter No. 26, was created the 16th day of May, 1842, under a dispensation from the Most Excellent Comp. G. D. Hines, Dept. G. H. P. of the Grand Chapter of the State of Ohio.

First Officers.—J. N. Burr, E. H. P.; B. F. Smith, King; James Huntsbery, Scribe; ——— ———, Secretary; C. Delano, P. S.; B. H. Taylor, C. of H.; S. W. Burr, R. A. C.; A. Corbin, A. C. Rowland, J. Garrison, Masters of the Vails; Joseph Muenscher, Chaplain.

On the 20th of May, the above officers were duly installed by M. E. G. D. Hines, Dept. G. H. P.

Officers in 1862.—S. P. Axtell, E. H. P.; J. N. Burr, King; W. M. Mefford, Scribe; Dennis Smith, C. of H.; J. B. Beardslee, P. S.; W. B. Brown, R. A. C.; O. M. Arnold, G. M. 3d Vail; C. S. Pyle, G. M. 2d Vail; R. D. Huntsbery, G. M. 1st Vail; James Huntsbery, Treasurer; S. P. Warden, Secretary; J. R. Wallace, G.

Standing Committee, 1862.—J. N. Burr, O. M. Arnold, J. B. Beardslee.

Clinton Encampment No. 5, of Knights Templars and Appendant Orders, was instituted at Mount Vernon on the 12th of October, 1843, by virtue of authority and a letter of dispensation granted for that purpose by William James Reese, General Grand Generalissimo of the General Grand Encampment of the United States of America. The grant was to B. F. Smith, Joseph Muenscher, Isaac Davis, J. M. Smith, and A. D. Bigelow.

First Officers of the Encampment.—Sir Joseph Muenscher, G. Com.; Sir B. F. Smith, Gen.; Sir A. D. Bigelow, Capt. Gen.; Sir J. N. Burr, Prelate; Sir C. Delano, S. W.; Sir Isaac Davis, J. W.; Sir James Huntsbery, Treasurer; Sir T. Winne, Recorder; Sir Adam Randolph, Standard-bearer; Sir Joseph Hildreth, Sword-bearer; Sir E. W. Cotton, Warden; Sir D. D. Stevison, Sentinel.

Present Officers.—Sir J. N. Burr, G. Com.; Sir Dennis Smith, Gen.; Sir J. B. Beardslee, Capt. Gen.; Sir Adam Randolph, Prelate; Sir William Mitchell, S. W.; Sir S. P. Axtell, J. W.; Sir James Huntsbery, T.; Sir S. P. Warden, R.; Sir Wm. Sanderson, Jr., Standard-bearer; Sir W. M. Mefford, Sword-bearer; Sir E. W. Cotton, Warden; Sir J. R. Wallace, Sentinel.

Number of Sir Knights, 31.

CHAPTER XV.

THE OWL CREEK BANK OF MOUNT VERNON.

ITS PUBLIC AND PRIVATE HISTORY.—LET IT BE RELIEVED FROM ODIUM!

THE history of Knox county would be incomplete without a faithful and true account of an institution with the above euphonious name, located upon the banks of Owl Creek, and within the sacred precincts of Mount Vernon. The engraving above gives a view of one of "the owls" issued by this bank. They were of every denomination from the shinplaster form of 6¼ cents up to $10. The paper, engraving and finish of the notes, although not so perfect in every respect as those issued by banks in the present day, nevertheless is of a higher order than those put forth by the so-called "Confederate States of America," of which Cotton is king, and Jeff. Davis vicegerent. From the journals and old files of that day, as far as accessible, we have compiled the following.

There being great complaint of the scarcity of

money after the war, large numbers of people in various cities and towns in the United States, and more particularly in the West and Ohio, conceived the idea of multiplying the quantity of paper in lieu of money by manufacturing what is called a "currency." Among other points, those of Mount Vernon determined to engage in the business of making money. As early as December, 1814, a meeting was held, and articles of association for the organizing of a bank, to be called the "Owl Creek Bank of Mount Vernon," were entered into, fixing the capital stock at $150,000, divided into shares of $50 each, payable in installments of not exceeding $5 each, and appointing certain commissioners to open stock books, &c. Petitions were then presented to the Legislature, praying for a charter; and after having petitioned the Legislature for an act authorizing such an association, and been denied the grant, determined to "go it alone," on their own hook.

On the 10th day of April, 1816, the first meeting of record of those who inaugurated the Owl Creek Bank was held at the court-house in Mount Vernon, and as this is the most important of all events in the early history of Knox county, we give the proceedings entire of this the first meeting, and also of the first meeting of the Board of Managers on the 17th inst.

"Agreeable to previous notice, there was a meeting at the court-house on April 10th. Jonathan Miller was called to the chair, and Joseph Brown appointed Secretary. The following independent sentiments were set forth:

"*Resolved,* That we have by the Constitution of this State guarantied to the people of this State a full and fair right and privilege to have charters granted when we shall petition the legislative body of this State for that purpose. We, the undersigned, having complied with the requisitions of the Constitution, and will continue so to do, without waiving our rights and privileges.

"*Therefore be it resolved,* That we do form ourselves into a company for the purpose of establishing a bank in the town of Mount Vernon, Knox county (Ohio).

"2. *Resolved,* That the following named gentlemen be appointed managers of said bank, and to draft articles of association and by-laws for the future government of the company, viz.: James Smith, Wm. Mitchell, M. Merritt, Abraham Darling, Hosmer Curtis, John Warden, Gilman Bryant, Jonathan Miller, L. S. Silliman, Benjamin Martin, Joseph Brown, John Green and Jacob Young.

"From this number a committee was appointed to draft the articles, who met at the house of Joseph Brown on the 17th April, and adopted the following:

ARTICLES OF ASSOCIATION OF THE STOCKHOLDERS OF OWL CREEK BANK OF MOUNT VERNON.

"BE IT KNOWN, That we, the subscribers, having formed a company and limited partnership, do hereby agree and associate with each other, to conduct banking business in the manner hereinafter specified, under the name and title of the *Owl Creek Bank of Mount Vernon.*

"And we do hereby covenant and mutually agree, that the following are and shall be the fundamental articles of this our association, by which all persons who are parties hereto, or may in future transact business with this association, shall be bound and concluded :—

"ARTICLE 1. The capital stock of the company shall be two hundred and fifty thousand dollars, current money of the United States, with the privilege of extending it to five hundred thousand dollars, and of commencing business so soon as twenty-five thousand dollars is subscribed—to be divided into shares of fifty dollars each.

"ART. 2. The books for the subscription of said stock, shall be opened on the first Monday in March next, at such places and under such agents as the commissioners may think proper, at the hour of ten o'clock in the morning, and continue until three o'clock in the evening of the same day, and from day to day during said hours, until the whole number of shares are subscribed for. The books thus to be opened, are to be under the direction of the following named commissioners, viz: Jonathan Miller, James Smith, Gilman Bryant, John Warden, Benjamin Martin, H. Curtis, W. Mitchell, M. Merritt, A. Darling, Jacob Young, John Green, L. S. Silliman and Joseph Brown. At the time of subscribing, there shall be paid to the commissioners or their agents, on each share subscribed for, the sum of one dollar; the further sum of two dollars and fifty cents shall be paid on each share, within ninety days thereafter, at such place as the commissioners shall appoint, of which due notice shall be given; the residue in such portions and at such places as the directors hereafter to be chosen shall appoint; they giving at least sixty days notice thereof in the public newspaper of the county: Provided, such installments shall at no time exceed two dollars and fifty cents; neither shall any subsequent installment be called for until a previous one has become payable.

"ART. 3. No person or persons, body politic or corporate, shall be permitted on the first day to take more than *one hundred shares*, and if the shares are not all taken on that day, the foregoing part of this article is not to operate.

"ART. 4. If it shall so happen, that more than the stipulated number of shares may be subscribed for, the commissioners shall apportion them by deducting from the highest subscription; and if more persons subscribe than there are shares, the commissioners shall determine by lot to whom such shares belong; and as soon as may be thereafter, receipts shall be issued to the stockholders, and certificates of the amount of stock held by each.

"ART. 5. If any stockholder shall fail to pay his, her, or their installment, to the amount of *three dollars* on each share at the time or times, or in the manner heretofore specified, such stockholder shall forfeit to the use of the company all monies paid antecedent to such failure or default; however no forfeiture of stock shall take place, after *three dollars* on each share shall have been paid. But to secure the regular payment of any installment or call, after five dollars on each share hath been paid, such stockholder shall not be entitled to a dividend until such installment or call shall be fully paid; and the dividend thereafter to be paid to such stockholder (as well upon the money regularly paid as upon the money paid after default) shall be calculated only from the time when said installment shall be fully paid.

"ART. 6. The affairs of the company shall be conducted by thirteen directors, and a president, whose place, if chosen from among the number of directors, shall be supplied by the choice of that body, the whole of which is to reside within the county of Knox; and five directors, together with the president, shall form a board or quorum for the transacting of all business of the company. Each director shall be a stockholder at the time of his election, and shall cease to be a director if he should cease to be a stockholder; and the number of votes to which each stockholder shall be entitled, shall be in proportion to the stock he may hold, as follows, viz: For the first five shares, one vote; for ten shares, two votes; and for each additional ten shares, one vote; and no stockholder shall be entitled to vote, who has not held his stock six calender months next preceding the election, except as to the first election—all stockholders, residing within five miles of Mount Vernon, shall vote by ballot in person, and those who reside a greater distance from Mount Vernon than five miles may vote by proxy, which at all elections is to be made in such form as may be directed by the board.

"ART. 7. The first election for directors shall be on the fourth Monday in May next, under the superintendence of the commissioners, four of whom shall form a quorum. The directors so elected shall take their seats at the board the day following their election, and they, or a majority of those present, shall proceed immediately to the choice of a president, all of whom shall continue in office for one year, and until their successors shall be regularly elected and qualified. All future elections for directors shall be held annually on the fourth Monday in May, under the superintendence of three persons, being stockholders, to be appointed by the president and directors for the time being, of which at least four weeks notice of the time and place shall be given by advertisement in the public papers in Knox county. The bank shall be established as near the court-house, in Mount Vernon, as may be thought most convenient by the board of directors,

"ART. 8. As to vacancies.

"ART. 9. The president, directors, and superintendents of elections, before they enter upon the duties of their respective offices, shall take the following oath or affirmation, as the case may be:

I do solemnly swear (or affirm) that I will impartially, faithfully, diligently and honestly execute the duties of a of the Owl Creek Bank of Mount Vernon, conformably to the constitution and articles of association of the same, and the trust reposed in me, to the best of my skill and judgment. And the cashier, the tellers, book-keepers and other officers, shall also take a similar oath or affirmation, and shall besides give bond with security to the satisfaction of the president and directors for a faithful discharge of the duties in their respective stations.

"Art. 10. The board of directors are hereby fully empowered to make, revise, alter or annul, such rules, orders, bye-laws and regulations for the government of the company, and that of their officers and others whom they may think proper to employ, as they or a majority of them shall, from time to time, think expedient, not inconsistent with law or these articles of association, and to use, employ and dispose of the joint funds or property of said company (subject only to the restrictions hereinafter mentioned) as to them or a majority of them may seem expedient.

"Art. 11. As to signatures to bills, &c.

"Art. 12. As to books.

"Art. 13. The board of directors shall have power to appoint a cashier and such other persons as they may think proper to employ for executing the business of the company, and to establish the compensation to be paid to the president, cashier, and others respectively; all which, together with all other necessary expenses, shall be paid out of the joint funds of the company.

"Art. 14. Two-thirds of the directors shall have power to call a general meeting of the stockholders, for purposes relative to the concerns of the company, giving at least two months notice in the public newspapers of the county, and specifying in such notice the object or objects of such meeting.

"Art. 15. The shares of the capital stock at any time, owned by any individual stockholder, may be transferred on the books of the company, according to such rules as (according to law) may be established in that behalf by the board of directors; but all sums for which the stockholder is liable, as drawer, must be satisfied before such transfer can be made.

"Art. 16. No transfer of stock in this company shall be considered as binding on this company, unless made in a book or books to be kept for that purpose by this company. And it is hereby further expressly understood that any stockholder who shall transfer in manner aforesaid all his stock or shares in this company, to any person or persons whatever, shall cease to be a member of this company, and that any person or persons whatever who shall accept a transfer of any stock or share in this company, shall become a member of this company according to these articles of association.

"Art. 17. It is hereby expressly and explicitly declared, to be the object and intentions of the persons who associate under the title and firm of the president and directors of the Owl Creek Bank of Mount Vernon, that the joint stock or property of the said company (exclusive of the dividends to be made in the manner hereinafter mentioned) shall alone be responsible for the debts and engagements of said company, or to whom they shall or may become indebted by such engagements, and no person or persons to whom this company may in any wise become indebted, shall on any pretence whatever have recourse against the separate property of any present or future member of this company, or against their persons, further than may be necessary to secure the faithful application of the funds thereof to the purposes to which by these presents they are liable. But all persons accepting any bond, bill, or note, or other contract of this company, signed by the president and countersigned or attested by the cashier of the company for the time being, or dealing with it in any other manner whatever, thereby give credit to the said joint stock or property of said company, and disavow having recourse, on any pretence whatever, to the person or separate property of any present or future member of this company, except as above mentioned. And all suits to be brought against the president for the time being, and in case of his death or removal from office, pending any such suit against him, measures shall be taken at the expense of the company for substituting his successor in office as defendant, so that persons having any demands upon the company may not be prejudiced or delayed by that event; or if the person suing shall proceed against the person first named as defendant (notwithstanding his death or removal from office) this company shall not on that account, take advantage of such proceedings by writ of error or otherwise; and all recoveries had in manner aforesaid shall be conclusive upon the company, so far as to make the funds or joint stock of this company liable for such amount, and no further; and the company shall immediately pay the amount of such recovery out of the joint stock, but not otherwise; and in case of any suit in law, the president shall sign his appearance upon the writ, or file common bail thereto, it being expressly understood and declared that all persons dealing with said company agree to these terms and are to be bound thereby.

"ART. 18. Dividends of the profits of the company, or so much of said profits as shall be deemed expedient and proper, shall be declared half yarly in every year, and shall from time to time be determined by a majority of the directors present, at a meeting to be held for that purpose, and shall in no case exceed the amount of the net profits actually acquired by the company, so that the capital stock of the company shall never be impaired by dividends; but the directors shall be at liberty to retain at least one per centum upon the capital, as a fund for future contingencies.

"ART. 19. If the directors shall, at any time, willfully and knowingly make or declare any dividend which shall impair the capital stock, all the directors present at the making or declaring such dividends, and consenting thereto, shall be liable in their individual capacities to the company, for the amount or proportion of said capital stock so divided by said directors; and each director who may be present at the making or declaring such dividends, shall be deemed to have consented thereto, unless he does immediately enter in writing his dissent on the minutes of the proceedings of the board, and give public notice to the stockholders that such dividend has been made.

"ART. 20. These articles of association and agreement shall be published three times in the public newspapers of the county, at least two months before the books are opened; and for further information, to all persons who may transact business with, or in any manner give credit to this company, every bond, bill, note, or other instrument or contract, by the effects or terms of which the company may be charged or held liable for the payment of money, shall specially declare in such form as the board of directors shall prescribe; that payment shall be made out of the joint funds of the Owl Creek Bank of Mount Vernon, according to the present articles of association, and not otherwise; and it is hereby expressly declared, that no engagements can be legally made in the name of said company, unless it contain a limitation or restriction to the effect above recited.

"ART. 21. The company shall in no case be owners of any real property, except a site for banking business, or directly or indirectly be concerned in trade, or the purchase or sale of any goods, wares or merchandise whatever (bills of exchange and bullion excepted), except such lands, goods, wares, or merchandise as may be truly pledged to them by way of security, or conveyed to them for debts due, owing or growing due to the said company, or purchased by them to secure such debts so due to said company.

"ART. 22. This association shall continue until the fourth Monday in May, one thousand eight hundred and thirty; but any number of stockholders, not less than fifty, who together shall be proprietors of not less than five hundred shares, may, for any purpose, relative to the institution, at any time apply to the president and directors to call a general meeting of the stockholders, and if by them refused, the same number of stockholders, proprietors of not less than that number of shares, may and shall have power to call a general meeting of the stockholders, giving at least two months' notice in the public papers in Knox county, specifying in such notice the object or objects of such call.

"ART. 23. Immediately on the dissolution of this association, effectual measures shall be taken by the directors then existing, for closing all the concerns of the company, and for dividing the capital and profits which may remain among the stockholders, in proportion to their respective shares.

"In witness whereof, we the undersigned have hereunto set our names or firms, this —— day ——, one thousand eight hundred and ——."

Shortly after the opening of subscription lists, the following notice was published:

"NOTICE.

"It is requested that all persons holding books for the sale of shares in the Owl Creek Bank of Mt. Vernon, will be pleased to receive the installments due thereon, and forward the same by the 20th day of the present month.

B. MARTIN,
JOS. BROWN,
JAMES SMITH, } Bank Commissioners.

"MOUNT VERNON, July 3d, 1816."

The preliminaries having been arranged, the bills are ready to circulate, and the officers publish the following in the *Register*, page 175, which explains the *modus operandi:*

"MOUNT VERNON, Sept. —, 181—.

"Sixty days after date, for value received, we promise to pay JAMES SMITH, at the house of *L. S. Silliman*, the sum of ——— ——————— without defalcation.

"*Credit the Drawer.*

"A. M.
"C. D. } Endorsers.

"J. P., *Drawer*."

[L. S.] "THE STATE OF OHIO,
County, ss.

"Before me (A. B.), a Justice of the Peace for the county of—— aforesaid, came C. D., who, being duly sworn, deposeth and saith, that, whereas, he has thrown a note into the *Owl Creek Bank of Mount Vernon* for discount; saith, that, if discounted, he will take no advantage of any statute law of this State; and farther this deponents saith not.

"*Signed*, C. D.

"Sworn and subscribed before me the —— day of ——, 181—
"A. B., J. P."

"The above form of a note you will please to insert in your paper, which note must be executed with two good endorsers, without a blot or interlineation. The endorsers' names must appear written on the back of the note as well as at the foot. The form of an affidavit is given, which must be made by the drawer, and accompany the note. *By order of the Board of Directors.*

"JAMES SMITH, *President.*

"L. S. SILLIMAN, *Cashier.*

"September 13th, 1816."

On the 20th November, 1816, L. S. Silliman, Cashier, notifies the stockholders of the *Owl Creek Bank* of Mount Vernon that an installment of $2 on each share is requested to be paid within sixty days.

March 6th, 1817, a dividend of six per cent., on account of stock actually in Bank, was declared.

At a meeting of the Directors of the Bank, the following resolutions were unanimously adopted, viz:

"WHEREAS, Unfavorable constructions have been put on the twentieth section of the Articles of Association; Therefore,

"*Be it Resolved,* That no Director, or any other person, shall have a right to draw any money out of said Bank, without giving their notes with sufficient endorsers.

"*Resolved, secondly,* That a preference shall at all times be given to the Stockholders, in the accommodation of loans, to double the amount of all money by them actually paid in.

"B. MARTIN, *Chairman.*

"G. BRYANT, *Secretary.*

"June 3d, 1816."

July 9th, 1817.—All persons indebted are notified that they must pay "at the rate of from 10 to 50 per cent., in proportion to the amount of their loans."

As showing the feeling existing in regard to such Banks in the winter of 1816–17, when the Owl Creek Bank was applying for a Charter, we give this anecdote: Two persons of color, at Columbus, quareled; one, wishing to make his antagonist as contemptible as possible, called him "*a d—d* UNCHARTERED *son of a b—h.*" And it became very fashionable at the Capital to apply the term unchartered to all evil doers.

In these times of evil talk, and while the public were busy crying down this institution, there were occasionally to be found parties willing to "give the devil his due." The following extract from the Zanesville *Express* of December 16th, is an instance in point:

> "Notwithstanding so much has been said against the Owl Creek Bank of Mount Vernon, we are assured that two gentlemen, a few days since, presented bills at that bank for a large amount, which were redeemed with chartered paper and specie."

About this time an enemy of the Bank killed a tremendous big Owl, and brought it into the town and rudely threw it down upon the counter, exclaiming, "There, d—n you, I've killed your President."

The Bank building was located where Adam Weaver's hardware store now is. It was a rough, yet substantial piece of workmanship, a mixture of the Doric and Corinthian styles of architecture, weather-boarded, with four-penny nails thickly driven through its batten-door and window-shutters, so thieves should not cut in and steal. On the ground it covered about fourteen feet square, and was one low story in height, and painted *red!*

The bills rapidly depreciated under the heavy blows given. There seemed to be no stopping the clamor against the Bank.

The principal circulation in Knox county was Owl Creek, and we find very many advertising for it. Of the merchants advertising for it were James Miller, and Burr, Green & Co.

"William Stanbery offers to sell 'The Craig Farm,' at present occupied by Major Joseph Brown, to the highest bidder for Owl Creek Bank paper.

"J. Brown offers to sell 156 acres of land near the town of Mt. Vernon, in the Hamtramick section, for such paper.

"OWLS.—All persons indebted to the subscriber, are requested to make prompt payment, for I am in want of OWL CREEK PAPER.

JOHN SHAW.

"N. B. Those indebted for taxes, for 1817, are also requested to pay with the same."

The paper when presented was at first redeemed by the Bank with chartered paper, and the stockholders and parties interested endeavored to sustain its credit by various devices. Among other plans adopted to keep up the paper was the following, which we give as showing the disposition of stockholders to pay, and the strenuous efforts resorted to:

"OWLS.

"OWL CREEK BANK OF MOUNT VERNON,
January 1st, 1818.

"Whereas, several reports have been circulated, some of which are false, and injurious to the credit of the Bank, with respect to certain measures adopted by the Directors: Therefore, for the purpose of suppressing the further propagating of such false rumors, the Directors have thought proper to exhibit to the public, and to the stockholders, a fair and accurate statement of the measures actually determined on by them, and which has been the subject of such reports. The Directors have observed with regret the depreciation of the Owl Creek paper of late, and particularly in Knox county; they have been fully convinced that the principal cause of the sudden fall of the Owl Creek paper is owing to the circumstance of the difficulty, or almost the impossibility of obtaining such goods as are wanted by the citizens with this kind of paper.

"With a view, therefore, to obviate these difficulties, and at the same time to draw out of circulation the paper of the Bank, we have entered into the following contract with Burr, Green & Co., viz.: Said Company, on their part, have undertaken to bring on a complete assortment of goods, and to retail the same for Owl Creek paper, at prices as low as they can be purchased for in chartered paper, and to take assignments on judgments in favor of the Bank, or wait until the Bank can with convenience exchange; and for all paper thus collected, the only privilege granted to said Company is a loan of $700 of such money as will pay carriages, to be made use of for that purpose, and to be paid back in good chartered paper, in installments, within one year. Given under our hands.

"James Smith, William Mitchell, Jonathan Miller, Benjamin Martin, John Warden, John Hawn, Jr., John Shaw, Gilman Bryant, Hosmer Curtis, Wm. Y. Farquhar."

"PUBLIC NOTICE IS HEREBY GIVEN,

That a meeting of the stockholders of the OWL CREEK BANK OF MOUNT VERNON, will be held at the Banking House in Mount Vernon, on the 12th day of March, 1818, for the purpose of taking into consideration the propriety of closing the business of said Company, and to transact any other business relative to said Company which may be thought proper when met. Dated at Mount Vernon, this 6th day of January, 1818.

"Nathaniel Johnson, Jonathan Miller, Godleib Zimmerman, Benjamin Rush, I. N. Richardson, John Shaw, John Hawn, Jr., William Douglass, Samuel Mott, John Wilson, J. M. Banning, James McGibeny, James McGibeny for Joseph S. Newell, James Miller, Joseph Brown, L. S. Silliman.

"N.B. All the stockholders are particularly solicited to attend on said day."

The course of true love never did run smooth. In the career of banks as well as of nations and individuals, there are "ups and downs," drawbacks and obstacles to prosperity; and parallels in history are always to be met with. Jackson throttled the United States Bank; Sam Williams seizes the gullet of the Owl Creek Bank: Jackson denounces

Nicholas Biddle; Williams attempts to play the tyrant over James Smith: Jackson removes the deposits; and Sam Williams refuses to deposit.

The banking question gets into the papers, and the public mind becomes much distracted thereat. Several communications appear in August and September of 1816 in regard to the Owl Creek Bank. The office of Bank President was no sinecure in those days, at least of the Owl Creek Bank, for we find that the chief owl was compelled at all times to defend his institution from the stump and the press. The Lancaster, Zanesville, Mt. Vernon and other papers of those days, contain many articles from the pen of James Smith in reply to attacks of Dr. Moore B. Bradley, Sam'l Williams and others. Some of the papers show much acerbity and bitterness of feeling; but, from our standpoint of observation, we must say that our old friend James Smith beat them all.

In a communication of August 6th, 1817, replying to an article in the *Ohio Spectator*, in regard to a meeting of the farmers, mechanics, merchants, and innkeepers of the town of Mansfield, county of Richland, and State of Ohio, on the 11th of July, 1817, James Smith pointedly says:

"If, sirs, your sympathy has been awakened for unfortunate persons who have received the paper, I hope you will shortly be prepared to discharge your engagements with the *Owl Creek Bank of Mount Vernon.* It would be an insult upon your good sense for me to tell you, that for you to refuse the paper of this bank, while you are in debt to the bank, is a full sacrifice of every spark of honor. If you, sirs, and such characters as yourselves, would pay your engagements, or one half thereof, the Owl Creek Bank of Mount Vernon would be completely prepared to pay and give satisfactory exchanges for their notes in circulation. Your honors, sirs, we look after no longer, but your purses and property will have to be tried. Tavern bills and pills* ought to be paid for in this paper as well as in the Mansfield.

"* * * * * I would advise you to be industrious in collecting the paper, as you know you soon, or at the next court, will have judgment against you. The Owl Creek paper will answer *you* as well as specie. * * * * * I censure no person, not in debt to the bank, for rejecting the paper; both the principle of moral justice and honor enjoins on every person indebted, to receive it. The sooner, sirs, you procure this paper, it will be the better for you. This bank will shortly be prepared to make general and satisfactory exchanges. JAMES SMITH.

"P.S. The editors of the *Ohio Register* and the *Ohio Spectator* will confer a favor on Messrs. Bradley and Williams, as well as myself, by giving the above a place in their respective papers.

"J. S."

Samuel Williams replies in the *Ohio Register* of August 20, in a very long article addressed to James Smith, President of the Owl Creek Bank, &c., in which he evidently lets his temper get the better of his judgment by such expressions as these:

"You, sir, are President of the Owl Creek Bank of Mount Vernon, you are Clerk of the Court of Common Pleas, a Justice of the Peace, and, sometimes, preach the Gospel of Jesus, as I am informed—in politics a professed republican; all of these callings you profess to fill with fidelity, nay, in some you have sworn to discharge their incumbent duties according to the best of your abilities. * * * You have prostituted the official duties and obligations as a Justice of the Peace to subserve its interest by administering unconstitutional oaths. Were you not sworn to support the constitution of this State and of the U. States in the oath of office? Yet swearing individuals not to take advantage of the statute law to prevent the collection of your illegal demands. * * * You loaned us your bills in order

* Bradley was a doctor—Williams a tavern-keeper.

to destroy those rights you profess to admire, the rights of managing our pecuniary concerns. That when we assert our independence, like freemen, you threaten us with destruction and tell us we are in your net, and at your mercy, the mercy of your religión, your integrity, your republicanism—your official virtue, the potent demand of one great Owl debt."

To this communication of great length—the bank President replies with vigor—we have space to extract but a paragraph which may be called a clincher:

* * * "I think it unnecessary to answer your charges against me, when you charge my official, political and religious principles; all you say about it only exposes yourself. Had you kept silent the public had not known your baseness. Truly, Samuel, you was one of the persons that took a solemn oath to take no advantage of any statute law to prevent or stop the payments of your bank engagements. You brag of your full purse; you are then without excuse if you imagine you took an unconstitutional oath. Will you violate that oath to atone for the crime? You ought to be ashamed to let any person impose on you so far as to publish your black crimes with an idea of injuring me. If your purse is so full and heavy pay up your bank engagements. Strangers, citizens, and your neighbors too, will have much more confidence in you. FIVE HUNDRED DOLLARS of the trash you mentioned will be received of you in place of gold and silver."

On the 28th February, 1822, a paper was drawn up and signed by certain of the subscribers, binding themselves to give their notes, with security, by the last of March next, to John Shaw, John Trimble and Samuel Mott, trustees, whenever the sum of $15,000 shall be subscribed, for the purpose of settling up the affairs of the Owl Creek Bank. As every thing calculated to throw light upon this mysterious subject may be regarded as worthy of preservation, we give the names of the parties subscribing, and the amounts and conditions affixed:

Gilman Bryant	$600
Allen Scott	200
Joseph Talmage, in trade at trade prices	150
Henry Markley, in trade at trade prices	700
Eli Miller, ½ in Owl Creek paper and ½ trade	200
Jonathan Miller, in good trade or Owl's Creek paper	300
Wm. Mitchell, in Owl Creek paper or cash	400
Hosmer Curtis, in something as good as the debts	400
Moses Merritt, in Owl Creek paper or trade	150
Jacob Young, in Owl Creek paper or trade	300
Robert Giffin, in good trade at cash price	300
Jas. Shaw, in property	300
John Trimble, in good trade at cash price	250
Jonathan Hunt, in good trade at cash price	150
Jos. Brown, in good trade—say whisky	100
Samuel Mott, in trade	100
Henry Davis, Owl Creek paper or cash	400
John Hawn, in property	70
John Hawn, jr., $300 in *traid* and $500	
John Troutman, in good trade or Owls	200

THE FAMOUS OWL CREEK BANK CASE.

Robert Giffin, Joseph Talmage, Jacob Young, William Douglass and others, on the 21st of August, 1829, by Thomas Ewing, their solicitor, filed a Bill in Chancery in the Supreme Court of Ohio for the county of Knox, against Jacob M. Banning and others, claiming the defendants whose names were set up in said Bill as Stockholders in the Owl Creek Bank, and demanding that they should be decreed to account, pro rata, for their shares of stock held to apply in payment of a certain suit prosecuted by one Luke Walpole upon the paper of said bank, and upon which a judgment thereon was recovered by said Walpole at the September term, 1826, against the parties complainants and Abraham Darling, John Ewalt and William Mitchell, for $8,445 20, and costs of suit. Upon said judgment executions having been served out and levied upon the lands of complainants, and they demanded that those who were with them in equity alike bound for payment of the same should be required to liquidate their proportion of the same, and for such other further and complete relief as they were in equity and good conscience entitled to at the hands of the court.

These parties admitted themselves to have been stockholders to the amounts following, to wit:

Robert Giffin, 25 shares, contributed $200—cash deposited in bank.
Joseph Talmage, 10 shares, contributed $250.
William Douglass, 70 shares, contributed $600.
Jacob Young, 10 shares, contributed $500.

Of the other judgment debtors to Walpole, Wm. Mitchell had 25 shares, and paid $500; Abraham Darling 25 shares, and paid $500; and John Ewalt had 20 shares, and had paid nothing.

The stockholders to the bank were never fully known by reason of the mutilation or alteration of the books, which took place pending a suit between Luke Walpole and some of the stockholders. The bank was entered one night, and the large box that contained the papers carried off, and subsequently the box was found in a thicket of hazel, east of town, broken open, and the books and papers scattered about with several of the names of stockholders obliterated. The testimony in this case, the proceedings of the court, and reports of the Receiver, exceptions to his report and final decree, make one of the largest volumes of record in the Clerk's office of Knox county—duly labeled "The Owl Creek Bank Case." From this official, and authoritative record we copy the names and shares of stock of parties alledged to have been partners in the firm, name and style of the "Owl Creek Bank."

Hosmer Curtis	50	shares, paid	$500 00
Jonathan Agnew	20	"	30 00
William Scritchfield	5	"	......
Insley D. Johnson	5	"	......
Joseph Critchfield	10	"	133 00
James Barkhurst	5	"	66 00
Robert Dalrymple	12	"	380 00
James M. Gibeny	15	"	725 00
Allen Scott	10	"	250 00
Joseph Mann	10	"	......
Gilman Bryant	50	"	900 00
John Green	10	"	......
John Hawn	15	"	150 00
Philip Melker	50	"	510 00
John Stilley	25	"	200 00
John Shaw	10	"	316 00
Wm. Darling, of Richland county	10	"	......
James Boltom	20	"	160 00
George Davis	20	"	......
John J. Tulloss	10	"	50 00
Jonathan Hunt	24	"	150 00
Abel A. Webster, of Richland	50	"	......
Eli Miller	50	"	250 00
Benjamin Rush	10	"	266 00
Henry Markley	25	"	375 00
Nicholas Riley	25	"	500 00
Henry Davis	20	"	625 00
Jacob M. Banning	50	"	150 00

Gotlieb Zimmerman	20 shares,	paid	$345 75
W. Y. Farquhar	20	"	125 00
Nathaniel Scritchfield	10	"	133 00
Francis Wilkins	25	"	100 00
Eli Gregg	10	"	58 00
Jacob Lepley	20	"	......
Samuel Mott	30	"	125 00
Aaron Hill	10	"	......
Thomas Irvine	20	"	......
Jonathan Miller	50	"	350 00
John Trimble	15	"	316 00
James Smith	50	"	......
Isaac Richardson	5	"	66 00
John Hibbits	10	"	200 00
Jacob Draper	10	"	200 00
Henry B. Carter	10	"	100 00
Wm. Robeson	20	"	......
James Severe	8	"	......
Rebecca Harris	25	"	......
Jonathan Rapp	10	"	......
Wm. Bevans	20	"	......
Wm. W. Farquhar	15	"	265 00

All of the county of Knox—

James M. Taylor, 10 shares.
John Cully ..... 10 "
A. H. Caffee .... 10 "
Noble Landon... 10 "
A. Warthen .... 10 "
Silas Mead ..... 10 "
Joseph Fulton....... 10 shares.
Jonathan Conard .... 10 "
Wm. Robinson ...... 70 "
Wm. W. Gault ...... 50 "
John Houston .... 67 "
Benj. Warner........ 10 "

All of the county of Licking—

Jacob Been....... 10 shares.
Hiram Ball .... 9 "
Benj. Mochaber.... 8 "
John Badger .... 6 shares.
Matthew Kelly ...... 10 "
Henry Vaught....... 10 "

Buckingham, Sherwood and Eben P. Sturges, traders, under the name and style of Sherwood & Sturges, 20 shares, all of whom are of Richland county, and

Yours truly

Middleton, Strobridge & Co. Lith. Cin. O.

Elijah Newcomb, 17 shares; Thomas Butler, 50 shares, paid $350—both of Coshocton county.

John Beckwith, 8 shares, of Perry county.

Jacob Morris, 5 shares, of Perry county.

Samuel B. Carpenter, 15 shares, of Huron county.

John Leyland, 10 shares, of Huron county.

Enoch Harris, 15 shares, colored man, of Marion county.

John Morris, 20 shares, of Wayne county.

John Shrimplin, 20 shares.

Adam Johnson, of Coshocton county, 50 shares.

Isaac Dillon, of Muskingum county, 50 shares.

George Reeve, of Muskingum county, 50 shares.

Robert Dalrymple, 50 shares.

James Barcus, 50 shares.

Wm. Critchfield, Sr., 50 shares.

Wm. Darling, 50 shares.

James Rightmire, 50 shares.

Insley D. Johnson, 50 shares.

Jacob Cook, 50 shares.

The above named were claimed, as above represented, by the bill of complainants, to have been interested in the concern; and having been duly subpœnaed and brought into court, their own answers and testimony, of much extent, was given as to who the partners were, &c. While some few plead the statute of limitations, in addition to other testimony, the greater number—to their credit be it said—confessed the soft impeachment, and expressed themselves ready to stand the consequences.

Henry B. Curtis was appointed Master Commissioner, and, after a thorough and searching examination, he made, on the 18th of September, 1837, a very elaborate and able report. Having, upon his appointment, caused publication to be made by newspaper to all interested, either as creditors or partners, of his appointment to close, and finally settle, as far as practicable, the concerns of said Bank, and having before him all the testimony, he determined the relative position of the parties defendant, and discharged from liability, as stockholders, of that number Jacob M. Banning, Wm. Bevans, Isaac Dillon, George Reeves, Sturges and Sherwood, Francis Wilkins and Matthew Williams for insufficiency of proof.

At the said September term of Supreme Court, A.D. 1837, Judges Reuben Wood and Peter Hitchcock approved said report, by which it appeared that the sum of $26,796.20 was required to be raised to meet and discharge the present unpaid debts of the Company, in Owl Creek Bank Bills, commonly called; and the liabilities of the parties defendant being established equal, it was further ordered that said sums, as assessed by said Master Commissioner's report, be paid by said parties to him, and the cause was continued for further report.

Several of the parties defendant, by their Attorneys, filed exceptions to said report, and, as to their rights, and for further examination, the papers in the cause are referred to H. H. Hunter, Esq., of Lancaster, as Special Master, who, at the September Term, 1838, submits a partial report, as to certain parties referred to him, and still further reports, as by testimony, the following additional stockholders equally liable, viz: Solomon Geller, owner of 20 shares; John Hawn, Sr., 15 shares; Nathaniel Johnson, 60 shares (50 of which being transfers from Jonathan and Eli Miller); William Blackburn, 20 shares; Matthew Merritt, 4 shares; G. B. Maxfield, John Troutman and N. M. Young, 10 shares each. At the same time the Special Master concludes with this statement:

"It is believed that no man can, at this time, possess himself of the facts necessary to *do* exact justice in the case. Though it is believed that much additional evidence, with proper exertions, may be collected, to render the case more perfect. All which is respectfully suggested.

"H. H. HUNTER, *Spl. M. C.*

At the September Term, 1839, Judges Peter Hitchcock and Frederick Grimke allowed the complainants leave to amend their bill, and make the newly-discovered stockholders parties, &c.; and the Court continued H. H. Hunter Special Master for further investigation, and with more extensive powers.

At the September Term of 1840, Master Commissioner Hunter submitted his final report, concluding with a statement of accounts and an aggregate amount remaining due—$17,457 27; and the Court, upon further hearing of exceptions by counsel and arguments for their respective clients, decreed accordingly, and continued the appointment of Henry B. Curtis as Receiver, to collect from the parties the sums assessed against them, and to pay off the judgment creditors, &c.

At succeeding terms of the Court, various orders were made, as necessary in the progress of the cause, and upon the reports of the Receiver of his action had in the premises.

And thus the case "dragged its slow length

along," until the final report of the Receiver was filed, and the cause finally disposed of upon exceptions taken by Miller & Dunbar, of attorneys for certain defendants, which were overruled by the District Court in chancery, 16th of June, 1859—and an entry upon the journals expresses the satisfaction of the Court at its termination—by the Receiver in having disposed of the remaining assets by sale under order of Court, for an amount sufficient to liquidate all outstanding indebtedness.

"It is now, therefore, ordered and decreed, that said report be forthwith approved, and sale fully confirmed," * * "and this whole case is accordingly discontinued."

"The undersigned, now, therefore, regarding substantially all interests adjusted and settled in behalf of party creditors, and the assets for that pupose exhausted, recommends that the suits pending be finally dismissed from the docket, without prejudice to the rights of the assignee to collect the balances against party creditors, standing unsatisfied, agreeably to former reports and decrees in this cause. The undersigned reports all costs paid, as far as known to him, and, as he believes, in full.

"In taking leave of the case which, for more than thirty years, has occupied a conspicuous position on the docket of this court, and in closing the trust which, for more than twenty years, has been confided to the undersigned, he takes leave to congratulate the court on the final adjustment of the whole matter, and to express his profound thanks for the confidence so long continued, without which, the vexed, complex, and protracted labors of the case would have been rendered much more onerous, and the results obtained proved far less satisfactory.

"To the parties (many of the original of whom have departed this life since the commencement of this suit) and to their heirs and representatives, the full record of this case—while it may recall some reminiscences of an unfortunate enterprise and its calamitous results, will also remind them of many incidents, and profitable lessons in the school of experience, and be, for all time to come, the veritable history of 'The Owl Creek Bank of Mt. Vernon.'"

Such is, in brief, the history—more particularly the legal history—of the Owl Creek Bank; an institution which, in part from its outre name, has acquired more notoriety than any other that has ever existed in America—if not in the world! The fame of the "United States Bank" was not more widely extended. Its failure created no greater dismay. Nations civilized and tribes savage have seen and handled its money. In its brief life, yet protracted existence, it has been cursed most by those whom it befriended, and wronged most by those who professed to be its friends.

The evil day came upon it—even in its early youth; before it had become full grown, the keen frosts nipped it. Its crest fell and its petals closed in, because too much light struck in on it suddenly. Its head wilted; it fell; and great was the fall thereof. Its sunshine friends deserted when the cloud portended the coming storm—some who had received its money and upon whom it had showered benefits, and some who had lent their credit and volunteered their names to the infant, deserted its cause, and attempted to plead infancy and limitation in bar. As with the human kind, when life is almost extinct, doctors are often called in only to attend upon the corpse; so, in this instance, lawyers were brought in at the eleventh hour to the wake. In the last pangs opiates were sought to be administered, and the sleep of forgetfulness was invoked by a few; but to their credit be it said, that less than a half dozen of all the defendants in Knox county invoked the aid of the act of January 25th, 1810—pleading, accordingly, the statute of limitations; or that other plea, in bar, of like character—that the partnership or association they had formed, to make themselves rich, was contrary to an act to prohibit the issuing and circulation of unauthorized bank paper.

To their honor be it said that the stockholders of the Owl Creek Bank of Mount Vernon—the hardy old pioneers—the Darlings and Youngs and Mitchells and others, who knew so well how to fell the forest; to hunt the wolves, deer and bear; to till the soil; to clear off the wilderness, and so little of banking as not to be classed as experts by financiers of more modern date, yet came up "to the scratch," and redeemed "the promises to pay" of their bank officers.

It is true, that the arbitrament and final settlement of its affairs went to law; but, under the circumstances, it was a matter of necessity that the equities should be adjusted by the courts. Almost every one of the parties were willing to pay their proportion of the debts at the first; but each thought it but right to pay his own proportion and no more. Hence the ablest of the men learned in the law at that time accessible, were "called" to take a hand in the Owl Creek Bank case. Among the number thus employed were Thomas Ewing, Henry Stanbery, H. H. Hunter and W. W. Irwin, of Lancaster; C. B. Goddard, C. C. Converse, C. W. Searle, Wyllis Silliman and Geo. James, of Zanesville; David Spangler, of Coshocton; Judge Orris Parish, of Columbus; W. Stanbery, G. B. Smythe and I. Dille, of Newark; Jacob Parker, of Mansfield; Benjamin S. Brown, R. C. Hurd, J. C. Hall, C. Delano, H. Curtis, J. K. Miller, W. Dunbar and M. H. Mitchell.

Of the entire number of parties defendant named in these pages, but five, so far as known, survive, to wit: our venerable townsmen, Aaron Hill and Eli Miller; our noted countymen, John Troutman and Nicholas Riley; and H. Curtis, Esq., now residing in Keokuk, Iowa. And of the 24 attorneys engaged in the case, but 13 are now living.

Of the Judges who have heard this great cause at different stages of its progress, Calvin Pease, Joshua Collett, Peter Hitchcock, Jno. C. Wright and N. C. Read, are dead.

Finally, after thirty years in the courts, this case, noted as that famous one of *Jarndyce* vs. *Jarndyce*, was brought to a close, the last dollar of its issue presented redeemed, and, forty-three years after its birth, "all that was of earth and earthy" of the Owl Creek Bank of Mount Vernon, was consigned to its final resting-place—the Great Book of Records.

CHAPTER XVI.

INCIDENTS AND EVENTS OF 1816.

THE FIRST PAPER AT MOUNT VERNON.—GLEANINGS FROM THE OHIO REGISTER.—SOME ACCOUNT OF THE BUSINESS MEN OF THAT TIME.—OF THE MARRIAGES, INCREASE OF POPULATION, ETC.—SOME OF THE DEATHS.—ADDRESSES OF CANDIDATES.—KING CAUCUS APPEARS.—ELECTIONS.—PRICE OF SALT, ETC.

ON Sunday evening, April 28th, the people were thrown into great consternation by "*A Phenomenon.*—A dark place appeared on the north part of the Sun; it appeared gradually to move towards the centre. What wonderful event this is the forerunner of is yet unknown, whether it be the fall of empires, kingdoms, or of more important events." This appeared on the evening of the 4th day after the first paper was issued at Mt. Vernon. Wonderful circumstance!

Rattlesnakes were quite common, and their bites frequent about these times—hence the *Ohio Register* publishes, May 8th, an efficacious remedy for the bite. An application of kali preparation to the wound, and a lump the size of a hazel nut dissolved in vinegar to be swallowed during effervescence every twenty-five or thirty minutes.

"COLD WEATHER FOR THE SEASON." "5 DOLLARS REWARD?"—Taken from the OHIO HOTEL, in Mt. Vernon, on or about the 15th of April last, (either *intentionally* or through mistake) a dark colored GREAT COAT, with a cape somewhat larger than ordinary, and the collar lined with snuff-colored velvet. If said Great Coat was taken through design, the subscriber will exchange small clothes for it if returned to him by the person who took it away; or the above reward will be given to any other person who will deliver it to J. Brown, in Mt. Vernon, or to

JOHN FRANK.

May 15, 1816.

Samuel H. Smith gives notice, April 23, 1816, that he has for sale 7,800 acres which he has just "subdivided into LOTS, from 100 to 300 acres to accommodate actual settlers."

"John Wilson, with the greatest respect, would inform his customers and the public in general, that he has just received a fresh supply of NEW GOODS, consisting of Morocco slippers, &c., all of which he will dispose of on the most moderate terms for cash or approved country produce." On the 24th of July he advertises himself "west of the court house and next door south of Mr. Anthony Bannings, where he will sell salt by the barrel at $2 per bushel, or $2.25 by the single bushel," &c.

"Dr. Robert D. Moore, engaged in the practice of Medicine. from his medical attainments, hopes to render general satisfaction."

As showing the wild nature of our county seat, at that time, and the difficulties of raising children in a new country, we insert the following obituary notice as we find it in McArdle's style of publishing—the first article under the editorial head, May 22d, 1816:

"SUDDEN DEATH.—Departed this life on Friday afternoon, the 17th inst., Samuel Zimmerman, son of Gotleib and Eve Zimmerman, of this town, aged eleven years, one month and twenty-nine days. His death was in consequence of eating a small portion of the *root of a wild parsnip,* said to be rank poison. His illness was short, but pains excruciating, which terminated his end in about 40 minutes—leaving behind him an affectionate father, tender and loving mother, two brothers and three sisters, who greatly lament the irreparable loss of a dutiful son and brother.

In youth's bloom day I'm called away,
  My parents are behind;
Of this fine boy who would have been their joy,
  Had he been spared to live.

But God in mercy called me home,
  His wisdom to fulfill,
He gave me birth and gave me breath,
  And blessed be his will.

O! look on me and you will see
  A youth knip'd in the bud,
Here I can't stay, I must away
  To appear before my God.

My Pappy and Mamma I fear will fret
  At loosing of their Son;
But dry up your tears, appease your fears,
  My time was fully come.

An accident it seemed to be,
  Which brought about my end;
But God does all things for our good,
  And Christ is our sure friend.

Then why should I fear death's stern looks,
  Since Christ for me did die;
For all in Mount Vernon, old and young,
  The force of death must try."

Bryant and Burr, under date of May 1st, 1816, give notice that they "have just received a fresh supply of new goods, consisting in part of fine and coarse cloths, cassimers, velvets and cords, vesting, bombarzets, factory muslins, silk for dresses and bonnets, silk and cotton shawls, silk and Madrass handkerchiefs, cotton and worsted hose, a few *fashionable* bonnets, &c., &c., all of which will be sold cheap for wheat, rye, oats, sugar, bacon, homemade linen, rags, furs and CASH. Ready for trade and barter—sell is the word!"

Having formed this arrangement, another partnership is about this time entered into, which continued for life. It is thus published in the *Ohio Register* of May 8th:

"HYMENIAL.

"Lovers, you well may envy them,
Whom such fair joys adorn;
His hand receives a Diadem,
And she has lost a Thorn.

"*Married.*—On Sunday last, (May 5th, 1816,) in this town, by the *Rev. James Smith,* DOCTOR TIMOTHY BURR to MISS RACHEL THRIFT, daughter of the Rev. Wm. Thrift of this county."

"Married, June 2d, 1814, by the Rev. Mr. George, Mr. Daniel Conger, to Miss Elizabeth Roberts. 'And God said unto them, *Be fruitful, and mutiply and replenish the earth.*'"

John Garrison, having laid off the town of Edwinburg on an elevated spot of ground, six and a half miles west of Mansfield, on the State road, offers lots for sale May 8th, 1816, and advertises the public that a large spring of water is in the center of the town. Poor Edwinburg! alas, death stole gently upon the innocent, and not a mark of the place is now visible upon any map!

The following specimen from the *Ohio Register* of June 12th, 1816, is the first effusion of a lovesick swain on Owl Creek's stormy banks. It is to be hoped that the "youth" was "relieved:"

"MR. M'ARDLE—By inserting the following Acrostic, you will particularly oblige your friend and well wisher,

ALPHONSO.

"TO MISS M   S   .

"M ay Heaven on thee her choicest gifts bestow;
I n thy dear breast may every virtue glow:
S edate and modest, wise, kind, and free—
S uch may thy character forever be.

"M ost charming fair, the loveliest of your kind,
A nd most accomplished, both in form and mind,
R eceive this humble tribute to your fame,
Y et far beneath what your just merits claim.

"S uch winning sweetness decks your beauteous face,
N o other maid possesses half such grace;
Y our unaffected beauty, free from art,
D elights and captivates each youthful heart;
E ngaging fair, then let thy pitying breast
R elieve a youth whom love has robb'd of rest."

"Miss Mary Fulton respectfully informs the inhabitants of Mount Vernon and its vicinity, that she has opened a MILLINERS SHOP at H. Curtis', Esq., second door Sow West of the Court House on High street, where she intends keeping on hands an elegant assortment of fashionable bonnets, caps, &c. * * * * Plain sowing done in the neatest manner and on the shortest notice. May 22d, 1816."

" A gentleman who arrived at Xenia, O., about the 15th of April, from Vincennes, states that seven soldiers belonging to Fort Harrison, had been killed by the Indians. It was unknown to what tribe they belonged."

"On the 18th of April last, the Steamboat Maria, Captain Lovell, arrived at Cincinnati from Marietta, bound to Boston, Mass., with a cargo of pork, flour and lard."

Another store is opened at Mount Vernon by A. & T. Gormly, from Pittsburgh, in May, 1816. They advertise "*an assortment of the manufactures of Pittsburgh*, to wit: two stills, iron in the bar, &c., &c."

At about this time the principal travel was to Zanesville. J. Reeve advertises that he keeps tavern at the sign of the BEAR, formerly occupied by Col. J. Perry, on Main street, Zanesville, and closes with the following notice:

"N. B.—Travellers will be supplied with a Way Bill, giving an account of the Roads and Distances to the principal towns in the United States."

At this time John Hamm, Marshal of the District of Ohio at Zanesville, paid Invalid Pensioners of the United States at his office in that place.

William Kattle, living in Clinton township, near Charles Cooper's one mile West of Clinton, lost "one pretty good chunck of a grey horse, and a chesnut sorrel with a Roman nose and a white strip inclining down one of his nostrils."

In July, John Sawyer and Adney Coleman commenced butchering in Mount Vernon, and keeping beef at their slaughter-house every Tuesday and Friday morning at reduced price.

Thomas Irvine also advertises as a butcher, and wants to purchase hides and fat cattle.

Alexander Elliott found, on Saturday morning, Sept. 21st, on Market street, six dollars in bank bills, which he advertised as wanting an owner.

James Moor, acting Sheriff of Richland county, Sept. 25th, 1816, proclaims through the *Ohio Register* that the people of Jefferson township are expected to vote at the house of *Mr. Bell, on the Clear Fork* on the second Tuesday of October next.

Six cents reward is offered, September 16th, by J. & S. Selby for George Huntsbery, an apprentice to the hatting business (through the persuasions of some intriguing persons) induced to run away; but no charges paid for returning said boy.

Andrew Thompson & Co. carry on the Woolen and Coverlet Weaving at Henry Oldacre's, near James Dunlap's, on Licking Creek.

The firm of A. & T. Gormly is dissolved September 11th, and Thomas Gormly continues the business.

In September, B. Bentley opened for Jos. S. Newell an extensive assortment of goods, which were for sale or exchange for butter, beeswax, linen, grain, rags, bags, or feathers.

"To substantial citizens a credit will be given without any enhancement of prices."

"TO ALL WHOM IT MAY CONCERN.—You are hereby notified that a petition will be presented to the next Court of Common Pleas, for the county of Knox to vacate a certain part of the town of Mount Vernon, viz: Lots No. 29, 30, 31, 32, 33, 34, the property of L. S. Silliman, together with the streets and alleys adjoining."

Nathaniel Herron wants immediately two or three *Journeymen Carpenters;* also one or two apprentices.

Alexander Enos has for sale one first rate and one second rate wagon.

The members of the Mount Vernon Polemic Society met at the court house October 17th, at 6 o'clock, P. M.

On the 23d of November Wm. Y. Farquhar, Clerk, exposed to sale, at 12 o'clock, "sundry works and repairs to be done to the court house," by order of the Commissioners.

Huron and Wayne, Coshocton and Richland county advertisements are inserted in the *Ohio Register*.

Jonathan & Eli Miller, Nov. 27th, advertise that they are receiving new goods from Philadelphia: groceries, imported liquors, morocco leather shoes, queensware, &c.

J. & S. Selby, hatters, on the 7th September, at public vendue, disposed of all their traps. Among the articles enumerated were a two wheeled pleasure *carriage ;* also a handsome *sleigh, a rifle gun,* a number of first quality *hats,* &c.; and the following choice tit bit for our early citizens : ☞ "*Epicures, here is something for you!*—A PET CUB BEAR will also be sold to the highest bidder! You seldom meet with such a chance as this."

George Dickenson, in November, offered a reward of one cent for the return of a runaway apprentice boy, named Michael Fairchild, between 18 and 19 years of age, short thick set, light complexion, cunning and rogueish.

John Greer, Collector for Knox county, on the 7th December, at Major Joseph Brown's tavern, offered for sale 47 lots for taxes, amounts due ranging from 4 cents to $1.50.

Samuel H. Smith, August 7th, advertises as just finished a lot of LEATHER—*sole* and *upper, kip* and *calf,* for sale wholesale or retail, at Clinton.

James Miller, August 21st, opens a new store in Mount Vernon, in the room lately occupied by Mr. John Wilson.

Hugh McMahon carries on a tanyard at Clinton, and he warns people against purchasing leather of Samuel H. Smith, as he has a claim on it. Whereupon Samuel comes back upon him in the following unique style :

"Mr. McARDLE—*Sir* : In your paper I observe a caution to the public, by *Hugh McMahon,* forewarning them from meddling with his property. I would ask Mr. McMahon how far his claims extend ? Does he still hold a claim to the store of goods in the town of Delaware, into which he entered by the window, in the night, in the absence of the store kepeer ? Or has he relinquished his claim to the goods in hopes of having better success with *Leather* I would advise said McMahon to go to work and endeavor to obtain a livelihood by honest industry, and shun the counsel of the man who would advise him to thieving or perjury in order to gratify his revengeful passion.

I am, sir, your obedient servant,

S. H. SMITH."

A meeting of citizens of Richland county was held at the house of Samuel Williams, Esq., in the town of Mansfield. John Garrison, Esq., was called to the Chair, and C. R. Pollock appointed Secretary; and they resolved to support Thomas Worthington for re-election as Governor, Peter Hitchcock, Esq., for Representative in Congress, and Joseph Brown, Esq., for Senator, to represent Knox, Richland and Licking counties. The proceedings were ordered to be published in the *Trump of Fame*, in Trumbull county, and the *Ohio Register*.

"*Was found*, on the Main street, Mt. Vernon, a calico dress pattern. The owner, by giving an accurate description thereof, and paying for this advertisement, may have it again. Enquire of the printer.

Mt. Vernon, July 10, 1816."

From a song of these times we extract the following hits at members of Congress for voting to increase their pay, which, since the passage of the great tax bill of June, 1862, will be read with a lively interest:

Our stills you tax most dev'lish high,
You promised that it should die
When wars were o'er one year gone by
That you'd relieve us;
But here you told a thumping lie,
A thing most grievous.

Ye tax our whisky day by day,
That you may riot, sport and play—
Perhaps on Sunday ye do pray
To make amends;
Whether or not, ye are on the way
To have no friends.

We're told you sport and drink and game,
If true, dear sirs, do blush with shame—
If true or false ye have the name,
And more's the pity;
Rise quick, and tell us who's to blame,
In some committee.

There are many verses, but the above will suffice as showing the spirit in resistance to the tax on spirits, &c.

About this time, Nov., 1816, aristocratic notions entered the heads of some of our citizens, and an advertisement appears—

"A BARBER WANTED.—A Barber will, probably, meet with good encouragement in this place (Mount Vernon.) It would make it an object well worth the attention of any one who could devote part of his time to any other business."

Population in the county began to increase quite rapidly by immigration, and in the natural way. As showing something of the stock in those times, we take from the *Register* a statement in regard to David Wilson, Sept., 1816, in his seventy-eighth year, who "has had four wives and by them forty-two children. His oldest child is but sixteen years younger than himself. His second wife had five children, at two births, in eleven months. Mr. Wilson is a native of Pennsylvania—drinks grog freely—converses with ease and affability—and supports his family by labor. He has worn a hat twenty-two years, which is still passably decent."

Old Captain Wilson was well known to his neighbors as one of the liveliest old pioneers. Some of his stock yet survive in old Knox.

That there was unexampled fecundity at this time among our people, we may still further note the fact that, on the 9th of December, a petition from the west was presented to Congress, by Mr. McCoy, from an honest couple, who represented that they had been united in wedlock's happy bonds for 27 years—in which time they have added to our population 20 children, 19 of whom are living, and whom they have maintained by the product of their manual labor. On that score they pray Congress for a donation of public lands to make their declining years more easy. The Journals show its reference to the committee on Public Lands.

We still further find by the *Ohio Register*, Vol. 2, No. 11, that a "Mrs. Contzeu was delivered of *four* children—three boys and one girl, all likely to do well."

From the publication of Marriages, by McArdle, we take the following of parties well known to the citizens of the county:

"July 30th, 1816, by Rev. James Scott, Mr. John Frank to the amiable and accomplished Miss Sarah Hickman.

"July 4th, by Abner Ayres, Esq., Mr. *Isaac Williams*, of Richland county, to Miss Sally Bartlett, of this county.

"October 26th, by Jacob Hanger, Esq., Mr. Nathaniel Davis to Miss Patsey Doty.

"October 26th, by Benjamin Barney, Esq., Mr. William Wager to Miss Margaret Bixler.

"December 4th, by James Smith, Esq., Mr. John Strain to Miss Maria Craig.

In the issue of August 14th, 1816:

"HYMENIAL.

'The laws enacted by our God,
Peremptorily bind
Man to unite in silken ties,
With lovely womankind.'

"MARRIED—On Sunday evening last, by the Rev. James Smith, Mr. Daniel S. Norton, of Connelsville, Pa., to Miss Sarah Banning, daughter of Mr. Anthony Banning, of this town."

"Though Heaven had made him such another world
Of one entire and perfect Chrysolite,
He would not exchange her for it."—*Shakspeare.*

"Married—On the 26th of December, by John Young, Esq., Mr. *James Harris* to Miss *Mary Logan;* also Capt. John Stiltz to Miss *Margaret McCulloch.*

"On the 12th December, by Rev. Henry George, Mr. *William Bryant* to Miss *Elizabeth Norton.*

"At Frederick, by Abner Ayres, Esq., Mr. *George Ayres* to Miss *Jane Garrison.*

"At Mansfield, Mr. *Henry Ayres* to Miss *Jane Hoy*, daughter of Capt. Wm. Hoy, of Richland county.

Samuel Mott, candidate for Senator, Sept. 11th, sends out to the electors of Licking, Knox and Richland, the first printed address we have been able to find. He says, among other things, that he has "been induced to become a candidate from the encouragement of many substantial and respectable citizens in the district."

In the *Register*, of Sept. 11th, we find tickets announced as the choice of Chester, Morris, Morgan and Miller townships.

There were many aspirants for political promotion. Among the number we find, for Governor—

Thomas Worthington, Ethan A. Brown, James Dunlap.

For Congress—Peter Hitchcock, John G. Young, David Clendenan.

For Senate—William Stanbery, Esq., William Gavitt, Esq., Major Joseph Brown, Samuel Mott, Esq., Benjamin Martin, Esq., Waitstill Hastings, Henry Smith, Mordecai Bartley.

For House of Representatives—Jonathan Miller, William Mitchell, Munson Pond, John Warden, Alexander Enos, Judge Thomas Coulter for Richland county, William W. Farquhar.

The *Ohio Register*, of August 28th, having contained this notice:

"There is another gentleman who very kindly offers his services as Representative in the State Legislature; he is extremely modest, though very *popular;* he, therefore, believes that it will amply suffice, at this time, to make public the initial letters, only, of his name. They are "R. B."

Expectation, on tip-toe, was gratified by the following explanatory card:

"September 5th, 1816.

Mr. *McArdle:* After my respects to you, as you have been so good as to insert the two first letters of my name, (I presume it has been from the solicitations of my friends) I wish you to insert my name in full, as I am a candidate, and determined to oppose Wm. Mitchell; and forward your bill to me, and you will much oblige yours, &c.

ROBERT BUTLER.

J. P. McArdle."

Col. John Greer, about this time, felt the importance of his military commission, and issued an order to the commandants of companies in the county of Knox to send two men from each company to Mr. Boalse's inn, to nominate suitable persons to represent the counties of Knox, Licking and Richland. Whereupon there appeared, on the 13th September, the following persons:

From Captain Parcel's company, *Truman Strong* and *David Shaw*. From Captain Cook's company, Capt. *John Cook* and *Isaac N. Richardson*. From Captain John Venom's company, *Josiah B. Day* and *John Trimble*. From Captain A. Emmet's company, *William Bevans* and *Benjamin Warner*. From Captain Cooper's company, *Jacob Hanger* and *Jonathan Burch*. From Captain Squire's company, *James Miller* and *John J. Tullos*.

The result of this caucus—or military dictation—the first of the kind ever known in this county, was the nomination of Waitstill Hastings and Jonathan Miller.

Nominating caucuses were also held in Richland and in Licking counties this year. The contest waxed very warm; circulars and handbills were much circulated, and all manner of electioneering was resorted to at this election. The result, however, was that out of 485 votes for Governor cast in the whole county, Thomas Worthington received 424 majority. Peter Hitchcock had 463 majority for Congress; and the county gave small majorities for Martin for Senator and Miller for Representative.

Samuel Mott received 1 vote in Clinton, 3 in Morris, 8 in Miller, and none in Chester, Wayne, Jackson, Union and Morgan. Connected with this election is the following anecdote, which is altogether too good to be lost: Gideon Mott, the brother of Sam, who was a very plain man, yet full of wit, was responsible for it. He said that he dropped in to see Mrs. Mott on the night of the election, and while there Samuel got home from Richland county, where he had been electioneering, and asked how the election had gone in Clinton, and when he replied "He got one vote," Mrs. M. exclaimed—"That's always the way it is—if *you* had only been at home, Samuel, *and voted*, you would have got two!"

Josiah L. Hill, of Green township, offers himself as a candidate for Representative of Richland county in the following pithy address:

"The usual theme of candidates, in my standing, are many loud swelling words full of legislative wisdom, or rather of their own egotism, and to harangue every neighbor in their way with the prospect of a State road or a turnpike, by measures of which one-half of our citizens will become wealthy inn-keepers, and the other half their happy customers, with their pockets flushed with money drawn from a new country bank to be erected on a new fangled system, and thus all are to be ritch and happy. But such language as this hath never fallen from my lips since the days of my youth, when under the passions of love and addressed to females of my age, and I shall not again resume this theme until I become a widower; but while I speak for myself to men of understanding and discernment, and not to women, I have only to say that I stand a free will offering at the alter of your good pleasures. * * * Should I succeed in my election I shall feel it incumbent on me to use my feeble endeavors, by lawful incense, to gratify my constituents, and this is all the flattery I have to make use of. My abilities are too small to boast of, which, with my character, are now for you to enquire into.

So I remain the public's devoted servant,

JOSIAH L. HILL.

Green Township, Sept. 15th, 1816."

Whereupon Thomas Coulter withdraws his name from the list.

At the election, this year, 470 votes were cast in Richland county—of which Worthington had a majority of 353, Hitchcock 433; and for Senator Mordecai Bartley received 339, Wm. Gavitt 77, Joseph Brown 23, Samuel Mott 10, Benjamin Martin 6, Waitstill Hastings 6. And Samuel Williams was elected Representative.

Benjamin Martin, for Senator, puts forth the following address:

"*To the electors of the district composed of the counties of Licking, Knox and Richland:*

GENTLEMEN—As I am offering myself as a candidate to represent the inhabitants of the above district in the State Senate, I think it my duty to lay before the public a copy of official papers, which I hope you will read, and thereby satisfy your minds in regard to my political character. The first of my certificates of the oath of allegiance.

I do hereby certify that Benjamin Martin, of Bedford county, hath voluntarily taken and subscribed the oath of Allegiance and Fidelity, as directed by an Act of General Assembly of Pennsylvania, passed the 13th day of June, 1777. Witness my hand and seal the 10th day of October, A. D., 1783.

JAMES MARTIN.

Bedford county, State of Pennsylvania, ss.

We, the subscribers, Justices of the Peace, &c., in and for the county of Bedford, do hereby certify to all who it may concern, that we have been acquainted with the bearer hereof, Benjamin Martin, son of James Martin, Esq., of the county aforesaid, for these several years past, and that we have not heard of anything to operate against his character as an honest young man; but on the contrary, that he has behaved himself as a good WHIG and a friend to his country. And he being desirous to go from here to the lower parts of this State to transact some business and see his relations; therefore, all persons are requested to permit the said

Benjamin Martin to pass and repass, he behaving himself as a good and faithful citizen ought to do.

Given under our hands and seal, the 20th of April, in the year of our Lord 1784.

[L.S.] BARNARD DOUGHERTY,
DAVID ESPY.

SIRS—Having always in view, as my polar star, the principles contained in the above oath and certificate, I have with a steady mind, either as a private citizen or as a public servant, pursued that kind of policy which would best promote the interests of our country, as the principles of general suffrage; for I always have and ever shall be of opinion, that when a man has enrolled himself in our militia muster-rolls, and has paid State and county tax, that in consequence thereof, he is, and ought to be entitled to all the privileges and advantages of the government; and any policy or law, which, in its operation, would tend to lessen those privileges would be an invasion on the natural and inherent rights of man. Those, gentlemen, are the principles which I ventured my life to establish, and the remaining part of my days shall go to maintain.

Written by the public's humble servant and real friend,

BENJAMIN MARTIN."

The difficulty of collecting debts, in part at this time, may be judged of by the following unique notice of sheriff Shaw:

"PUBLIC NOTICE.—My friends and the public are hereby informed, that should they have large sums of money to collect, not to bring suit in the Court of Common Pleas, in expectation of thereby obtaining their just demands in a reasonable time, I have been induced to publish this friendly caution that the public may not censure me for neglect in my official capacity. In order to show where the fault lies read the following plain statement:

"I have been assiduously endeavoring to collect the amount of an execution ever since I have been sheriff of this county, and have as yet received no money. The associate judges grant bills of injunction successively, after I have had the property ready for sale, which has procrastinated the collection of the money. There have been two on the aforesaid execution; the judgment was rendered at December term, 1815, for ERKURIUS BEATTY. Therefore, if the laws of this State will keep a man out of his money three years after judgment is rendered, I would seriously advise my friends not to bring suit for debts due them, but rather remove to some other State or country where they may obtain justice.

JOHN SHAW, *Sheriff of Knox Co.*

September 4, 1816."

The fall term of Court of Common Pleas came on December 24, 1816.

"*Grand Jury.*—Isaac Vore, sr., foreman, Abednego Stephens, Thomas Townsend, Zebulon Ashley, David Jackson, Robert Work, Wm. Lepley, Wm. Kittle, John L. Lewis, Samuel Durbin, Robert McMillan, Anthony Banning, Francis Wilkins, Francis Blakeley and Thomas Fletcher.

"They found six bills of indictments. Tavern license was granted to Anson Brown and Jonathan Hunt. Store license to John Williams, James Rigby, James Miller, John Shrimplin, Bryant & Burr, Eli & Jonathan Miller, and Anthony Banning. Shadrach Ruark, of the Methodist church, was licensed to marry, and James Craig was fined $15 and costs for assault and battery.

"A HINT—*Promises, without performances, are like clouds without rain.*—The subscriber finds it indispensably necessary (these hard times) to call upon those of his friends who are indebted, lest they should forget him. He feels very sorry that a few broken promises should interdict all social intercourse: therefore, he earnestly solicits them to come forward and enable him, like an honest man, to meet those who have reposed confidence in him.

"J. BROWN.

"N. B. I have a quantity of whisky for sale, either by the barrel or gallon, at my tavern in Mount Vernon. J. B.

"MOUNT VERNON, June 12, 1816.

"J. Brown's tavern, called the 'Ohio Hotel.'"

"Mr. John Mecabee gives notice that he has commenced tavern keeping in Clinton, at the well known stand of the "Rising Sun," formerly occupied by Mr. E. Ogle. That the house is large and commodious for the reception of ladies, gentlemen, *and travelers.* June 19."

The 4th of July was celebrated in becoming style

at several points in the County, as will be seen from the following notices:

"At a meeting of a number of the inhabitants of Knox county, held at the house of William Mitchell, Esq., June 12th, to make arrangements for the Fourth of July, William Mitchell, Esq., was appointed Chairman, and Doctor G. B. Maxfield, Secretary. The following resolutions were unanimously adopted:

"1st. *Resolved,* That a committee be appointed to conduct the business of the day. Accordingly the following gentlemen were chosen, viz: Wm. Mitchell, G. B. Maxfield, Job Allen, N. M. Young, John Garrison and John Lewis.

"2d. That the day be kept as a day of *Thanksgiving*, and all ministers of the Gospel living within a reasonable distance be invited to attend, and that they meet at the house of Captain Job Allen, about three-quarters of a mile south of Fredericktown, at 9 o'clock A.M.

"3d. That an invitation be given to all that wish to unite with us. The business of the day to commence at 9 o'clock A. M.

"4th. That the following named gentlemen be a committee to superintend the singing, which is to be part of the performance of the day: Benjamin Jackson, Sen., Jacob Young, John Mefford and Benjamin Jackson, Jun. All those who are completely acquainted with all or either of the parts of vocal music are requested to make it known sometime previous to forming for the march, as it is intended to practice certain tunes.

"WM. MITCHELL, Chairman.

"G. B. MAXFIELD, Secretary."

In the issue of July 10, 1816, we have a notice of the proceedings celebrating the Fourth, in pursuance of the arrangements made at the meeting before noticed:

"Agreeably to previous arrangements to celebrate the 41st anniversary of American Independence, a respectable company of between three and four hundred persons met at the house of Captain Job Allen, and having formed a procession, they moved in regular order to the place appointed for public worship. A very suitable and impressive discourse was delivered by the Rev. Henry George, from Gallatians v: 13; and, after a short intermission, the attention of the audience was again called by the Rev. James Smith, who delivered an excellent and comprehensive discourse from Luke xx: 25. The singers took their seats by themselves, and the greatest decorum was observed throughout the day. The devout exercises being ended, a highly gratified audience dispersed in harmony, nothing having occurred to mar the pleasures which a decent commemoration of the birth day of our National Independence is calculated to produce."

The paper of July 21st contains a communication giving an account of a celebration "by a very respectable number of citizens in Wayne township, at the dwelling house of Mr. William Drake. The day was ushered in by the discharge of musketry from a volunteer company commanded by Captain Israel R. Dalrymple. The Declaration of Independence was read by Mr. Jabez Beers, and a patriotic and very animated oration delivered by Mr. Truman Strong." Some of the toasts are rather spicy. Witness the following:

"*Each Monarch of the Earth*—The Island of St. Helena their dominion, and Bonaparte their landlord."

"*The factious Americans, or English devotees*—Dartmoor prison their cradle, and Captain Shortland their nurse."

"*George Cabot, President of the Hartford Convention*—May the warm sun of Republicanism melt the tory frost from off his head and heart; and may he cast off his pernicious principles as the reptile doth its skin."

"*John Bull*—Twice has he attempted to destroy the liberties of America, and twice has he witnessed the futility of his attacks on the sons of freedom's soil."

CHAPTER XVII.

KNOX COUNTY IN 1817.

ILLUSTRATIONS OF THE SPIRIT OF THE TIMES.—THEATRICALS.—MISSIONARIES TO BE SENT TO CONNECTICUT.—SMALL-POX EXCITEMENT.—TRIALS OF INTEREST.—PATRIOTIC OUTGUSHINGS OF POPULAR FEELING.—COMBINATION OF MECHANICS.—BILL OF PRICES.—FIRST DELEGATE TO THE STATE INSTITUTION.—ANOTHER TOWN.—MORE WHISKY AND MORE MARRIAGES.

THIS year was introduced by a grand Theatrical exhibition by the young gentlemen of Mount Vernon. Of the performances, the following were a part: 1. An Address to the audience; 2. The Conjurer—A Dialogue; 3. The Dispute between a Merchant and his Wife; 4. Clownishness and Awkwardness, in 2 Acts; 5. The Lap-Dog—A Dialogue of two Ladies; 6. Douglass, or the Noble Shepherd—A Tragedy; 7. The Knight's Dream; 8. Cowardice and Knavery; 9. A Dialogue between a Schoolmaster and School Committee, &c. For several years the young gentlemen continued their theatrical exhibitions, and often acquitted themselves handsomely.

The following "furwan" we copy verbatim from the *Register* of January 29th, 1817:

"TAKE NOTICE—That eye have left my wife Iselbelah irelands bead and board and eye know furnwan eny person or persons creeaditing hir on my account as eye shall not be acountable for eny of her deats or contracts from this date likewse eye furwan eny person or persns from purchasing eny property whatever til her former deats is all paid up JOHN IRELAND."

The following entry upon the Court minutes, shows that the people were minus a term of Common Pleas. The reason, we learn from the oldest inhabitant, was "high water"--one of the "biggest" spring floods ever known by the old settlers:

"The Court of Com. Pleas was opened at Mount Vernon the 24th March, 1817. The Sheriff appeared and called the Court, who failing to appear, the Sheriff adjourned the Court until to-morrow morning, 9 o'clock. The Sheriff appeared and opened Court agreeable to adjournment, and called the Court, and Judges Young and Trimble, and no other Judge; whereupon, by order of the Judges, ordered the Sheriff adjourn the Court until to-morrow morning. JACOB YOUNG.

"9 o'clock, according to adjournment, the Hon. Jacob Young and John Trimble, Esq., Associate Judges, appeared. There not being a quorum, the Court being opened, the said Judges ordered the Court adjourned until Court in course. JACOB YOUNG."

This month a Yankee peddler, named Giddings, passed through the county bound for Columbus, who sold to several of the merchants wooden nutmegs, having a few genuine ones for them "to sample."

The old settlers of the county became charitably inclined, and determined to send Missionaries to convert "the everlasting heathen of Connecticut." Accordingly they formed a society for this purpose, and published on the 9th of April the following notice:

"OHIO MISSIONARY SOCIETY.

"☞ We are authorized to state, that a Society has been formed in this State for the purpose of propagating the Gospel among the everlasting Heathen of Connecticut and the parts adjacent. The first meeting of the Society will be held in Zanesville on the 20th of May next, for the purpose of electing suitable Missionaries for the performance of the arduous undertaking. It is hoped that all who are favorable to the cause, will contribute their mite to effect so desirable an object.

"☞ Printers favorably disposed towards the Ohio Missionary Society, are requested to give the foregoing one or two insertions."

At this period Zanesville was the great town of Central Ohio, and at that place and Putnam the principal shipping and other business was transacted by the citizens of Knox county.

In May, 1817, John S. Dugan having opened the Green Tree Hotel in Zanesville, advertises that he has a number of German servants (redemptioners), "who are attentive and honest; one of which is a regular bred horse Doctor, and served six years under Bonaparte as such; and 'tis said by travelers, he is one of the best hostlers in the United States. ☞ My whole study is to please, and I hope the public will give me a chance to do so."

The little log school-house on the public square had served its time, and at private houses schools had for some time been kept, when the public-spirited men in Mount Vernon started subscriptions to build another.

June 7th. The subscribers to the new school-house proposed to be erected, met at Richardson and Vore's tavern to choose managers, &c.

June 18th. The small-pox having made its appearance at Newark, caused a great excitement in the quiet village of Mount Vernon. The inhabitants ran to and fro, not knowing what to do. A public consultation was had, and Dr. R. D. Moore wrote and published a little treatise on the subject, giving the origin of the disease, the views of "the immortal JENNER" upon "*the grease*," "cow-pox," "small-pox," etc., and concluding as follows:—

"☞ The small-pox has been for some months past traveling northward, and is now within a short distance from this place. The subscriber will attend on every SATURDAY, at his house in *Mount Vernon*, for the purpose of vaccinating (those whose pecuniary means will not warrant application), *gratis*."

Anderson Searl, of Mount Vernon, on the 18th of June, publishes that he will not pay a certain note given to William Shinnibery for a certain black and white muley cow, to be delivered to him next harvest; "the said note being given in part consideration of a certain horse sold to me by said Shinnibery for a sound horse, which I have since found to be unsound."

NOTABLE PROCEEDINGS OF COMMON PLEAS COURT, JUNE 23D.

"At this term, the Indictments vs. John Strain, were read, and he was fined on the first $20 and costs—and on the second, assault and battery, $10 and costs.

"The *Grand Jurors*—Royal D. Simons, foreman—returned seven bills of Indictment. Albert Sherwood, by verdict of jury, recovered $75 off of Wm. Williams for assault and battery; and in suit of the State Wm. Williams was fined $15 and costs. Thomas Wilkins and John Roop are, each, fined $5 and costs for assault and battery; and John Strain and John Roop, each, fined $5 and costs for an affray, and Robert Butler was fined $15 and costs.

"James Trimble renews his tavern license; also Michael Harter, John Davidson, Gotleib Zimmerman, and Richardson & Vore.

"On application of Anthony Banning and Samuel Kratzer for the vacating of a part of the addition of the town of Mount Vernon. The application is overruled at the cost of the applicants.

"Samuel H. Smith's application for vacating part of the town of Clinton was continued; and also continued Oct. term, 1817.

"Ordered that a certificate issue to pay expense of Coroner's inquest over the body of Wm. Conaway, jr.; also of N. Butler.

PATRIOTIC OUTBURST ON THE NATIONAL ANNIVERSARY.

The 4th of July was celebrated by the Mount Vernon Artillery Company, under Capt. Joseph Brown, with all the pomp and circumstance of war. The day was duly ushered in by a national salute—a grand parade came off—a sumptuous dinner at Richardson & Vore's inn—and toasts, speeches, and wine made it a merry occasion. The Declaration of Independence was read by Doctor Robert D. Moore. Among the toasts were the following:

"*The Constitution,* the grandest work of human genius—May it long stand the proudest monument of Republican solidity.

"*The memory of our departed American heroes from Warren down to the brave Pike and Lawrence.*

"*Faction,* the bane of republican governments—May it never be suffered to impair confidence in our legally constituted authorities.

"May the words Federalist and Democrat be exchanged for the prouder appellation of—'I am an American citizen.'

"*The Fair Daughters of Columbia*—Always lovely, but more divinely enchanting when attired in homespun, smiling on the patriot brave.

"By Capt. John Shaw—May *brother Jonathan* watch *John Bull* with the eye of an Eagle."

A *quarterly* or *sacramental meeting* was held on Friday, the 4th of July, at the Dry Creek school house. All christians and ministers of the gospel were earnestly solicited to attend and assist in the various exercises of the service.

THE STORE SET UPON CAMPBELL'S POEMS—THREE DOLLARS OF ADVERTISING A $1.50 BOOK.

"Hope deferred maketh the heart sick."

"In the month of November, 1815, I advertised a volume of Campbell's poems, which I had lent some considerable time before to an acquaintance of mine. The principal poem in this work is entitled "*The pleasures of Hope*," and I had entertained a *hope* of obtaining it long ere this; but this hope, like some other of my expectations, has perished. I now only *wish* it may be returned to me.

ROBERT BUCHANAN.

June 18th, 1817."

This notice not having the desired effect, on the 16th of July the following pointed addition is made to it: "If Mr. J—n W—k—r, who was entrusted to deliver the above volume to me, by the person to whom I lent it, does not return it within two weeks from the date hereof, I will give his name to the public, together with some traits of his character, which have not much the appearance of *honesty!*

"As I am credibly informed that you have refused *five dollars* for those poems, I think you ought not to object paying me $1.50 for them. You may send or bring me this amount, or the book, at your own option. I am determined to have it or its worth from you—*peaceably if I can, forcibly if I must.*

R. B.

"The pleasures of Hope"——*again.*

"*To Mr. John Walker:*

Sir—The two weeks in which I allowed you to return the above poems, have now elapsed unheeded by you. At the expiration of that time, I promised to give the public your name and an exposition of your conduct in retaining this book in your own possession after having *politely* proffered your services to convey it to me from the young lady to whom I had lent it; but being blessed with a pretty good share of *charity,* I have omitted the exposition for the present, and inserted your *name* only—giving you one week further to decide whether or not '*honesty is the best policy!*'

ROBERT BUCHANAN.

July 3d, 1817."

MISCELLANEOUS ITEMS SHOWING THE KIND OF CURRENCY, BUSINESS VIEWS AND INCONVENIENCES.

John Frank & Co., July 17th, offer "iron, castings and salt, being both *chartered* and *cash* articles in this place, and solicit their friends to whom they gave a short credit last winter to come forward and discharge their respective accounts. * * * * They are informed that the paper of the *Owl Creek Bank of Mount Vernon*, and that of *Canton*, and the *Farmers & Mechanics' Bank* of Steubenville will be taken," &c.

Luke Walpole brings to Mount Vernon a quantity of salt, leather, and castings to exchange for beef and pork, delivered in Zanesville the coming winter.

Oct. 16th, Frederick Falley, proprietor of Venice, has 1,000 lots for sale, and invites all classes of mechanics and business men to locate there. About this time it was the supposition that Venice would become the future shipping point for Knox county, and Norton & Banning established a storage, commission and mercantile house at Venice, on the Sandusky bay. As evidence that this belief was general, we may cite the act of the Legislature of 1817, declaring that the road to be made by the Knox, Richland & Huron Turnpike Company shall terminate at the town of Venice, on Sandusky bay.

Robert D. Moore, as agent for the Mary Ann Furnace, situate on the Rocky Fork of Licking, brings to the notice of our citizens a large assortment of castings of superior beauty and quality, and asks them to encourage manufactories.

Daniel S. Norton notifies those who were in debt

to him on the 16th of August last, to pay up while they can in the paper of the country.

Anthony Banning advertises a large lot of *leather*, which he will sell for hides or chartered money—or chartered money will be given for hides.

Jesse B. Thomas cautions "*all persons* (indiscriminately) against cutting, destroying, or removing timber from or otherwise trespassing upon his lands on the Hamtramck section, as I have given my agents (Messrs. *John Roberts* and *John Warden*) positive instructions to prosecute all."

THE FIRST COMBINATIONS OF MECHANICS, WHO THEY WERE, AND THEIR BILLS OF PRICES.

"TAYLORS PRICES.—We, the subscribers, of Mount Vernon, have agreed to establish the following prices for Tayloring, viz: *Great coats*, $4.50; *broad cloth coats*, $4.00; *common homespun*, $3.50; *common pantaloons*, $1.25; *vest*, $1.25; *pantaloons with buttons on the* legs, $1.75; *ditto welted*, $1.50; *cherrivallies laced*, $3; *plain ditto*, $2.25; *ladies' coats*, $3.50. *Any extra work* on the above articles shall be priced according to the work.

WM. W. ALEXANDER,
WM. PETTIGREW,
WM. CROUCH.

May 20, 1817."

William Giffin and Peter Zarly got up a meeting of Millwrights, at Zimmerman's inn, on the 26th of August, for establishing a bill of prices for their work. At this meeting John Williamson, Samuel Pyle, Peter Zarly, James King and William Giffin were present. Among the items we find—"For a double geered grist-mill, $300; for a double geered saw-mill, $200; for a meal spout, $2; meal trough, $3; hopper, $4, &c."

Jacob Myers, Patrick Nellans, Robert Robertson, Samuel Hoppers, Samuel Vance, John Byan, John Cottle, John Kinsey and David Poter; agree, upon honor, to support the said bill of prices.

PETTY THIEVING AND OTHER RASCALITY.

Michael Click offers one cent reward for Michael Teadrow, an apprentice to the brick-making business, but no charges paid. September 3d.

James Miller publishes the following notice:

"The person who took away a *Mattock* from my building, without leave, is requested to return the same immediately, or his name will be given to the public (besides prosecuting), as it is well known who purloined it."

"TAKE CARE.—The person who was so kind as to take away without leave, a pair of *stretchers* and a broken *singletree*, on the 29th of August; they were laying on the green between *Messrs. Bryant & Burr's* and *Mr. J. Frank & Co.'s* stores, are requested to return the same immediately to the subscriber, and save themselves trouble, they had better return them before they are troubled with a call from Mr. Constable.

"Mt. Vernon, Sept. 5, 1817. *James Thompson.*"

Noah Rude has a chesnut sorrel horse stolen from James Bryant's pasture on the night of the 5th of September, and offers a reward for him.

At the District Court of the United States, held at Chillicothe on the 9th of September, Samuel Bunting was indicted on a charge of robbing the mail between Newark and Zanesville, and was sentenced to the Penitentiary for one year.

Horse thieves about this time became so bold that Joseph Berry had, on the morning of the 19th of September, a mare, saddle and bridle stolen from the door of James Thompson in Mount Vernon, just after he had hitched her, and gone into the house.

At the October term of Knox Common Pleas, John McFarland was tried for feloniously stealing a five and two one dollar notes on the Owl Creek Bank of Mount Vernon. The jury found him guilty of stealing the five dollar note; as to the other counts in the indictments, not guilty. The court sentenced him to one year imprisonment in the penitentiary at hard labor, but no part of said term to be kept in solitary cells of the prison. The prisoner was a boy, 14 to 15 years of age, the son of a poor man, who, from want of restraint and of care in his tuition, had been led to crime.

PROCEEDINGS OF FALL TERM (OCT. 13TH) COMMON PLEAS.

"On the petition of sundry inhabitants of Mount Vernon for incorporation of said town, the sheriff made proclamation thereof according to law. Store license was issued to Daniel S. Norton and P. M. Weddle. Tavern license issued to Wm. Ayres, Seth Knowles, Richardson & Vore. S. W. Culberson was allowed $10 for defending Jacob Kyser, a criminal now in court."

Patrick Moore had 81 cases at this term upon the docket vs. John Green. Thus many bank cases make their appearance, and add greatly to law business in this county. Among others were the noted Owl Creek ones; Patrick Moore vs. James Smith, John Hawn, jr., Jonathan Miller et al.; the famous Luke Walpole case shows its head, and the "Granville Alexandrian Society" brings suit vs. Enos, Farquhar et al. The first money made by process of law, for military purposes, was in the noted cases of C. Langworthy for use of George Downs vs. Alex. Enos and Samuel Kratzer. In which it was "ordered that in both these cases the money be paid to Dr. Timothy Burr, the present Paymaster of this Regiment," &c.

The State case vs. Alex. McKee was disposed of by fining him $5 and costs; vs. Wm. Henry by fine of $3 and costs; John Watt $3 and costs; George Lybarger $10 and costs. Assault and battery was coming to be regarded in a more serious light.

ANOTHER TOWN ON PAPER.

A new competitor for public favor springs into notice in September bearing the name of FLORIDA. It is a town laid out by Samuel Hardenbrok, Geo. Vennemon and Plum Sutliff, on the ⋈ roads from Mansfield to Columbus, and from Mount Vernon to Upper Sandusky—on a handsome eminence surrounded with springs of elegant water and rich soil, convenient mill seats on the waters of Owl Creek and Whetstone. Of this as of another city it may truthfully be said—"*Ilium fuit.*"

"*IO TRIUMPHE*"—A NEW INSTITUTION ESTABLISHED.

Joseph Brown starts a distillery near Mount Vernon, and gives *sixty-two and a half cents* for every 56 lbs. of good clean rye delivered at the distillery, or at Capt. Douglas' mill; he also gives one gallon of whisky for every five pecks of good clean rye. Thus in October, 1817, did the second large manufactory of fire water go into operation.

THE MARRIAGES REGISTERED.

"On January 2d, 1817, by Rev. James Smith, Mr. *John Dwyer* to the amiable Miss *Sally Martin*, both of Mt. Vernon.

"On January 7th, by the same, Mr. *Reasin Yates* to the accomplished Miss *Nancy Boalse*, daughter of Capt. N. C. Boalse, both of this town.

"On Tuesday February 4th, by the same, Mr. *Obadiah Tatman* to Miss *Peggy Severe.*

> "What joys they both receive and both bestow,
> Virgins may guess but wives, experienced, know."

"On same day, by Rev. James Scott, Mr. *David Newell,* of Richland county, to Miss *Juliet Cooper* of Knox.

> "There seems no goose so gray, but soon or late
> She finds some honest gander for her mate."

"On Saturday evening, 22d February, by Wm. Douglass, Esq., Mr. Elijah Webster to Miss Elizabeth, disconsolate widow of— Mr.— *Ask,* alias —— alias—— Simpkins.

"Married, April 10th, by Wm. Douglass, Esq., Mr. Isaac Hollister to Miss Hannah Kattle.

> "A matchless pair—
> Hers the wild lustre of the rising morn,
> And his the radiance of the risen day."

"Married, on May 15th, 1816, by Rev. James Smith, Mr. *Alpheus Chapman* to the amiable Miss *Amy Ward.*

"On May 7th, 1817, by Rev. James Scott, Mr. *Edward Marques* to Miss *Elizabeth Newell.*

"On June 19th, by Rev. James Smith, Mr. *Leonard Simons* to Miss *Sally Boyles.*

"On July 17th, by the same, Mr. *Isaac Vore,* jr., to Miss *Polly Martin.*

"On July 10th, by Rev. George Vennemon, Mr. *Ensley D. Johnson* to Miss *Sarah Petton,* near Lexington, Richland co.

> "Love, friendship, honor, truth and pure delight,
> Harmonious mingle in the nuptial rite."

"On July 17th, by Rev. James Smith, Mr. *Alexander McKee* to Miss *Tabitha Waddle.*

"The following good play is made on occasion of the marriage of James Strong to Miss Sally Strong:

> "It has been said in former times,
> Too sacred to be wrong;
> The battle is not always won,
> Or given to the STRONG.
> Grant this assertion may be true,
> As on the sacred page;
> Who'll gain the battle, I will ask,
> Where two that's STRONG ENGAGE?"

CHAPTER XVIII.

CONDITION OF THE COUNTRY IN 1818.

RUIN IMPENDING.—MUCH SUFFERING.—A FEW QUAINT ADVERTISEMENTS.—EFFORTS TO START A SABBATH-SCHOOL, AND TO SELL YOUNG LADIES!—HORSE-THIEVES AND COUNTERFEITERS ABOUND.—A JAIL-BIRD ESCAPES.—A CRIPPLE RUNS.—HABEAS CORPUS TRIALS.—A GRAND CIRCULAR HUNT.

THE palmy periods of Knox county, prior to 1820, were from 1808 until 1812, and from 1815 until 1818. In the intermediate time there was much depression and suffering caused by the war of 1812; and from the beginning of the year 1818, there was another period of deep gloom and distress caused by the scarcity of money, failure of banks, &c. For several years there was but slight influx of population, but little addition to the wealth of this section. The productions of the country were almost valueless in exchange for money, and it was with difficulty that they could be bartered for goods at the stores. The unfortunate speculation in which many of the most substantial citizens engaged, under the name of the Owl Creek Bank; the depreciation of the paper money making up the principal circulation, and the general lack of confidence throughout the country in all kinds of business operations, prevented much improvement being made in Knox county. Many of the then settlers became entirely discouraged and out of heart, pulled up stakes and returned to their old homes eastward, or sought better chances elsewhere in the new country. Almost all whom we have conversed with, say that the most dull and gloomy times they have witnessed since the last war with Great Britain, were between the years 1818 and 1825.

During this period we find numberless suits instituted, and judgments obtained, by "The Granville Alexandrian Society," "The German Bank of Wooster," "The Owl Creek Bank," and other like institutions, against the Vores, and Farquhars, and Strongs, and Smiths, and Browns, and Martins, and Hawns, and Winships and others, of the older class of settlers. The mere mention of this fact, in connection with matter developed in our Owl Creek Bank history, will be sufficient upon this subject to convey an idea of the sad condition of affairs at that period. To other matters, then, we will revert.

And first, as to the other business disposed of by the Court in 1818. The Grand Jury, at the April term, found bills of indictment against fourteen persons. For affrays, the Court fined Wm. Wright $1, and costs; Wm. Herrod and Simon Anderson $3 each, and costs. At the July term, six bills were returned by the Grand Jury; and for fights, Sylvester Buxton and Daniel Baxter were each fined $3, and costs. Except Michael Harter, no new person makes application to keep tavern, and none to sell goods—the houses of Burr, Green & Co., and Moody and McCarty, being simply alterations in style of firms. And for six years so few changes were made in these or other branches of business, that we desist from further detail of Court proceedings.

The legal termination of Clinton's existence is the only court matter left to be recorded on this page. The Court, on the 17th of April, heard the petition of Samuel H. Smith, Ichabod Marshal, Elihu S. Webster, Lathrop Shurtliff, John P. McArdle, Benjamin Barney and Richard Ayres, for vacation of a part of the town of Clinton, and granted the prayer. Shortly after this the Post-Office at Clinton is discontinued, and it rapidly goes into decline.

Miss Ann Davis is the second milliner advertised in Mount Vernon. "She is to be found at the house of James Smith, Esq., on Gay street; and will alter straw hats of old date to any fashion, and has straw on hand for a few hats."

As the people are becoming still more fashionable, another milliner makes her appearance—and she has the advantage over the others of being "*Mantua-maker*" and "*Florist.*" Mary Lindsey is at the house of Benjamin Martin, corner of Vine and Market streets. March 18th, 1818, witnesses the opening out of the first "Man-tor-mentor," as the natives then pronounced the word in Mount Vernon.

Burr, Green & Co., having bought a stock of goods of Mr. Norton, in January, advertise that they will sell as low as formerly for *Owl Creek paper*, or approved country produce, but no credit given.

In April, 1818, a two-column address was published in favor of establishing a Sabbath School in Mount Vernon—arguing that "it would be much better for young men to instruct the children, instead of haunting the taverns from morning till night;" and saying that "a respectable company of young ladies in town intend to associate themselves together for the purpose of forming a Sabbath school."

James Smith issues an advertisement so characteristic of himself, and characteristic of the times, that we give it in his own words:

> "NEW GOODS FOR SALE.—James Smith has just received and offers for sale a general assortment of Merchandise. In the house of Mr. Gilman Bryant, he will sell low for CASH in hand, or country produce delivered, but no credit given. OWL Creek paper will be received at par; Granville, Wooster, New Lisbon, and Canton will be received at the present. Clerk's Office removed to this stand, and
>
> YOUNG LADIES FOR SALE
>
> at seventy-five cents each."

About the time the Owl Creek Bank was in its glory, sundry citizens of the northern part of Knox county and of Richland and Huron concluded to grow suddenly rich in like manner. Accordingly they met at Mansfield in September, 1816, and associated themselves as the Bank of Richland and Huron. Having consulted upon the subject, in October they put their schemes into articles, and Daniel Ayres, John Garrison, Winn Winship, Wm. Webster, Wm. B. James, Wilson Elliott, Matthew Kelly, Alexander McGaffick, Plum Sutliff, Samuel Williams, Wm. W. Cotgreave, Wm.

Dean Mann, Geo. Venneman, Jacob Ozenbaugh and Joseph Williams take stock, and act as Commissioners.

They got fairly to work in Owl Creek style, and gave through the paper frequent notices reading thus—

"Wilson Elliott, *Cashier*, notifies stockholders to pay *ten per centum on the amount of stock subscribed*, being the fourth installment, within 60 days. Also those who have been accommodated with loans, will be prepared to pay in 25 *per cent. on the renewal of their notes.*"

The paper of the "Granville Alexandrian Society" had, about those times, a large circulation among our citizens, and as this institution has subsequently acquired almost as great notoriety as the Owl, we give a few lines of our history to its origin.

A number of the *Granvillians* having become desirous of handling money faster than the hard money allowed, associated themselves together in 1806 to make paper money. Among this number were Timothy Rose, Timothy Spelman, Elias Gilman, Samuel Thrall, Job Case, Samuel Rose, Samuel Bancroft, John Duke, Hiram Rose and Jeremiah R. Munson. On the third day of January, 1807, an act of incorporation was obtained, and the persons first named were constituted the first Board of Directors; and for many years this organization manufactured what they called money.

The country was filled with other worthless and irresponsible bank paper, and a great deal of that counterfeit, too. "Shinplasters," as now termed, were manufactured wherever type and printing-ink could be got. We have one of the kind made at the *Register* office in Mount Vernon, by McArdle, to fill an order from a stranger named *Isaac Foster*. They were printed on common letter paper. Two quires of eighty-seven and a half cents and two quires of seventy-five cents were issued.

Mr. A. Liggett, Teller of the Farmers' and Mechanics' Bank of Pittsburgh, wrote to L. S. Silliman, Cashier of the Owl Creek Bank:

"There is no doubt but the person getting the checks you mention printed is doing so without the knowledge of Mr. Ross, for the purpose of defrauding the public. If you can, without any trouble, put a stop to it, be good enough to do so."

McArdle had printed them the 7th of December, and it was not until January that the Cashier had been heard from. Excitement ran high "on change," and with those who had taken these change tickets. Those were terrible times on Owl Creek!

Just before this occurrence, the men of commerce had been greatly alarmed by counterfeit silver dollars being put in circulation in the county, and in preference paper had assumed a prominence in the public estimation.

A man named *Daniel Wolgamott* was arrested, and lodged in the jail of the county, for attempting to pass twelve base and counterfeit dollars, purporting to be silver. And Robert Walker was arrested for having attempted to pass one counterfeit dollar. A warrant was also issued for one *William Coffran*, for being concerned in making and passing counterfeit dollars, purporting to be silver, founded on an affidavit of the prisoner, Wolgamott. *Coffran* was a shoemaker by trade, and, notwithstanding he was quite lame, made his escape. The community believed him guilty.

Wolgamott, or *Vulgamott*, as Sheriff Shaw called him, remained in his lodgings (the jail) about a month, when, between dark and daylight one night, he "left his bed and board;" and the Sheriff offered $45 reward for the capture of a "man six feet high, dark complexion, dark hair, and has a downcast look"—but all in vain; the place that had known him shall know him no more forever!

Horse-thieves abounded more in Knox county at this time than at any other period of its history. Scarcely a day passed without an account of some new depredation. Among the number were two fine mares stolen from the stable of Elijah Adams, in Morris township, for which he offered $40 reward; also a reward for the thief, "who no doubt belongs to the gang of thieves who have so long *labored in their vocation* of taking away horses from their honest owners *without leave*, and passing counterfeit money through this State."

Two shoemakers by trade, who passed by the names of Richie and Ryan, alias Austin and Scott, were of this gang; and also one John Crawford, who was caught with a horse stolen from Fairfield county, tried, and sentenced to six years imprisonment in the Penitentiary. A horse-thief was followed till near Hanary's Block-house; but by leaving the horse, rode down and made good his escape. Another horse-thief, followed beyond Radnor, left a horse dead in the road from hard driving. It was the custom then for men to make common cause, and hunt for each other's horses as soon as they heard of a theft being committed; for no one knew then but what it would be his turn to suffer next. Anti-horse-stealing associations were got up, and neighbors sympathized with each other, upon the principle that "a fellow-feeling makes us wondrous kind."

HABEAS CORPUS.

The first writ of habeas corpus was allowed "by the Honorable John H. Mefford, Esq.," April 26th, 1819. John Shaw, Sheriff, brought into the Courthouse the body of Amos Yarnall, with the mittimus, showing the cause of his caption and detention. Saml. Mott, Esq., appeared as his attorney, and on his motion, after the attorney for the State had duly considered the matters in law arising, the Court let him to bail in the sum of $50. James Smith his security.

The second case, that of Wm. Knight, who, on the 8th of July, 1819, was brought to the Courthouse, and by Judge Mefford admitted to bail in the sum of $50; Alexander Elliott becoming his bondsman.

The third case occurred April 3d, 1820, when Judge Joseph Brown set at large Abel Fowler, upon Artemas Estabrook and Alfred Manning becoming his security for his appearance at the May term of Knox Common Pleas, in the sum of $50.

In this year an interesting case was presented in allowance of a writ, on the 20th of November, by Judge Brown, requiring John Bird and Judah Bird to bring into Court the body of an Indian child, daughter of Rachel Conkapote, deceased, by her husband, Elisha Conkapote, both Indians of the Stockbridge tribe. Judges Young and Chapman also appeared, and the whole Court lent itself to an impartial examination of the case, which resulted in their leaving the little Indian in the hands of the Birds, John and Judah. This little Indian was daughter of the squaw killed, as related in chapter xxi.

This was perhaps the most interesting case heard upon writ of this character, until the great military case of Col. Warden, which was tried upon writ issued in name of the State vs. Wm. E. Davidson.

"*By Judge James Elliot, September 27th,* 1837.

"W. E. Davidson, Provost Marshal of the 2d Brigade, 3d Division, Ohio Militia (late 4th Brigade, 7th Division, O. M.), in pursuance of an order by Brigadier-General Wm. Bevans (commander of said Brigade), and upon action of a Court Martial, now in session in Mt. Vernon, convened by order of said Gen. Wm. Bevans, on Monday, Sept. 25th, 1837. Col. H. W. Strong, President of Board. Discharged by said James Elliott, Judge, &c."

Another case, of much interest, at a still later period, was about the two dwarfs—of Porter's wife—held, it was claimed, illegally by Warner. Upon hearing, however, the Court did not think so, and they remained in custody of the showman, at last accounts.

The writ of habeas corpus became a favorite resort in liquor cases, where parties were, as they thought, unjustly persecuted and cast into prison, by fines imposed upon temperance principles. During the administration of his Honor Judge Bevans, more writs of habeas corpus were granted than in all the rest of our history put together. To such an extent was it carried, that he acquired the *sobriquet* of Old Habeas Corpus. The venerable Judge always leaned towards the side of suffering humanity. If he erred in judgment, it was because no work upon the subject had been published at that date. Our townsman, Judge Hurd's work on Habeas Corpus, did not get into print until the year 1858.

SPORTS AND CIRCULAR HUNTS.

From the earliest period in our history, hunting, horse-racing, and athletic sports, were freely indulged in by our people. Many, very many of these festive occasions have been lost sight of or entirely forgotten by the great majority of those now living, who in these later days have become wholly absorbed in money-making pursuits, and have ceased to think that man was made to rejoice as well as to mourn. Our Owl Creek settlers, the old pioneers, bless their memories, believed that there is a time for all things, and that sports of the turf, circular hunts, etc., were not interdicted. In truth, we are constrained to say that very many of the old set believed in such sports all the time.

A grand circular hunt came off in 1818, wherein the natives of Knox and Coshocton vied with each other for the mastery. At an early hour of the day appointed for the frolic, the people commenced gathering in on the lower part of Owl Creek; and when the companies were formed under their captains, more than 1500 people were present. The drive was from our county towards the town of

Coshocton, and when finally the ring was drawn in, from 300 to 500 deer and many wolves were bagged. It was a glorious day that—remembered with pride by all who participated in it. Our old friend Joe Hull, of Monroe, was one of the captains, and it can well be imagined that he enjoyed it hugely.

CHAPTER XIX.

HISTORY OF THE PRESS IN KNOX COUNTY.

THE OHIO REGISTER.—THE AURORA—STANDARD—ADVERTISER—WATCHMAN—GAZETTE—DAY-BOOK—BANNER—TRUE WHIG—TIMES.—THE VARIOUS DAILY AND WEEKLY PAPERS, RELIGIOUS AND POLITICAL PUBLICATIONS, AND SOME ACCOUNT OF THE EDITORS AND THEIR ADVENTURES.

IN July, 1813, a press was put up in Clinton, and the first newspaper ever issued in Knox county then made its appearance, styled *The Ohio Register*, printed and published every Tuesday by Smith and McArdle. Samuel H. Smith was the proprietor of the town of Clinton, and he induced John P. McArdle, who was a good practical printer, to engage with him in the publication of a newspaper, and in the printing business generally, at that place. McArdle emigrated from Ireland, March 17th, 1801, and came to this county in 1809. He is now living, in his 78th year, at Fremont, in this State. Smith, as elsewhere stated, is alive, and surveying in Texas.

The waning fortunes of Clinton, and the rising greatness of Mount Vernon, caused the office, after two years of tribulation, to be transferred to the latter place, and accordingly, on the 24th of April, 1816, the first paper ever issued in Mount Vernon made its appearance, bearing the name of "*The Ohio Register*," and having the laudable motto—

"Aware that what is base no polish can make sterling." It was the prolongation of *The Ohio Register*, published for two years at Clinton by Sam'l H. Smith and John P. McArdle.

From the Editor's "Address to his Patrons," we extract the following:

"On moving the office and establishment of *The Ohio Register* to this place, it will be expected the editor (according to custom) will say *something* to his patrons.

"The editor, well awarė of the difficulties attending the task he has undertaken, to instruct, enlighten and please the public, must not only produce that which is excellent in its kind, but he must continually vary the matter and manner of his lucubrations; he must, to a certain degree, *be all things to all men.* The serious, the gay, the learned and the unlearned, not only expect that their tastes will be studied and their inclination gratified, but the same individual becomes dissatisfied with a long course of the same species of entertainment; he hopes to be delighted and surprised; he must find productions which are meant to be instructive, and novelty in those which are designed for amusement. How the editor will execute the duties of his employment, time will discover; he is not disposed to boast of his education, to make a parade of his abilities, or to seduce the public with a multiplicity of specious promises. It is too common for editors of newspapers to undertake more than they are able to perform.

"The editor is determined not to subject himself to accusations of the nature above-mentioned; and although he feels a considerable degree of diffidence, he would have it fully understood that he expects and desires to be judged by his work. One thing however he confidently promises, the most assiduous and persevering industry will be exerted to render his paper worthy of the patronage which he hopes he will meet with.

* * * * * *

"Finally, the *Ohio Register* shall not be a receptacle for party politics, or personal abuse. On those principles the publication of the *Register* is commenced in this town, and the editor hopes that he will receive that share of patronage which will enable him to continue it.

* * * * * *

"Terms: The *Ohio Register* will be published every Wednesday, and will be distributed to subscribers in Mount Vernon and Clinton, and forwarded to those at a distance by the first opportunity, at $2.00 per annum if paid in advance, or $2.50 if paid within the first six months, or $3.00 if paid within the second six months.

"Those who receive their papers by post, are to pay the postage. No subscription received for less than one year, and no paper discontinued until all arrearages are paid. A failure to give notice of discontinuance of a subscription, at or previous to the end of the time subscribed for, will always be considered as a new engagement."

The following good rule in regard to advertisements was set forth: "The COST must accompany all advertisements, otherwise they will be continued at the expense of the advertiser until paid for."

In those early times there were many who courted the muses, and among their effusions we find a lengthy piece which appeared May 1st, 1816, and we have heard it ascribed to John H. Mefford. We extract a few verses descriptive of "Mount Vernon walk" and "Owl Creek's fertile banks," gratified, that as Shakspeare has it—

"The poet's eye in a fine frenzy rolling,"

prophetically told in that early day, how

"For lovely nymph and gentle swain,
Its gentle stream shall long remain
A pleasing prospect for the view!"

And though fools wisdom's lovely ways
For want of sense, hate all their days,
May all MOUNT VERNON walk erect
In all the paths she may direct,

Then shall not war's furious guns
Bereave parents of faithful sons;
The cries of children we'll not hear
Whose fathers left them arms to bear;

Nor shall a true and loving wife
Mourn for losing a husband's life,
Who fell a victim to war's rage
Before he passed the middle age.

A fair damsel shall not complain
For a true sweetheart in war slain;
Nor citizens for faithful friends weep
Who gave life their country to keep;

But fields shall bear, and we be blest
With crops the choicest and the best;
And gentle cows shall come at will
Our pails with richest milk to fill.

Our barns shall be filled with plenty,
And Springs emit water gently,
Which shall in small clear currents flow,
To refresh man, or panting roe.

Abundance shall our tables spread,
And servants never long for bread;
But look up satisfy'd, and say,
"Lawful commands we will obey."

Then long shall Owl Creek's fertile banks
Be a peaceful walk for all ranks,
Where the sycamore tall does grow,
And where the elm its shade doth show.

For lovely nymph and gen'rous swain,
Its gentle stream shall long remain
A pleasing prospect for the view,
Where songs of birds are ever new.

On the 15th of October, 1817, the first six months of the second volume of the *Ohio Register* having been completed, the editor calls upon subscribers to pay up old scores—

"For without this one thing necessary, it is impossible to expect that we can live; money would be preferable, but if that is scarce with you, rags, wheat, rye, corn, and almost all kinds of market produce will be taken in payment."

On the 5th of November he proposes to "take for subscription, advertisements, hand-bills or book-binding, wheat, rye, corn, buckwheat, &c., delivered at Davis' mill in this town, in preference to *some* unchartered paper." (A sly dig this at the Owl Creek Bank, Mr. McArdle.) On the 8th of April, 1818, he says—

"*Peaceably if we can, forcibly if we must.*" HARD TIMES!! *So they are, but that is not my fault.*—The next number of the *Ohio Register* wil complete the 2d volume that has been printed in Mount Vernon. From many of our subscribers we have received nothing but *promises* for services rendered. But these will not always answer the purpose. Like the notes of some of our banks, they soon depreciate when thrown into market, unless it is known they are bottomed upon a specie capital; and like them "they will not pay debts abroad." But to be brief, "we want money and must have it." Remember the trite old saying, "*the laborer is worthy of his hire.*" As soon as this volume is out we intend altering the paper into a different form. As we expect on a large quantity of paper in the course of two or three weeks, (for which we must pay the cash) we hope those in arrears will call immediately and settle their respective accounts."

On the 15th of April, A. D., 1818, Vol. 2, No. 52, was issued. Those who were in arrears and so often and politely requested to call and settle did not do so; the large quantity of paper could not be paid for in cash, and John P. McArdle goes down under the debt of unrequited kindness—unrecompensed services. And the people of Mount Vernon, for a time, were without a newspaper because there were not enough among them having the high sense of honor to "pay the printer!"

From this period until 1844, there was no paper published uninterruptedly as long as the *Ohio Re-*

gister. Various new papers were started, and the editors became dissatisfied, the publishers discouraged, and, after a little experimenting with journalism, went to some more profitable business, engaged in some new enterprise, or left the country. And we regret to say that the people seemed to have no proper appreciation of their journals, for there is not in existence a complete file of any of the old papers, and in fact scarcely a number of either to be found.

During this time the ablest men who were connected with the press, and the most violent in opposition to each other, were Charles Colerick and William Bevans. They were arrayed against each other as candidates for office, and each for several terms held the position of Sheriff of the county. Both were from Western Pennsylvania—Bevans from Fayette, and Colerick from Washington county—and well skilled in the political wire-working and manœuvering for which the politicians of that county have ever been famous. In the division of parties, the former was for Adams and the latter for Jackson. The great bone of contention, however, was the county printing, and that might with much truth be said to have been the only principle at issue between them.

About 1822, Charles Colerick with his brothers, John and Henry, made their appearance in this county, while Bevans was Sheriff, and they set about establishing a small printing-office. In 1824 Edson Harkness, a printer, surveyor and schoolteacher, emigrated from "Down East" to Mount Vernon; and in 1825 he started a very small newspaper, which he styled *The Western Aurora*, and, after publishing it two years, he sold out, in 1827, to James Harvey Patterson, from Fayette county, Pa., and William Smith, from Washington county, Pa., who, under the firm of Patterson & Co., continued its publication until 1829, when they transferred the establishment to William Bevans, who carried it on until 1831, when he disposed of it to Wm. P. Reznor, who had learnt his trade in the office and lived with Bevans. In 1832, C. P. Bronson became associated with him, and for a time the paper was published by Bronson & Reznor, until, in October, 1833, Dan Stone buys out the office and carries the paper on a few months alone; and then Dr. Morgan L. Bliss is associated with him, and it continues, under the style of Stone & Bliss, until November 29th, 1834, on account of severe and protracted illness, the latter withdraws, and Dr. Lewis Dyer, in a salutatory of two mortal columns, enters the list as editor, as a permanent business; but in January, 1835, he disappears, and Dr. John Thomas succeeds him, who, being like his immediate predecessor, of a philosophical turn of mind and inclined to treat upon physiology, hygiene, temperance and the laws of health, found the age unsuited for moral reform, and, seized by one of his fits of "azure devils," suddenly abdicated the tripod, leaving Dan Stone alone in his glory, who continued "solitary and alone" until May 16th, when he too published his valedictory, and the paper fell into anonymous hands; and it had thenceforth a very short and precarious existence, and has passed from memory forever.

The first name of the paper published by this press was the *Western Aurora*—the last name was the *Mount Vernon Gazette*. This office was first set in operation at a small frame house where Dr. Thompson's residence now stands, on lot No. 113, Main street; subsequently it was on the lot where General Jones now resides, on the west side of the Public Square, Mount Vernon, and from thence was moved into the second story of the Market-House, where Mefford's saddler shop now is. Among the hands who worked in it were John Borland, now of Hocking county, Patterson, Reznor, and Wm. Crosby. Elliott C. Vore was the carrier-boy in 1825–6, and Lewis Lindsay in 1827–8.

About these times the rhymester of this office was Dan Jewett, a brother of Cynthia, wife of Ira Babcock. He wrote the Carrier's Address of the year 1828, and, as the first verse is worthy of consideration in these times of disunion, we give it for consideration:

"Ye lovers of Freedom, I pray you attend,
And listen awhile to the post-boy, your friend;
Lay aside all disunion, United let's stand,
The friends and supporters of our happy land."

One of the political songs of that time will occur to the mind of our old settlers by the first line:

"Jackson fought Duff Green like ——."

Another will be remembered by suggesting the chorus:

"O, Johnny Q.. my Jo John, since last I wrote to you,
I have been disappointed, John, and that I s'pose you know."

In 1838 a new office was established here, and a paper called the *Western Watchman* published by Samuel M. Browning, and for a few months John Teesdale was connected with this paper as editor, and had bargained for the establishment; but being a philanthropic Englishman, happening to insert an abolition article, he found it advisable to leave and never complied with his engagement as to paying for it. In 1839, October, the paper was published by S. Dewey & Co. but for a very short time. And a new candidate for public favor called the *Family Cabinet* was published for a few weeks, and then compelled to give up the ghost "under the pressure of existing circumstances." And thus we have traced the one side up to 1840, now let us retrace our steps and bring down the other.

The Colericks, as heretofore stated, had come from Washington, Pa., where their father had a printing office at a very early day, and they had been brought up to the business. No copies of their papers are extant. They were intelligent and energetic men and labored under great disadvantages for many years, as did other newspaper men in this county.

In 1827 their paper was called *The Democrat and Knox Advertiser.*

The early carriers for their paper were Ignatius Colerick, their nephew, and Henry Estabrook.

In March, 1831, Samuel Rohrer purchased the office and published the paper.

In October, 1832, F. S. & P. B. Ankeny became proprietors, and enlarged its size and name—*Mount Vernon Democrat and Knox Advertiser.*

The name was changed the next year to *Looking Glass and Whig Reflector*, and in the campaign of 1834, between Cols. Peres Sprague and James McFarland, it was very bitter against the former, who ran on the Independent ticket, as may be judged from the following chorus, which we extract from a song of the times as showing the acerbity of the contest:

"Yankee Doodle, Sprague's the boy,
Yankee Doodle dandy;
He plays a good hand at cards
And loves a good glass of brandy."

The people did not regard these vices as disqualifying Sprague for office, for he received, for Representative, 1,518 votes to 1,289 for his opponent!

This printing office was also migratory in its disposition, having been during its existence on Mulberry street, on the lot where H. W. Ball now lives, on the old Jeffres lot where Barnes' marble factory is, and in the second story of the frame where Robert Irvine's shoe store now is, on Main street.

In June, 1835, Charles Colerick established *The Day Book*, which was conducted by him with much energy and spirit until he volunteered as a soldier and went to Texas, when the office was bought by Delano and Browning, and the paper continued by William Byers until in the winter of 1837–8 it was transferred to S. M. Browning.

When the campaign of 1840 opened, the Whigs having become dissatisfied with the abolition article of John Teesdale and caused him to give up the publication of that paper, found it necessary to pass resolutions in their county convention inviting Whig editors to view this location, and appointed a committee, of which Johnston Elliott was chairman, to advertise in the leading Whig journals in the State for some one to come on and publish a paper. Under this call James Emmet Wilson, a son of Judge James Wilson, of Steubenville, came and started the *Knox County Republican*, and in about six months associated with himself as publisher Milo Butler, his brother-in-law. He was a poor stick; and this paper which started under the most favorable auspices in the triumphant campaign of 1840, in the fall of 1841 was discontinued by reason of the inertness and inability of the said Wilson and Butler to give the patrons a "live Whig paper," and because they were too much of the Teesdalian order.—— A hiatus ensued—Wilson and Butler went to preaching. And in 1842 Wm. H. Cochran, who was teaching school in Newark, came up and chartered the office and issued *The Times*; and from that office has been continued a paper, under different names and editors and proprietors, until the present day—the *Mount Vernon Republican* brings up the list.

This paper has been known to its readers as *The Times—The Republican Times—The Ohio State Times*, etc., as conducted by Cochran and Silmon Clark; G. E. Winters, J. H. Knox, O. B. Chapman, Witherow, J. W. Shuckers, the Republican joint stock company, and H. M. Ramsey. At present it is under the editorial management of W. C. Cooper, Esq. Other names may have been omitted who, for short periods, edited the paper.

After the Day Book office had been bought up and merged in *The Western Watchman*, an effort was made to establish another paper; and *The Democratic Banner* was started in April, 1838, by Chauncey Basset and —— Robb. During the summer it was edited by C. J. McNulty; but upon its sale to Edmund J. Ellis, it was continued without an editor in 1839, and, until it was sold to John Kershaw, in 1841, it was issued without an editorial, except as some partisan, able to write, would furnish it an article gratis. Kershaw edited and published it until, in June, 1844, he sold it back to E. J. Ellis, and then it was edited by G. W. Morgan, until, in 1845, it was sold to D. A. Robertson, who after a short time resold it to Ellis, who continued its publication until its sale, in November, 1847, to William Dunbar, who had associated with him in its publication for some six months George W. Armstrong; and for the remainder of his time edited and published it himself, until, in December, 1853, he sold it to Leckey Harper, then of the Pittsburg *Post*, who has since edited and published it. During Mr. Dunbar's management, a daily *Democratic Banner* was published in the winter of 1852 for thirty days.

Upon the nomination of General Taylor for President, in 1848, the editor of the *Times* refused to support the Taylor and Fillmore ticket, because Zachary Taylor lived South and owned slaves; whereupon another printing-office was brought to Mount Vernon that should advocate Union principles, and, to distinguish it from the *bogus* article, it was styled *The Mount Vernon True Whig*, and was published for seven years—edited during the campaign of 1848 by Joseph S. Davis, Esq.; in 1849 by John W. White, and the remainder of its existence by A. Banning Norton. With the exception of a brief period, when it was published by Higgins and White, the foreman of the office was that excellent printer, George Smith, now in the *Keokuk* (Iowa) *Daily Gate City*.

For three years *Norton's Daily True Whig* was published with the motto of Davy Crocket—"Be sure you're right, then go ahead;" and having become satisfied in that time that this place would not sustain a daily, unless out of the pocket of the publisher, and hence that it was not "right" to continue it, in March, 1855, its diurnal appearance ceased.

The motto of the *True Whig* was taken from Washington's Farewell Address, and would in these times be somewhat original:—"Frown indignantly upon the first dawning of every attempt to alienate any portion of our country from the rest, or to enfeeble the sacred ties which now link together its various parts." It was adopted as expressive of the determination to stand by the Constitution and the Union, and to oppose abolitionism and sectionalism of every form and description.

Several short lived newspapers have made their appearance in the county within the past eight years, which, by being named, may be kept fresh in the memories of some of the people. They were the *Rainbow*, which was of the nature of the "Nashville, Bowling Green, Louisville Courier" of these war times—migratory in disposition, and altogether fleeting. It was opened out at Mount Vernon by Rev. A. Laubach, sojourned a while at Fredericktown where the Reverend editor was sold by a vile acrostic; then tarried a brief space at Belville, and the last heard of was among the Senecas, at the city of Tiffin! *The Lilly*, which advocated short frocks and emigrated to the far west with Amelia Bloomer—the *Universalist Advocate* at Centerburg, which Daniel Wolfe found must proclaim glad tidings to *all* people without price, or not at all, and *The Western Home Visitor*, which was too large for Mount Vernon and could not find a home at Columbus. After these came *The National*, when its publishers, Agnew & Raguet, found it without a *nationality*, and after three months search in the exciting times of 1858 it gave up the ghost! *The Knox County Express* was started by Agnew & Tilton, in December, 1860, and is now published by C. M. Phelps & Co., and edited by Judge J. S. Davis.

The Banner, *Republican* and *Express* are the papers published in Mount Vernon in July, 1862, and *The Western Episcopalian* at Gambier, in this county. The *Episcopalian* is devoted to the interests of the Church, and of Kenyon College more particularly. It was first started as *The Gambier Observer*, upon the Acland Press, at Gambier, in 1827, and has been continued from that time to the present under different editorial and financial managers. George W. Meyers was for many years its publisher, and its present publisher is R. M. Edmonds. It has been ably edited by Dr. Sparrow, Dr. Wing, Dr. Muenscher, Dr. Colton, the Rev.

Norman Badger, and George Denison, and has been favored with many very able articles from the pens of professors of the college and other friends.

The first book printed in Knox county was "The American Revolution," written in scriptural, or ancient historical style—"Honi soi qui mal y' pense." "Clinton, Ohio. Printed by Smith & McArdle at the office of *The Ohio Register. Year of our Lord,* 1815." 170 pp. And the second was "The Columbiad, a poem on the American War, in 13 cantoes, by Richard Snowden." pp. 38. The next was "James Smith's Vindication."

There was also published at *The Ohio Register* office "A caveat against the Methodists, by a Gentleman of the Church of Rome." I have not sent these Prophets, yet they ran; I have not spoken to them, yet they prophesied.—*Jeremiah,* chap. 23, verse 21.

C. & J. Colerick published a directory of Knox county, compiled from the tax list, and showing the value of every man in the county as listed for taxation.

In 1835, the Laws and Ordinances of Mount Vernon were printed by the *Day Book* office and bound. And in 1852 the Charter and Ordinances of Mount Vernon were printed at the *True Whig* office and bound, making a work of 50 pages.

"An Essay on Justification by Faith, with particular reference to the Theory of Forensic Justification, by Joseph Muenscher, A.M., Rector of St. Paul's Church, Mount Vernon, 1847." pp. 63.

In 1858, John W. White published George Seymour, or Disappointed Revenge—a drama in 3 acts. 88 pp. And the Book of Chronicles, humorously illustrated, being a history of the dissensions among the harmonious democracy of Knox upon the Kansas question, written by Telegraphic Inspiration! pp. 32.

From the Acland Press a number of pamphlets and small works have been issued pertaining to Church and College affairs. Among others, Tissue's Greek Forms, a very valuable book, by one of the Professors.

The Rev. Dr. Muenscher has now in press "A Commentary on the book of Proverbs," which will make about 400 pp. duodecimo; and "A Treatise on Biblical Interpretation," 350 pp. duodecimo. We have seen a portion of the proof sheets of each—they are neatly executed, and from the acknowledged ability and learning of the author will be of much value.

Our young friend Charles H. Scribner, Esq., has prepared for the press an excellent Treatise on Dower—which will be a Law book of much size, and of very great value to the legal profession and the public generally.

The pioneers of the press in this county, who, a half century ago, spread the first information before the people in the columns of a paper, are both living, having passed the "three score years and ten allotted to man"—McArdle being almost a score over the time, and Smith over a century old. They are still hale and hearty, while the younger brothers of the press have not become "fat and forty;" and those who immediately succeeded them, have almost all passed to "that bourne from whence no traveler returns." Of the editors—Col. Charles Colerick, after having served a tour in the Texan revolution, and assisted in achieving, though he did not live to behold the recognition of her independence, is dead. Gen. William Bevans, after having served his fellow-citizens creditably in many official positions, has departed. Dan Stone, a quiet, unassuming man of much goodness of heart, died in this town, where his widow and two sons survive. Dr. M. L. Bliss died shortly after he left the paper. James Harvey Patterson moved to West Union, Adams county, and, after the death of his wife, went South. John Thomas was a very singular genius, well read, particularly in anatomy, geology, conchology, and herpetology et als. ologies, but was so much subject to the blues, or what he called "azure devils," as not to enjoy life; he would not drink out of a cup or saucer that had a flaw or crack in it, nor eat with a knife that he did not see scoured bright—consequently he worried himself out of the world before his time. W. H. Cochran and H. M. Ramsey died with the editorial harness on—the latter this spring—both much lamented by a large circle of friends, and their widows reside in Mount Vernon. S. M. Browning died at Burlington, Lawrence county, about 1852. Dr. Dyer resides in Iowa, Reznor in Illinois; Harkness also is in Illinois, where he is noted for his large nurseries of excellent fruit trees; Kershaw is an attorney in Philadelphia, Pa.; Morgan is a Brigadier General, with the army in Tennessee; Bronson is in Boston, Mass., making blood-food for curing consumptives; Robertson, after having served as U. S. Marshal for Minnesota, settled down there in the practice of the law; McNulty, the only editor of the county sued for libel, from whom Elder Power recovered a large verdict, after having volunteered as a soldier in the Mexican war, died and was buried at Helena, Ark., by his brave comrades. Ellis had better have been dead than to have become a traitor to his country, and been driven beyond the lines. He was publishing the Boone County *Standard*, at Columbia, Mo., when he sinned against light and knowledge. Three of the old set—Smith of the *Clinton Register*, Smith of the *Western Aurora*, and Norton of the *True Whig*—a few years ago found themselves residing in the same district in Texas. Two of them yet remain there, while the third is writing these lines, having, from love for the Constitution and the Union, found it necessary to seek once again the shores of Owl Creek. Such are life's changes.

CHAPTER XX.

EVENTS FROM 1820 TO 1830.

WHITE MALE INHABITANTS AND VOTERS AT VARIOUS ELECTIONS WITHIN THIS TIME.—SOME ACCOUNT OF THE FINANCES AND REVENUE.—THE LAST OF THE INDIAN.—A WARNING.—THE OLD COURT-HOUSE FALLS, AND A NEW ONE IS PROJECTED.—OTHER OCCURRENCES.

THE white male inhabitants of Knox county above the age of 21 in 1820, were 1290, located as follows: Hillier 21, Bloomfield 69, Morgan 152, Miller 72, Jackson 178, Chester 122, Wayne 168, Morris 157, Union 144, and Clinton 207.

The county gave its vote for Ethan Allen Brown for Governor; John Sloane for Congress; Wm. Gass for Senator; R. D. Simons for Representative; Wm. Bevans for Sheriff; Abner Ayres for Commissioner, and E. G. Lee for Coroner.

Among the orders issued by the county, June 6th, 1820, were—

No. 3928.	Paying Moody & M'Carty for articles furnished Overseers of the Poor for the squaw that was shot	$2.84 4
" 3929.	Hosmer Curtis and Mott for expenses incurred for the sick squaw	1.00
" 3930.	Jacob Martin, making coffin for squaw	6.00

This, in the Indian line, is among the last known in the county. This squaw was of the Stockbridge tribe, and one of a small party who, in traveling out of Licking county, was espied and shot by Hughes, when near Homer, and in Morgan township. Without provocation or just cause, but simply to gratify his private hatred of the Indian race, she was shot through the hip. Her comrades brought her on to Mount Vernon, where her sufferings became too great to admit of her being taken further. She was put in the old log gunsmith shop of John Earnhart, on High street, but the quarters being uncomfortable on account of cold November weather, she was moved to an old log house on the north-west corner of Mulberry and Vine streets, and there died. True to the Indian stoicism she never groaned or complained, although her sufferings were intense. Five or six of her tribe staid through her sickness, and then buried her in the north-east corner of the old graveyard. For several years afterwards her husband would return at the time of year when she died to view her grave and see that the body remained undisturbed.

From this same old log house, in October, 1826, a gun was fired which caused the death of Ben. Roberts. George Low then lived in the house, and Jim Low was staying with him, when on Hallow Eve night, several of the town boys were out throwing cabbages against the doors, as has from time immemorial been the custom, and as they threw against Low's door, Jim took down his rifle and fired between the logs, the ball lodging in Ben's leg. He was carried home, and, after laying for some time, it became necessary to amputate the leg, which was done one Sunday, and the next afternoon at 4 o'clock he died. Low was tried, and Sam Mott defended him, and he was acquitted. This shooting affair caused very great excitement, and ever since, on the annual return of Hallow Eve, the old settlers rehearse this story to their children and grandchildren, as a warning against following this ridiculous custom of throwing cabbage heads to the annoyance of quiet people.

In 1822, the county gave majorities for Daniel S. Norton for Congress; H. Curtis for Representative; Wm. Bevans for Sheriff; John Kerr for Commissioner; W. Y. Farquhar for Auditor; James McGibeny for Coroner.

In 1824, majorities were given for Jeremiah Morrow for Governor; Wilson for Congress; Colerick for Sheriff; Stilley for Commissioner; Rigdon for Representative; Runyan for Coroner, and Farquhar for Auditor.

In October, 1825, the jail built by Solomon Geller is found according to contract, except "he is yet to put in a stove, and the door above going into the debtors' apartment."

In 1826, the whole number of votes cast was 1828, and the county gave majorities for Trimble for Governor; Norton for Congress; Robeson for Representative; Colerick for Sheriff; Runyan for Coroner; Elliott for Auditor; Leonard for Commissioner.

At the June session, 1826, of the Commissioners, upon petition of Francis Wilkins and others, a road was ordered to be opened up Dry Creek, beginning on the farm of Daniel S. Norton, to intersect the old road on the corner of Frederick Carey's orchard. Jonathan Miller, R. D. Simons and James McGibeny were appointed viewers, and J. W. Warden, surveyor.

On the 30th of September, the county jail is received in full satisfaction by the Commissioners. Wm. Bevans was allowed $5 for crying sale of the jail.

VALUATION OF KNOX COUNTY IN 1826.

Land, 301,695 acres, valued at	$716,070
Town property	81,362
Mercantile capital	60,000
Houses	26,340
Horses, 2467	98,680
Cattle, 4483	35,864
Total	$1,018,376

At this time Mount Vernon is stated as containing 80 dwelling-houses, one printing office, a brick court-house and jail, a merchant mill, a saw mill, a cotton factory, and within six miles, 9 grist and saw mills and three carding machines.

In 1827, Patterson and Smith, of *The Western Aurora*, published the Delinquent List for the ordinary price, and refunded one-fourth of the whole amount for county use.

In 1827, March 29, W. Y. Farquhar was "appointed keeper of the Knox county standard and half bushel measure, and authorized to get a half bushel of copper!"

Martin Tracy then gave bond as county Auditor, with John Troutman, Solomon and Paul Welker as securities.

At the June Term it was ordered that the Auditor cause two blank books for county orders to be procured, and that C. & J. Colerick print the same, and that the Auditor furnish six quires of paper for that purpose.

At the December Term, H. B. Curtis' account for office rent and wood is allowed—office rent, 7 months, $84; and wood 3 winters for Recorder's office, $15.

"OLD THINGS SHALL BE DONE AWAY WITH AND ALL BECOME NEW."

October 18th, 1828, James McGibeny contracted with the commissioners to build a stone wall to support the Court-house bank, standing ten feet north and south of the Court-house.

But all efforts to save it were unavailing: it had been written, "*Carthago detenda est;*" and on the 2d of December an order issued to B. S. Brown for $40, in consequence of the loss of his office by the fall of the Court-house.

The Court-house was no sooner down than the commissioners ordered proposals to be published in the *Standard* and *Advertiser*, for the purpose of making donations for the building of a new Court-house, and for a plan of building, &c. On the 20th of January, 1829, they agreed with Thomas Irvine for his brick house for a court-house, at $25 per term, in orders on the county treasury. In April, James Smith is notified by Marvin Tracy that the commissioners have obtained Thomas Irvine's bar-room for an office. The levy for taxes in Knox county, June, 1829, was 1½ mills on the dollar, on the whole valuation of property in said county, for State purposes, and 1½ for canal purposes, making 3 mills upon the dollar for State and canal purposes; and the commissioners, by and with the consent of the Judges of the Court of Common Pleas, levied a tax of 3 mills on the dollar for county purposes, 1 mill for road purposes, and ¾ of a mill for school purposes; one of the three mills shall be assessed and collected and appropriated for the building of the Court-house, and for no other purpose whatever.

At the June session, the following entry is made: "The account of James Smith, presented to the Board of Commissioners, for one year, from June 1st, 1828, to June 1st, 1829, including the rent unpaid at last settlement, books and stationery for clerk's office, all of which was rejected by the Board. The charges for one year's fire-wood, which was $12. From which decision the said Smith prays an appeal to the Court of Common Pleas as to the fire-wood." That record is clear, is it not? The resolutions of the commissioners, published in the *Standard* and *Advertiser*, in reference to the building of a Court-house, represent that "they will meet on the 15th of July, for the purpose of receiving donations, &c.; giving the public square $1,000; preference for location, &c.; otherwise at any point in the town plat where $1,000 is subscribed," &c. On the 15th of July, the commissioners met, and adjourned till the 24th of August, to receive donations, &c., for new Court-house.

On the 11th of September public notice is given in the *Western Aurora* and in the *Advertiser* and

Standard, of sale of contract to build a Court-house, to the lowest bidder, on the 5th of October next, &c. Peris Sprague is authorized to get E. G. Carlin, or some other person, to make and draft a plat for the same. This plan, as agreed upon, appears on the journal, specifying that the building is to be erected on the west side of Main street and north side of High street, and that $1,000 is to be paid to the contractor on the 10th of January, 1830, and $1,000 annually thereafter, and all orders to be expressly understood to be paid when due and presented. Edward G. Carlin is paid county order for $10, for making plat of new Court-house, and describing timbers, dimensions, &c. Richard House, for assisting Carlin in describing the plan, is paid $1 50.

October 5th. The building of the Court-house is sold to John Shaw for $5,485, who enters into bond with Byram Leonard, Philo Norton, Charles Sager, Solomon Geller, Thomas Irvine and H. B. Carter, in the sum of $10,970. Such is the record of the second Court-house built in Mount Vernon, which stood on the public square until 1853. It was built of brick, two stories high, with a cupola, and a very imposing building in its time. It answered well its part for many years—may we not say for that generation, as almost all then upon the stage of action have passed "hence without day." The Supreme Court, District and Associate Judges, the Commissioners, Sheriff, Auditor, Assessor, Treasurer, Surveyor, and Coroner, the Contractor and his sureties—are all, all dead. Melancholy is the reflection that few of the men, who flourished here only thirty-two years ago, now survive.

In 1828, majorities were given for Campbell for Governor; Stanbery for Congress; Shaw for Sheriff; Colerick for Representative; Tracy for Auditor; Sprague and Beers for Commissioners, and Neal for Coroner.

In 1829 the population of the county is stated at 8,326. There were then eight post-offices, viz.: Danville, Darling's, Martinsburg, Mount Vernon, Miles ⋈ Roads and Sandusky ⋈ Roads in Chester township, Fredericktown and Houck's.

The state of the County Treasury may be judged of from the following entry, June 7th, 1830: "Ordered that the Auditor issue an order on the Treasurer in favor of Daniel Converse & Co., for the amount of principal and interest due on a certain county order, payable to Solomon Geller, for the sum of $275, dated February 10, 1824, endorsed not paid for want of funds by the Treasurer when the said order shall be presented;" thus paying an old order by issuing a new one. The original debt for building the first court house not having been paid until after the building itself had crumbled and fallen, and the county was compelled to erect a new one.

Artemas Estabrook is, at the same time, allowed an order for boarding, bringing up on Habeas Corpus and attending the Judges—Eli Losh—amounting to $11.60.

C. G. Allen makes his escape from the county jail after his board bill had amounted to $8.05.

In 1830, the county went for McArthur for Governor; Stanbery, Congress; Greer, Representative; Neal, Sheriff; Tracy, Auditor; McFarland, Assessor; Low, Coroner; Wilkins for Commissioner. The total vote cast was 2,086.

During this decade the foundation was laid and the commencement made of that institution of learning which has contributed so much to the advancement and prosperity of this county—Kenyon College. Under its appropriate head we have devoted a chapter to this subject, and hence will say no more here than has reference to the action of the County Commissioners on matters connected with it. On December 7th, 1829, the petition of Philander Chase and others was presented to the Board for the view of four roads. 1. From the junction of Wiggin and Gaskin streets towards James Smith's mill. 2. To Coshocton. 3. To Giffin's mill. 4. Around the foot of College hill south west to Frederick Rohrer's tavern stand. The Commissioners ordered Thomas Griffith Plummer to survey; and Jonathan Miller, Wm. Marquis and Joseph Critchfield to view. All of these parties are now dead.

CHAPTER XXI.

LITERARY AND OTHER SOCIETIES.

THE MOUNT VERNON POLEMIC SOCIETY.—THE THESPIAN.—THE LIBRARY SOCIETY.—THE LYCEUM.—THE FRANKLIN.—MECHANICS.—HISTORICAL, AND ITS LIBRARY.

THE first society of a literary character, established at Mount Vernon, was the "Polemic Society," in 1815, which was kept up until 1817, and included among its members the more talkative and social citizens. It was converted into a Thespian Society and well sustained for many years. Theatrical performances were generally gotten up every winter, until about 1840, and were very creditable to those concerned. The object was to spend the long evenings agreeably—not to make money. Lawyers, doctors, merchants and students lent a hand as occasion required. Among the active and valuable upon the boards were Dr. R. D. Moore, Philo L. Norton, Jacob B. Brown, Charles Sager, J. W. Warden, Wm. Bevans, Chas. Colerick, B. S. Brown, T. G. Plummer, Jacob Davis, S. W. Hildreth, Wm. Smith, S. W. Farquhar, Eli Miller, N. N. Hill, T. W. Rogers, Henry B. Curtis, Isaac Hadley, John Colerick, J. S. Banning, and Calvin Hill.

The exhibitions were usually at the court house, or at the "Golden Swan Inn." The clothing, equipments and scenery, were of very rich material. One of the old actors says—"it was most splendidly illustrated with gorgeous parahernalia in most profuse variety and transcends representation."

"The Mount Vernon Library Society" was formed in the year 1816. Among the members of this association were Joseph Brown, Hosmer Curtis, R. D. Moore, Gilman Bryant, Timothy Burr, Daniel S. Norton, John Warden, Samuel Mott. H. Curtis was its last Librarian. It had a very good collection of standard works, which, in the end, were divided among its stockholders.

"The Mount Vernon Literary Society" organized in the winter of 1821–2, by a number of young bachelors of the town, to wit: Dr. Norman Murray, David Wadsworth, Henry B. Curtis, John W. Warden and James Beebee. Members subsequently admitted—Benjamin S. Brown, S. Farquhar, N. N. Hill and Samuel R. Curtis. The organization existed for several years. The society fell through by reason of the young men becoming absorbed in the more active duties of life.

"The Mount Vernon Lyceum," in 1830, was formed and well sustained for many years. At the session of the Legislature, 1833–4, it was incorporated, and high hopes were entertained of its being a permanent organization. We have before us the inaugural address of Henry B. Curtis, Esq., delivered January 1st, 1834, in which he says:—"We have now assumed a different and more imposing attitude. Having adopted a public charter, we from this time become a part of the history of the State. And let us at least hope that the account which its faithful pages may hereafter give of us and of our transactions shall be such as would not make us blush, could we be permitted to see them." May the hope of President Curtis be gratified; for, although the Lyceum has long since been consigned to the "tomb of the Capulets," and the greater portion of his associates have departed hence without day, he yet lives to "be permitted to see" "the account which the faithful pages of history"—our history of Knox county doubtless predicted—"gives of its transactions."

It was the best literary association and the longest lived ever in Mt. Vernon. It continued in successful operation until 1842, and numbered among its active members many of the best citizens of Knox. Its regular meetings were held at the court-house, and the public generally and ladies particularly attended its sessions. Literary essays, orations and discussions were the chief entertainment.

Among the number of those who have died we may name Benjamin S. Brown, David Dunn, John A. Holland, S. W. Hildreth, M. A. Sayre, Daniel S. Norton, T. W. Rogers, W. A. Hoey, T. G. Plummer, and Dr. M. L. Bliss.

Among those living in other parts, Wm. Byers, J. F. Kinney, J. C. Hall, G. Hathaway, J. W. Chapman, H. Curtis, J. B. Foster, E. Sparrow, D. C. Dunlap.

Among the survivors in this county are C. Delano, M. H. Mitchell, J. W. Miller, Henry B. Curtis, Rollin C. Hurd, J. S. Davis, J. N. Burr.

The Lyceum established a very good library of several hundred volumes.

In 1834, a "Mechanics' Society" was formed, which continued till 1840, and enlisted J. B. Brown, G. C. Lybrand, E. Alling, D. McFarland, Abel Hart, and pretty much all the workmen in this vicinity.

In 1839, a society called the "Franklin" was organized for mental improvement, by John Lamb, Robert Thompson, Ben. McCracken, W. H. Oldham, Isaac J. Allen, W. P. Griffith, W. T. Curtis, R. S. Thomas, and others, which was well sustained for three or four years, and then went down.

In 1850, Zoar Blair, Noah Hill, Robert Thompson, Dan. Clark and Sam. Davis started the Mechanics' Mutual Protection, which after two years, was merged in the Brotherhood of the Union, and continued till 1854.

In December, 1849, several gentlemen of Mount Vernon set about getting up a Historical Society for Knox county, and in January, 1850, a constitution was drawn up and signed by Hosmer Curtis, Gilman Bryant, Joseph Muenscher, M. E. Strieby, Jesse B. Thomas, James Scott, Daniel S. Norton, M. H. Mitchell, Henry B. Curtis, R. C. Hurd, R. R. Sloan, A. Banning Norton, C. P. Buckingham, G. W. Morgan, C. Delano, M. W. Stamp, Walter Smith, N. N. Hill, G. Browning, Matthew Thompson, J. C. Ramsey, J. N. Burr, S. Israel, J. W. Vance, W. H. Smith, J. C. Stockton, D. Potwin, J. W. White, J. H. Peacock, W. Beam, Samuel Mower and John W. Russell. H. Curtis was elected President; G. Bryant, V. P.; R C. Hurd, Treas'r; Cor. Sec'y, Rev. J. Muenscher, D.D.; Recording Sec'y, Rev. M. E. Strieby; Cabinet-keeper, R. R. Sloan. Among other standing committees were the following: on Agriculture, M. H. Mitchell; on Manufactures, Daniel S. Norton; on Mechanic Arts, C. P. Buckingham; on Fine Arts, H. B. Curtis; on Education, R. R. Sloan; on History, R. C. Hurd; on the Medical Profession, J. N. Burr, M.D.; on the Clerical Profession, Jos. Muenscher, D.D.; on Diseases, J. W. Russell, M.D.; on Population, S. Israel; on General Biography, A. Banning Norton; on Geology and Mineralogy, Prof. H. L. Thrall, M.D.; on Meteorology, Rev. Prof. Geo. Dennison; on Literature, W. H. Smith. Twelve years have passed by, the society long since was numbered among the things that were—and this comes the nearest to being a report of anything that yet has emanated from any of its members. Following in its wake, however, is an institution which it is to be hoped will long continue in existence—"The Mount Vernon Library Society," which has collected, through the instrumentality, principally, of the Rev. Dr. Muenscher, its learned Librarian, several hundred volumes of valuable standard works, and may serve as a nucleus for a future large collection. It was started in 1856, and its rooms are in Huntsbery's building, Main st., Mount Vernon,

CHAPTER XXII.

HON. ANTHONY BANNING.

AMONG the old settlers whose names have figured conspicuously in the history of Knox county, was Anthony Banning. Connected with the business, the growth and prosperity of the county at every period of its history after the first, and concerned as he was in various industrial pursuits, in commercial operations, in temperance movements, in church affairs, in political actions; and as his name has been widely known in legal history, his memory is worthy of more than a passing notice. "Judge" Banning as he was called more frequently than "Parson," notwithstanding his monument states that he was a Methodist preacher sixty years, was born in Talbot county, Maryland, and was the only son of James Banning, a proprietor of much consideration and influence, who had but two children, the son, James Mansfield Anthony Banning, and a daughter who married Benjamin Chew, of Philadelphia, Chief Justice of the State of Pennsylvania, a lawyer of much distinction and a man of great wealth, who was a bosom friend of Washington and whose family were his most intimate associates.

His parents died when he was very young, and he was consigned to the care of an uncle, Henry Banning, a bachelor, who was a sea-captain and took Anthony with him several voyages. The family were members of the Episcopal church, but in his eleventh year Anthony joined the Methodists. When about sixteen he went to preaching as a circuit rider in Greenbrier, Virginia, and the wilderness mountain region. In consequence of the great length of his name, and its inconvenience in writing, he dropped a portion of it in early youth. He married Sarah Murphy, daughter of one of the first settlers on Redstone, near Uniontown, Pa., who was also a native of the Eastern Shore of Maryland, and had been raised near Ellicott's mills. The children, by this marriage, were Sarah, wife of Daniel S. Norton; Jacob M. who died in 1835, and whose widow and children reside in Hardin county; Rachel, wife of Rev. Elnathan Raymond; James S.; Mrs. Mary Caswell; Elizabeth, Mrs. Bronson; Priscilla, Mrs. Gray, and Anthony.

After his marriage he settled in Fayette county, Pa., and resided for several years near Mt. Braddock and in Connelsville, where he preached the gospel, carried on a tanyard, kept a store, officiated as a justice of the peace, (from 1790 until 1799) traded in stock of every description, and navigated the western waters.

During his residence in the Keystone State slavery existed there, and this good man thought it no sin to better the condition of negroes by holding them in bondage. Twenty-eight family slaves of the Maryland stock were thus held at his marriage, and he subsequently bought Hannah, Peter, Jim, Cass and George, in Virginia; and in moving west sold them to Daniel Rogers and Abraham Baldwin, two of the most respectable and worthy men in that country.

In one of his trading expeditions on the western rivers he sold a load of goods to Ebenezer Buckingham, of Putnam, for the fine farm now occupied by Nicholas Spindler, Esq., in Howard township. He made several trips up the Muskingum with goods and wares from 1808 till he moved out in 1812. After he had bought lands in the county he traded a lot of iron, leather, saddlery, &c., to Samuel Kratzer, Esq., for the principal part of his interest in the town of Mount Vernon, and then took up his residence here. During his long abode he was engaged, as elsewhere, in a diversity of pursuits; and by reason of his remarkable energy, industry, prudence and business tact, prospered in all and enjoyed, to a very great extent, the confidence of the people. He was for the greater part of his life concerned in merchandizing at Mount Vernon, Tymochtee, Danville, &c.—carrying on his mills at Clinton and his tanyard, farming extensively and preaching.

His name is found as President of the first Clay meeting ever held in this county; he was all his life an ardent admirer and friend of that great statesman and patriot. In principle, politically, he was a Whig—religiously, a Methodist—strictly moral and temperate—in all the relations of life a good example.

He was honest and conscientious—liberal and kind hearted—determined and resolute—never disguised his sentiments or harbored unkind thoughts; was not a fanatic in temperance, morals, politics or religion; but by his well balanced mind and daily walk exerted a great influence for good.

Among other public positions held by him was that of Commissioner to select the permanent seat of justice of Clermont county, under act of the General Assembly, January 25th, 1823, associated with John C. Wright, then of Jefferson, and James

Clark, of Stark. He served as one of the Associate Judges of this county from 1827 to 1834.

In every public enterprise and work calculated to benefit the town, county and people he was active, liberal and useful. Among the many incidents of his life the following most clearly shows the liberality of his mind: In 1836 he set about erecting a church near his residence, and upon his own land. The neat brick edifice had been inclosed and about completed, when the Rt. Rev. Bishop Purcel visited Mt. Vernon for the first time, and there being no Catholic church the followers of that denomination, of whom there were but two or three families then in the place, to wit—David Morton's, Wm. Brophy's and Tim. Colopy's, requested the use of one of the churhes for the Bishop to hold service in on the forenoon of a certain Sunday. The favor was denied. An effort was then made to procure the use of the court house, and that too was refused.

The writer, then a small boy, having heard the circumstances on his way home, stopped in at Judge Banning's and stated what had occurred, when he at once buttoned up his vest and coat, took his cane, went up to David Morton's, where the Bishop was staying, and tendered the use of the Banning Chapel for Catholic service. The offer was most gratefully and graciously accepted, and the first Catholic discourse ever delivered in this town was pronounced at the Banning Chapel. This, in the eyes of many bigoted and intolerant minds, was a very great sin; but the religion of Grandfather Banning was of that catholic spirit which enabled him to do acts of kindness and pour out heart offerings as becometh a true christian. And here we will record that this "bread cast upon the waters returned again after many days" in like spirit.

In February, 1844, Judge Banning was drowned in the dam of the Clinton Mill Company, when attempting to cross upon the ice to his farm, after some infernal fiend had burned up the Norton street bridge. His body was soon recovered and great efforts were made to resuscitate life, but in vain. He was in his 76th year, and remarkably vigorous and robust for one of his age.

The Catholic sect having increased to a considerable number, and having, by liberality of our citizens, erected a neat brick church, Bishop Purcel again visited Mt. Vernon to consecrate it—and most happily referred to the circumstances attending his first visit and the charitable and brotherly kindness of Father Banning, and devoutly offered up his supplications to the throne of mercy in his behalf. The incident was a most affecting one, and the eyes of many were suffused with tears as their supplications were offered up.

CHAPTER XXIII.

RICHLAND COUNTY DURING HER TUTELAGE.—DIVIDED INTO TWO TOWNSHIPS.—THE EARLIEST SETTLERS.—VOTERS.—OFFICERS AND MATTERS WORTH REMEMBERING.

IN pursuance of our purpose, as expressed on page 26, we devote a few pages of our history to the earliest matters of record on our journals in regard to Richland county. The Commissioners of Knox, on the 8th of June, 1809, declared the entire county of Richland a separate township, which shall be called and known by the name of *Madison.* At the present time a township of this name exists, and Mansfield, the flourishing county seat of Richland, stands therein. At the election of 1809, that whole region polled but 17 votes, and in the year following there were but 19 votes. The vote in October, 1811, for Representative, stood, Jeremiah R. Munson 14, Wm. Gass 3; Sheriff, Ichabod Nye, 17; Commissioner, John Kerr, 17; Coroner, Dr. Timothy Burr, 17. The Judges of election in 1810 were James Copus, Wm. Gardner, John Foglesong; Clerks, John C. Gilkison, James Cunningham. In 1811, Winn Winship and John C. Gilkison, clerks, certify as to the full vote of Richland. Among the names of these early settlers will be found several with whom our readers were acquainted in the olden time; we give them—Moses Adzet, George Ackley, the Baughmans,

Jacob and John Coon, Andrew Craig, Thomas Coulter, James Black, Hugh and James Cunningham, John Crossen, the Gilkisons, the Gardners, the Hulls, Moses Fountain, the Lewisses, the McClures, the Murphys, the Newmans, Pearces, Olivers, Wm. Lockard, Jacob Shaffer, Joshua Rush, Sam. Martin, the Slaters, Zimmermans, John Wallace, Joseph Middleton, James Hedges and Rollin Weldon.

The first Justices of the Peace were Archibald Gardner, elected in May, 1809; Henry McCart, in 1810; George Coffinbery and Peter Kinney, in 1812; James McClure and Andrew Coffinbery, in 1814. The whole return on the tax duplicate, in 1811, was 73 horses, 124 cattle and one stallion, valued at $150, and taxed at $35.

A rib is taken out of the side of Richland on the 7th of January, 1812, as the following entry on the Journal of the Commissioners explains: "Ordered, that Madison township be divided as follows, to wit: The division line of the township should be one mile east of the center of the 17th range, in the lower township, and shall be known and designated by the name of Greene." Brief entry that—is it not, for the formation of a township within the lines of which we now find the better part of Ashland county and some of the best lands in Richland. Whether it was named after the Rev. John Green, who had just been licensed to marry, "this deponent saith not," as the books show not, but we presume, as our people were eminently patriotic, that it was named after General Nathaniel Greene, one of the heroes of our revolutionary war. The

Mohican river passes through this township on its way to the Gulf of Mexico via the Walhonding, Muskingum, Ohio and Mississippi rivers. In the olden time men did navigate this route, if we are to put implicit confidence in traditions of the dead past. We have a work published several score years ago which asserts that "it is navigable (except being obstructed by dams) most seasons of the year." Beaver dams, it is presumed, or some other dams, usually obstruct. The Judges at the first election were Melzar Tanneyhill, Isaac Pierce, Samuel Lewis, and the clerks Peter Kenny and Thomas Coulter. Melzar Tanneyhill received a $6 county order for listing this township. At the election April 6, 1812, at the house of Abraham Baughman, jr., Philip Seymour, Henry Seymour and Martin Rufner, whose adventures with Indians have since been so widely known, were among the voters. John Murphy, Henry Naugh, John Pool, Wm. Slater, John Totten and Ebenezar Rice were other voters. Among the settlers, in 1814, were Josiah L. Hill, Trew Petee, Wm. Brown, John Shehan, Ahira Hill, Asa Brown, Jeremiah Conine, Lewis Crossen, Stephen Vanscoyos, Noah Custard, David Hill, Moses Jones, Silvester Fisher, John Crossen, H. W. Cotton, Lewis Pierce and Adam Crossen. The poll-book for the township of Greene, in the county of Knox, October 13, 1812, "shows 41 voters, but the names of Seymour and Rufner are lacking. The 14th of March, 1812, Knox Common Pleas Court allowed Greene township three Justices. Perryville was the principal business point, and the Browns W. & A. were the first merchants, and for many years the leading business men.

On the 10th of April, 1812, a petition of citizens of Richland was presented to the Commissioners of Knox for "a road beginning at the house of James McClure in said county, and run the nearest way to a mill seat belonging to Amoriah Watson; the same be granted, and Jacob Newman, George Coffinbery and Wm. Gass were appointed Viewers, and W. Y. Farquhar Surveyor of the same."

In February, 1813, Thomas Coulter, Wm. Gass and Peter Kinney were elected Associate Judges by the Legislature. Winn Winship, the first Clerk of the Court of Richland county, wrote an excellent hand, and was a quick business man. Several of his certificates are on file in our Clerk's office, containing election returns, &c., with a hole cut through a piece of paper showing a wafer, the county having no seal. The entire vote of Richland, October 12, 1813, for Representative was: Wm. Gass, 31; Sam. Kratzer, 14.

Mansfield was determined upon as the seat of justice of the county, April 2d, 1809, by Jno. Heckewelder, John M. Connell and Moses Ross, Commissioners. Winn Winship was the first Postmaster at the town; and among the early tavern keepers known to our citizens was Capt. Sam. Williams. Jabez Beers was appointed lister of this county in 1812. Until after the war of 1812, there was not much improvement in the county. A very large proportion of the early settlers were from Knox, and throughout our history the people have been quite intimate, and lived together upon the most friendly terms.

We have much material that we would like to present; but as the history of our sister county and its affairs do not, from the period to which we have carried this sketch, properly belong to our enterprise, we close by giving a view of the Mansfield Female Seminary, whereof Rev. C. S. Doolittle, A.M., and J. Lindly, A.M., are Principals; and inasmuch as the former is a native of Knox, and a son of one of our old teachers, it will not be thought out of place to say that here young ladies can acquire an accomplished education upon very reasonable terms.

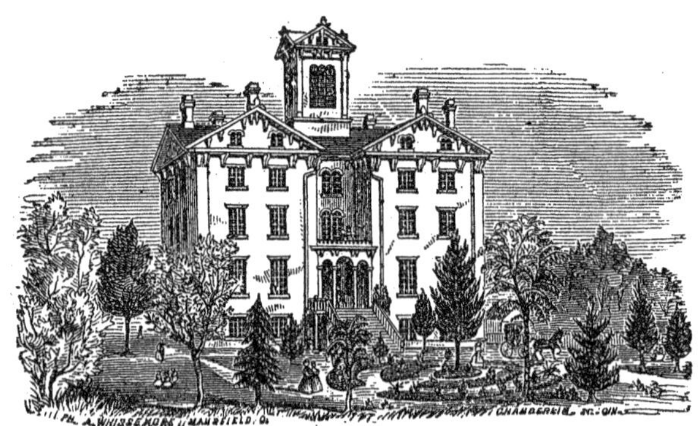

CHAPTER XXIV.

SOME ACCOUNT OF THE TOWNSHIPS SEVERED FROM OLD KNOX.—CHESTER, BLOOMFIELD AND FRANKLIN.—THEIR HISTORY UNTIL MORROW WAS CREATED.

THE territory of Knox remained entire, notwithstanding extraordinary efforts had been made time and again to erect new counties, taking a part of her territory, until, at the session of the Legislature in 1848, Morrow was created—taking from Knox Chester, Franklin and Bloomfield townships.

Chester Township, the oldest of the three, was laid off by order of the Commissioners at their session April 10th, 1812. The first election was held at the house of Wm. Johnson, on the 25th of that month. The Judges of election this year were Joseph Duncan, Henry George, Evan Holt; Clerks, Wm. Johnson and Samuel Johnson. Rufus Dodd, first lister of taxable property, received a $3 county order for his services this year. In addition to the above-named, we find other early settlers to have been Ensley Johnson, John Walker, David Miller, John Parcels, Enos Miles, Robert Dalrymple, Isaac Norton, James and George Irwin, Joseph Howard, Bartlet Norton, and Daniel Kimbel. Moses Morris, Henry George and a few other Welch families, were among the number of the best citizens of this township, and many of their countrymen located around them. The greater part of the original families were from New Jersey.

In 1813, at the October election, there were fifteen voters; among them were Joseph, William and Uriah Denman, Sam'l Shaw and Chism May. The vote stood, for Representative, Gass 15; Commissioner, Peter Wolf 9; Sheriff, John Hawn, Jr. 13, Wm. Mitchel 2.

The forks of Owl Creek passing through this township afford several good mill-seats a durable power, and furnish the people with facilities for getting breadstuffs at their own doors. Their lands are generally rolling and very productive. The citizens have ever been distinguished for industry and thrifty management. In 1830, the population was 778; in 1840, it was 1,297; and in 1850, 1,620.

Chesterville, the post-office and business point, was laid out by Enos Miles, deputy surveyor, ——. For many years the post-office went by the name of Miles's × Roads, and the good tavernkeeper's name seemed for a long time likely to absorb the other. It was on the main thoroughfare from Mt. Vernon to Mt. Gilead, and on the old State road from Johnstown to Paris and New Haven; distant from Mt. Vernon 14 miles, from Fredericktown 8, from Mt. Gilead 10, from Johnstown 23, and 30 from Paris. In 1830, it contained 250 inhabitants, 40 dwellings, 5 stores, 1 tavern, 1 flour-mill, 1 saw-mill, 1 tannery, 1 church, and several mechanic shops. This village has ever been distinguished for the attention paid to schools, churches, etc., and the general morality of its citizens; of whom we may name the Shurs, the Bartletts, and Hance, who have been heavily engaged in merchandise and trade, Abram King, Dr. Richard E. Lord, Dan. Miles and Judge Kinsel.

Evan Holt, as a revolutionary soldier, served six years; was a native of Chester, Pa., emigrated to this county in 1808, and lived for 39 years on land received for his services. He also was a pensioner until his death, in his 84th year, leaving a large family married and settled around him. Evan, Jr. was a great fighter—possessed of bone, muscle and pluck; he fought in Morris township, about 35 years ago, a fist fight with John Magoogin, where he displayed uncommon skill. They had a difficulty at a camp-meeting over the creek, on James Smith's farm, and then made up this fight, to come off at the first big muster at the Cross Roads, by Wm. Mitchell's. A great crowd witnessed it. Magoogin was a stout and brisk man of much courage; he died a soldier in the Mexican war. The fight was conducted fairly, and Magoogin carried the palm.

The Dalrymple family is one of the most respected, of whom Charles has long been a good justice of the township.

The poll-book of Chester in April, 1824, concludes as follows:—"We certify that John Stilley had 26 votes for Justice, Wm. W. Evans 26. Decided by draught in favor of John Stilley. John De Witt, John Beebee, Jas. McCracken, Judges; Enos Miles, Jas. F. Clapp, Clerks. We therefore do certify that John Stilley from Arrangements was duly elected a justice of the peace for Chester township, this 1st Monday, April, A. D. 1824."

SUCCESSIVE JUSTICES OF THE PEACE.

1812.	Wm. Johnson.	1833.	Enos Miles.
1817.	Rufus Dodd.	1836.	" "
	Joseph Denman.	1839.	" "
1819.	W. Van Buskirk.	1836.	Byram Beers.
1822.	" "	1839.	" "
1820.	Enos Miles.	1842.	" "
	Daniel Beers.	1845.	" "
1823.	" "	1835.	Henry De Witt.
1824.	John Stilley.	1838.	" "
1826.	John Beebee.	1842.	P. B. Ayres.
1829.	" "	1845.	" "
1832.	" "	1843.	Thomas Peterson.
1827.	Moses Powell.	1846.	Davis Miles.
1830.	" "	1844.	Charles Dalrymple.
1833.	" "	1847.	" "

Franklin, the most extreme township in the north-west corner of "old Knox," before she was shorn of her fair proportions by the erection of Morrow, was first known December 3d, 1823, by being created and named after the philosopher, statesman and printer, Benjamin Franklin. The first election came off on the first Monday of April, 1823, at the house of Thomas Axtell. The principal place of business is Pulaskiville.

Jamestown was many years ago a famous business place, projected by Allen Kelly, Esq., who emigrated from Northumberland county, Pa., at a very early day, and has ever been a prominent stock raiser and farmer. David Peoples, David Shaw, Wm. T. Campbell, Washington Strong, the Petersons, Hickmans, Blairs and Van Buskirks were among the early settlers. Of these Abraham Blair, of Perth Amboy, N. J., settled in 1811 upon the farm on which he died, in his 90th year, on the

2d of October, 1846. He served as a minute man during the Revolutionary War, and participated in the battles of Trenton and Monmouth. He was a good citizen, and much respected.

David Shaw served his fellow-citizens over twenty-one years as a Justice of the Peace, and was also Commissioner of the County nine years. He was a very clever, quaint old gentleman, whose name is ever associated with Franklin township affairs.

Colonel Strong was noted as a military character, and a democrat. His patriotic party ardor sustained him in walking all the way from home to the State Conventions at Columbus, and back again. And speaking of democracy reminds us of the zeal of Joshua Bickford, who, for many years, was one of the shining lights of Franklin. One little incident is worthy of note. He was selected once upon a time as Chairman of a County Convention, and among other business was the appointment of delegates to a district convention to be held at Johnstown to nominate a candidate for Congress. One of the legal gentlemen of the party arose, and moved the appointment of a committee to select delegates to the Congressional Convention, &c. President Bickford put the question—"Gentlemen, all you in favor of the motion just made about delegates to the Con*gregational* Convention will say aye." The gentleman who made the motion sprang to his feet somewhat excited, exclaiming, "The Congressional Convention," I said. "Exactly," said the President; "You've heard the motion, Gentlemen: the Con*gregational* Convention I said, and I say it again, and I know what Mr. M—— said, and what we all want—we want democrats to congregate at Johnstown, and *it is* a Con*gregational* Convention." Joshua was in earnest in whatever he undertook, and seconded by the efforts of Lieut. Bernard Fields usually carried his points. He was noted as tavern-keeper, merchant and horse-trader, and was always "bobbing around."

In addition to the prominent citizens enumerated as having held official positions, we may mention the Swingleys, from Hagerstown, Md., Sam. Livingston, Henry Weatherby, Anson Prouty, Wm. Faris, Wm. Gordon, Benjamin Corwin, Alex. Wilson, Jonathan Olin, Wm. Lavering, Caleb Barton, H. P. Eldrige, C. Sapp, Wm. Linn, B. O. Pitman, David Ewers, Ebenezer Hartwell, B. and E. Lyon, Ben. Hathaway and Thomas Morrison.

In 1830, Franklin had over 16,000 acres of land upon the tax list, and the census then showed only 800 inhabitants. In 1840, the inhabitants numbered 1,343, and in 1850, 1,456.

Upon the organization of this township, Wm. Van Buskirk, a Justice of the Peace within the territory, who had been re-elected in 1822, continued the functions until again elected in 1824. In 1824, John Truax was elected. In 1827, David Shaw was elected, and subsequently re-elected over and over again; and when the township was carried into Morrow county, it took the old Justice along to keep it straight. H. W. Strong was elected in 1834, and re-elected in 1837. Wm. Van Buskirk was elected in 1840, re-elected in 1843, and again in 1846; and during his term of service the connection with Knox was severed.

Bloomfield Township was created June 23d, 1817, and received its name in this wise: Several of the settlers were at the house of Sheldon Clark early in the Spring, talking about the new township, when John Blinn called attention to the coming of flowers upon the beautiful mound that they stood upon, and suggested that, as the field was in bloom, it should be called Bloomfield, which was accordingly done.

Benjamin H. Taylor was the first lister of property for taxation and made his return June, 1818, receiving an order for $5 for his services.

The family of Artemas Swetland emigrated to this State in 1808, and in 1812 located in this part of the county, where their name has ever since existed.

The next earliest settlers were the Clarks, Walker Lyon, Preston Hubbell, Seth Nash, John Helt, Wm. Ayres, John Blinn, Dr. Bliss, Samuel Whitney, Lucius French, Stephen Marvin, Samuel Mead, Lemuel Potter—all industrious and substantial men. The Clarks—Roswell, Sheldon and Marshal, were sons of Daniel Clark, of New Haven co., Ct. Lyon, Hubbell, Nash, Whitney, French, Marvin and Mead, were also from that county. Helt and Ayres were from Washington co., Pa.

The first post office established was called Clark's ⋈ Roads, at the intersection of the road from Johnstown to New Haven with the road from Mt. Vernon to Delaware—a central point—being 13 miles from Berkshire, Mt. Vernon, Chesterville and Johnstown. The post office was subsequently styled Bloomfield.

The next was Sparta, upon the old State road from Mansfield *via* Frederick to Sunbury and Columbus. It is considerable of a trading point. From 1840 to 1850 much mechanical and manufacturing was carried on. Benjamin Chase erected quite a large woolen manufactory and ran it for several years; upon his death the works stopped. Charles Osborne was the last at the business; he moved to Mt. Gilead and has since gone west, somewhere. Elisha Cook now operates a steam saw and grist mill in the old factory buildings.

In 1817 there were only 16 voters. In 1840, the population had increased to 1,252; and in 1850, 1,395.

Of the first settlers Sheldon and Roswell Clark, Walker Lyon, Stephen Marvin, Samuel Mead, A. W. and Giles and F. M. Swetland are yet living.

Roswell Clark came to the country in 1816, with his wife. They have had three children—Daniel, now in Xenia; Eliza married John Barr, in Bloomfield; Rev. Wesley died at West Liberty, two years ago, aged 46 years. He was a preacher of the Methodist Episcopal Church, and a man of much worth; his widow and children live in Bloomfield. Sheldon Clark was married when he emigrated, in 1819, and has two daughters—Victorine P., married Floyd Sears; and Rebecca Jane, C. B. Jackson. Preston Hubbell is dead, and his three children are in the west. Lucius French is dead; his son, Andrew, and daughter, Emeline, live in Bloomfield.

John Helt survives with two children—Casper, a son, in Bloomfield; and Lafayette, a soldier in the army. Wm. Ayres is dead, and left no children. Walker Lyon, in his 73d year, is in Bloomfield with his son, Smith. He has two daughters living—Harriet, wife of Rowland Rogers; and Sally Jane, wife of James Howe, of Fredericktown. Samuel Whitney died leaving two children—Wheeler, in Bloomfield; and Samuel, near Berkshire. Seth Nash is dead, and his children, three in number, are in the west. Artemas Swetland is dead; his three boys—Augustus W., Fuller M., and Seth, and his daughter, Mrs. Wm. Shurr, are living. Lemuel Potter moved into Bloomfield in 1819 from southern Ohio; he is dead, and left eight children—Cassandra lives in Bloomfield, Lemuel, jr., in Urbana, and two of the boys are doctors in Wayne.

Among the early items of this township was the separation of a man and wife, by public notice given, as follows: "By mutual consent James C. and Rebecca Wilson, of Bloomfield township, Knox county, have this day (Oct. 21st) agreed to dissolve as being man and wife."

Stephen Marvin is living. He had three children; two survive—Charlotte, widow of Wesley Clark; and Eliza, wife of Dr. Page.

The first brick house in this township was built in 1823, by Roswell Clark, a two story building in which he has so long resided. The first frame house was the two story frame in which Sheldon Clark resides, built in 1828. Prior to these houses they, like other settlers, lived in log cabins. The

Clarks burnt the first lime in this township on log-heaps. The price then was fifty cents per bushel unslacked—just double the present rate. Since that they have burnt many kilns, and made their support and fortunes. For many years they furnished the greater part of the lime used at Mount Vernon for building and other purposes.

Among the objects of sympathy, at an early day, was Samuel Collinfare, a poor little hunchback and ricketed spinner, who traveled from house to house and spun for the citizens. He was a native of the Isle of Man, and made his first appearance about 1819. The dwarf never would work for wages, but for clothes and food—was good society—well informed, and ever cheerfully greeted where he called. A few years since E. W. Cotton, obeying the prompting of a generous heart, erected a monument in the burying ground to mark the spot where his mortal remains were laid.

The first church in this township was the Methodist Episcopal, at Bloomfield, on Clark street, as it is called; it was erected in 1839. The next Methodist Episcopal Church was built at Sparta in 1846.

In 1846 the Christian Church was put up in Sparta. These churches are frame buildings. The first preacher in the township was Thomas Kerr, Methodist. A good man—long since departed. About 1817 Rev. —— Cooper, Methodist, officiated in the township; he is also dead. They were both local preachers.

The Rev. —— Britton, about 1817, preached the Christian or Campbelite doctrine. Rev. James Smith, about the same time, was a voice crying aloud in this wilderness the same gospel truths. They also have passed hence.

In 1850 the Wesleyan Methodists erected a small church about one and a half miles west of Sparta, at which the noted Edward Smith preached until he died at Harmony in 1859; his body was interred in the Bloomfield burying ground. The present preachers are John T. Kellum and Wm. Conant, Methodist Episcopal; Rev. —— Bainam, Wesleyan Methodist. The last Christian minister was the Rev. J. W. Marvin.

The Rev. —— Cleaver, a Cumberland Presbyterian minister of Bellville, occasionally holds forth in this township.

The first white person to die in Bloomfield township was Marshal Clark, brother of Sheldon and Roswell, who died in 1816.

Bloomfield deserves more than a passing notice for the respect shown to the dead. The cemetery is a sacred spot—neat and tastily kept. It is one mile north of Clark street, and contains many neat and costly monuments.

The trustees of the township have, from its first selection, had its keeping in charge, and they deserve credit for its management.

The first store in this township was kept by —— Carpenter. The second by Dr. A. W. Swetland, who is yet in business at Sparta.

The other parties selling goods at Sparta are Chase & Co., the brothers Wm., John & E. Byron, L. Swetland, and Antipas Dexter; and a stock of goods is kept at Bloomfield by Mann Lyon.

Among the residents of Bloomfield are the Conways. Widow Charlotte Conway, who died in 1859, moved from Fauquier co., Va., with her sons Joseph, Wm. and John. Joseph married a daughter of Wm. Sanford in 1842; Wm. lives near Mt. Liberty, and John in Knox co., Missouri. The Manvilles, the Barrs, the Sanfords, Lovelands, Sheldons, Burkholders, Searses, Ashleys, Craigs, Throckmortons and Higginses, are also among the well known names.

The Cottons were among the early settlers and as such deserving of notice at our hands, more especially since the name continues in the county and is familiar to our people. Harris W. Cotton, one of the commissioners of Fayette co., Pa., entered a section of land in Bloomfield, and upon his return home, while preparing to move, died. His sons, Emmet W. and Harris, brought out the mother and family. The old lady died in Union county in June, 1851, of cancer. The children were Nancy, wife of James Thompson, in Milford; Mary, wife of Michael Cramer, in Union county; Pamelia, wife of Elijah Crable, in Liberty; John W. in West Brownsville, Pa.; Harris W. who died in Liberty in 1835, Emmet W. in Mt. Vernon; Louisa, wife of Thomas Merrill, who died about 1852 in Columbus, Ill.; Charlotte, wife of Robert Butler, who also died in Illinois; and Elizabeth, first wife of M. Cramer, who died in Clinton township about 1833. The main dependence for errands and chores of the family, in early times, was Emmet, who has often carried two bushels of wheat on horseback to Mt. Vernon and exchanged it for one pound of coffee. At that time the only improvements on the road to Norton's mill were, first, a little clearing of —— Higgins; the next at the old Norton farm, now owned by Frazier; the next at Chapman's; next an old cabin, on the Gotshal place, where —— Wolford lives; and these were all on the now thickly settled road from Bloomfield to Mt. Vernon.

Idon V. Ball, born in Brownsville, Pa., in 1805, married Catharine Woods, of that place; moved to Bloomfield in Sept., 1841, and settled on the place he has since resided upon. He has had one daughter and eight sons; six of his boys now survive. For twenty years he has been engaged in farming and entertaining the public. Many a wayfaring man has fared sumptuously at his stand, and many have been the happy parties of pleasure-seekers from Mt. Vernon and other points, who have been hospitably entertained by Mr. Ball and his excellent lady.

William McKinstry and John Brocaw are among the prominent farmers of Bloomfield, both from Hunterton county, New Jersey, and came to Knox county with the family of Matthias McKinstry, in 1831.

John Lineweaver came in 1827, and still lives in it, with a considerable family. Harvey Lounsbery is another old settler. Antipas and Chauncey Dexter, good millwrights, are also among the present inhabitants.

Thomas Osborne and his wife Olive, emigrated from Rhode Island in 1818. He died in 1853, in his 74th year; she is at the old homestead, in her 74th year. They had nine children. Those now living are all in Bloomfield, but Orilla, wife of Jesse Severe, in Liberty. John H. married Nancy Severe; James M., Sophia Thatcher; Amanda is the wife of David Coyle; Sarah Ann the wife of John Dustin; Wm. N. married Harriet Dustin, and George R., Purilla Roberts. The old gentleman had been a sailor and soldier, and did good service in his day and generation.

Samuel Westbrook was a good rough carpenter and joiner; he moved to Michigan, and is now dead. The Westbrooks were among the old settlers of this township; none of the name now live in Knox county.

An aeronaut, by the name of F. H. Westbrook, met with a terrible end on the 4th of July, 1862. There was a large concourse of people at Sparta, in commemoration of the national anniversary, who were addressed by Rev. Mills Harrod, W. L. Bane, and A. Banning Norton, and at 5 o'clock P. M., as previously announced, a balloon went up with Westbrook to the distance of perhaps five hundred feet, when it burst in pieces and fell to the earth, killing the reckless navigator. It was a miserable rotten old fabric, and was the most foolhardy operation we have ever witnessed. About three thousand people were estimated to have been present, witnessing the sad termination to an otherwise joyful occasion. What a sudden transition from life to death! Within five minutes of the time he ascended, waving his hat amid the hurrahs and shouts of the people, he fell a corpse, leaving a wife and several children to mourn his exit. For their benefit B. L. Swetland at once started a subscription, which was liberally responded to by good citizens.

JUSTICES OF THE PEACE.

June 23d, 1817, the Court of Common Pleas allowed Bloomfield one justice, to be elected at the house of Timothy Smith, and Matthew Marvin was chosen in 1818.

1819. Walker Lyon.
1822. " "
1820. John Manville.
1823. Stephen Dodd.
1824. David Bliss.
1827. John Manville.
1830. " "
1834. David Bliss.
1837. " "
1840. " "
1843. Jared Irvine.
1846. " "
1824. James Thompson.
1827. R. Clark.
1833. James Thompson.
1837. John Beebee.
1840. " "
1836. James Shumate.
1844. Jacob J. Thompson.
1846. Wheeler Ashley.
1848. Charles M. Eaton.

CHAPTER XXV.

SYCHAMORE—AND THE TWO LAST SYCHAMORES.

"SEPTEMBER 4th, 1815, on petition, Morgan township is divided and the east part of it is placed into a township called Sychamore." Such is the brief entry upon the journal showing a name now unknown.

On the 15th of September, 1815, an election was held at the school house, in the township of Sychamore, for the purpose of electing three Trustees and a Township Clerk. Jacob Simons, William Claypool and Jonathan Hunt, sr., were the Judges, and John H. Simons and Alpheus Chapman, Clerks. William Bair, Jonathan Hunt, jr., and Lemuel Chapman were elected Trustees and John Mott, jr., Clerk.

At the election on the 10th of October 17 votes were cast, and among the number we find Riverius Newell, Otis Warren, Samuel Rowley, Gideon Mott, Riverius Newell, jr., Aaron Hill, Abner Hill, Alpheus Chapman and James Miller.

Of these parties but two now live, viz: Aaron Hill and Jonathan Hunt; both over fourscore years on earth.

The name of Sychamore, as a Township, is known to scarcely a man in the county at this time. When, or how it came to be lost the records give no information, except in the little extract at the head of this page; there is no mention of it on official records.

Of Jas. Miller's family—J. W., the old merchant in Mt. Vernon, who married Mary Bryant; Madison, of Miller, who married Mary Harris; Henry H., John F., Dr. Volney and Dana, were the boys. Mrs. Rosannah Sanford, Mrs. Harriet Knox, Mrs. Sally Sanderson and Mrs. Lucinda Ellis are living, and Mary is dead. The Chapmans, Motts, Warren, Bair, Simons, Claypool and Newell, have not one of their blood within the county limits. In 1812 Riverius Newell and Aaron Hill were blacksmiths in Mt. Vernon.

Jonathan Hunt, born in Somerset co., N. J., Oct. 23d, 1780, moved from Western Virginia to this county in 1806, and settled where he now lives. He learned the trade of wagon making of his father, and also worked as a gun-smith, and at this day works at the latter branch. After he located he did much work for the Indians, until the war broke out. In August, 1812, he started with the troops, under Maj. Kratzer, for the frontier, and upon reaching Mansfield was set to repairing guns with Andy Blair, from Belmont co., at $1 each per day and regular soldier's pay. They put up a little shop at Beum's mill, on the Rocky Fork of Mohican, and he recollects that Rufner called to see him the morning of the day that he was killed by the Indians. He was working there when Copus' family was attacked and Copus killed. After three weeks work he rejoined the company, and continued with them until discharged. When he first settled in this county he went to Bowling Green, below Newark, and bought grain and got it chopped there; and he afterwards went to Kerr's mill with his grist. When he moved here he had but one child, and his wife has had 11 children—four of whom are living in Pleasant township, and one in Illinois. In 1822–3 Jonathan lived in Mount Vernon and worked at wagon and plow making, &c. His wife, Honor Wells, born in Washington co., Pa., and of the old Wells and Dodridge families so widely known, is yet living in her 79th year.

Aaron Hill was born near Boston, Mass., emigrated to this county in 1811, and shared in the privations and toils of life in a new country. During his long residence he has worked as a carpenter and joiner, a blacksmith, and a farmer, and has, with true Yankee instinct, lent a hand at whatever work the wants of the country required. At the advanced age of 84 years he resides in Mt. Vernon, spending the evening of a well spent life in the society of friends. Of his family of five, Norman N. is the sole survivor. These twain—the last of the Sychamores—may their days be many in the land they sought out more than a half century ago.

CHAPTER XXVI.

MIDDLEBURY TOWNSHIP.

On the 3d of December, 1823, this township was established, and the first election was held at the house of Luther Bateman, in April, 1824. It is now the north-west corner of Knox, and on the score of improvement, the beauty of the country, and the intelligence of its inhabitants, ranks first. Its principal settlers at every period have been Friends, from Maryland and Virginia; and the influence of the Quaker element has been highly salutary. The increase of population and wealth has been steady. In 1830 the inhabitants numbered 705, and the amount of land returned for taxation was 13,000 acres; in 1840 there were 1,002 inhabitants; in 1850, 1,092; and in 1860, 1,040. The villages of Batemantown and Waterford are points for trading operations; the latter is quite a thriving little town, having the advantage of mills in its neighborhood. Here Josiah Fawcett and John Lavering for many years were rivals in business, competitors for the post-office, and the prominent men of their respective parties. When the Whigs were in power, Josiah held the post-office; and when the Democrats ruled, he was out and John in. The post-office and its name were mooted

Wm. Tinsley Archt.

Middleton, Strobridge & Co. Lithos. Cin. O.

ASCENSION HALL

KENYON COLLEGE, GAMBIER OHIO.

points in Middlebury. The Laverings were old settlers of this section. Of the old stock, Daniel and Mary were here in 1813 ; she died October 24, 1846, aged 85. Several of the name are in the county at this date ; John is yet selling goods at Waterford.

Samuel Wilson and Thomas Townsend emigrated from Frederick, Md., in 1808. The former is dead, and his son Joseph resides in Indiana ; the latter died March 18, 1859, aged 78, on the farm where he had resided over fifty years. Amos and Wm. Farquhar were early Maryland emigrants, and David and Robert Ewers from Virginia. The Wrights and Lewises, David Eaves, Jacob Zulman, Samuel Willett, the Comforts, Jesse Vore, Jesse Stevens, the Batemans, the Cravens, the Wagoners, the Grahams, the Fiddlers, the McPhersons, the Van Buskirks, the Walterses, have been long residents of this township. Josiah Fawcett, the old merchant, is in partnership with his son, in a store in Fredericktown.

Among the citizens of this part of the county in 1819, were William Watkins, from Stoney Creek, Somerset county, Pa. ; Warren Owen, from Vermont, who emigrated about 1817 ; Philo Doolittle and Zebulon Ashley, also from New England. Asahel Ashley, only son of Zebulon, is living in Missouri ; and his son-in-law, Frisbee Owen, also lives there.

Charles Strong emigrated from Frederick county, Md.; he died in 1850. Mrs. Strong is living. Of their eight children, the following survive : G. W.

and Lewis, at Fredericktown; John W., sheriff of Richland county; Peter, station agent, Bellville; and Mrs. Mary Parke, of Mt. Vernon.

The Denman family is one of the oldest and best in Middlebury and Chester. James Johnson, the old Justice, died a few years ago, leaving a considerable family in this township; his son Orlin is a prominent citizen. Lawrence Van Buskirk is another noted citizen, having served as State Senator. James Martin and his family have long occupied a front position among the good citizens; he has lived in the county since 1811.

Jacob Ebersole was an eccentric old settler, of miserly disposition, who lived close and mean to accumulate money to look at. After his death, over $2000 in coin was found hidden away by him—some under an old anvil block in a smith shop, and another lot in an old chest, under some rubbish.

SUCCESSIVE JUSTICES OF THE PEACE.

The first Justice in 1824 was James Johnson, who was regularly re-elected and served until 1848. The second was James Graham, elected in 1831, and served three terms. In 1842 Stephen McPherson was elected, and re-elected in 1845. Ezra Marvin and John W. Loofborow were elected in 1848, and re-elected in 1851; G. Wash. Ewers and Thomas Craven in 1852; Daniel Ayres in 1855; and at the same time J. D. Burke, who was re-elected in 1858, and again in 1861; Isaac Lynde in 1858, and re-elected in 1861.

CHAPTER XXVII.

BERLIN TOWNSHIP.

THIS township received its name from some of its earliest settlers having emigrated from Berlin, Connecticut. It was created March 9th, 1825. Stephen Cole proposed the name. Among the first voters were A. H. Royce, Ed. Richardson, the Markleys, George Wolford, James Traer, John Brown, Sr., Jno. C. Brown, John and Peter Kereghers, Fred. Ogg, Jeremiah Brown, Richard and Asael Roberts, John Long, Jacob Leady, Joseph Lane, Daniel Hedrick, the Joslins, and John Moltzbaugh.

Palmyra, during the days of our vassalage to stage and wagon transportation, was its sole town, and for many years a noted place of refreshment for man and beast, voyaging by mud or snow from Mt. Vernon to Mansfield. Since the construction of the railroad, it has dilapidated.

The township in 1830 had 520 inhabitants, and 11,674 acres of land were entered on the tax list, at a value of $34,724. In 1840, the population numbered 1,100; in 1850, 1,156; and in 1860, 1,012.

Ankenytown, or "Squeal," as it is more commonly called for the sake of euphony, is noted from the fact that when the steam-horse first made his appearance there, his "squeal" so terribly alarmed the natives that they came out armed capapie with gun and blunderbuss to capture him, and some worthy German denizens attempted to stop his travel on the iron track by tearing up the rails; the history of which fully and at large appears in the records of Knox Common Pleas.

Shalerville, so called from Shaler's Mills, is quite a trading point, where Henry W. Greggor officiates as Postmaster and Merchant.

Among the earliest settlers in this township were the Robertses, Richardsons, Wrights and Farquhars—all Friends, and from Maryland; the Browns, Pinkleys, Leedys, Hedricks, Coles, Wm. Van Horne, Peter Wolf, David McDaniel and Henry Markley, an intelligent Pennsylvania German, and his brother-in-law, Michael Harter. Markley had been a merchant, and was a quick and sprightly business man, and hence was selected for one of the first Commissioners. He was generous, and well liked by the people.

John Lewis and his family, Quakers, were here in 1808. November 14th, 1857, John, Jr., died. Casper Fitting, in 1808, lived with his family on the place, since known as the Harter stand. He is dead, and his sons, Frederick and Solomon, are living; the former a successful merchant at Bellville.

The Harters are worthy of special notice. Their tavern, at an early day, was the best in northern Ohio. The old people were kind and hospitable, and the society of the amiable Miss Christina made it uncommonly interesting for sleighing and other parties. The fame of Aunt Christina's cookery, pronounced by connoiseurs the best, caused travelers to ride long miles after night to get there. The Harters moved to Canton, where some of their descendants reside.

In 1849, a Postoffice was established at the residence of Richard Roberts, Esq., called "Maple Grove," and he was appointed Postmaster, and continued as such till 1860, when it was discontinued by his request.

Among the present settlers, we find Joseph Baker and wife, who emigrated from Virginia in 1819, the Elliotts, Joel and Amos, the Gibsons, the Foots, the Dennises, and the Loves. Amos H. Royce, the first Justice, is yet living in the enjoyment of health and plenty. We can not but commend the character of Henry Miller, Esq., the upright man; Alexander Menzie, the energetic old Scotchman; and others we might name, had we the space.

SUCCESSIVE JUSTICES OF THE PEACE.

1821. Amos H. Royce was elected, and re-elected in 1824, '27, '30, '33.

1823.	Richard Roberts.	1848.	George Shaffer.
1836.	Elijah McGregor.	1849.	Gideon Elliott.
1836.	George Ankeny.	1850.	Joseph Ankeny.
1839.	"	1853.	"
1842.	"	1852.	Michael Hess.
1838.	Alex. Menzie.	1855.	J. C. Auten.
1838.	J. N. Richardson.	1856.	Alfred Royce.
1841.	"	1858.	Joseph Ankeny.
1841.	Joel Elliott.	1859.	James Comings.
1844.	Richard Roberts.	1859.	J. W. Condon.
1845.	Henry Miller.	1860.	George Irwin.
1847.	Alfred Royce.	1862.	Issacher Rowby.

CHAPTER XXVIII.

BROWN TOWNSHIP.

THIS township was laid out March 9, 1825, and "attached to Jefferson until it shall be ascertained that there is inhabitants enough in Brown to have it organized." March 6, 1826, "ordered by the Commissioners that Brown be hereafter considered a separate and distinct township, and the election be held at the house of Josias Ewing, for township officers, on the first Monday of April, and Jefferson be henceforth attached to Union." The name was given to perpetuate the memory of Major-General Jacob Brown, the hero of Chippewa and Fort Erie, who had but recently become commander-in-chief of the U. S. Army.

The first post-office, called Phifer's × Roads, was where Brownsville now is, and of late has borne the name of Jelloway, after the stream of this locality.

The present merchants are, Wm. Patton, Sam'l Beeman, Pinckley & Watz; doctors, E. Booth, L. D. Whitford; wagonmakers, Thomas Thompson, Emanuel Storer; blacksmiths, Smith & Hagerman, D. Thompson; tailor, F. Schuch; shoemakers, E. Waddle, W. Stull and Knee; tavern, Mrs. Phifer; tanner, Henry Frazier; gunsmith, Henry Raisin; grocer, J. H. Burriss. The Methodists have a meeting-house, wherein Rev. Mr. Ball preaches.

In 1840 the inhabitants of Brown numbered 1,204; in 1850, 1,535; and in 1860, 1,440.

The most numerous families in this township are the McKees, Waddles, Halls and Blairs, descendants of early settlers, who cleared the way for the present.

Charles McKee emigrated from Ireland, with fourteen children, about 1808. Alexander McKee settled in this county in 1809; he resides on his old place on Big Jelloway, where was once an Indian camp; and when he first settled there, sixty-five Indians called at his hut, drank metheglin with him, and they had a jovial time all round.

The Halls, Sovernses, Pinkertons, Waddles, and Stewards have also been plenty in Brown. John Carghnan (pronounced Carnahan) was a wild Irishman of much note about 1826; he was a warm-hearted, impulsive creature; and "faith, an' he was a knowledgeable mon." Many anecdotes are quoted of him, which we have not room to produce.

Jacob Phifer from Strasburg, Germany, located in this township in 1818, when all was wild and new. He died Oct. 9, 1846, aged 89. He had served ten years a soldier in Europe, three years in the Revolutionary War, and three months in the war of 1812. The old soldier was the father of Freeman, John, James and Michael.

James Blair, our old friend, "God bless you," was one of the early stock. In 1816 he tended the old Shrimplin mill; moved to Brown in 1820, and has been one of its most prominent men, having served as justice long enough to entitle him to vote, and his decisions have been generally approved of by his fellow citizens. He has been engaged in milling, farming, raising children, writing "poetry" and making himself generally useful. His memory will endure in Brown forever.

Zephaniah Wade, who commanded a company of Riflemen from Loudon co., Va., in 1777, moved to this county in October, 1816, with his son, Thomas. Zephaniah and his wife, Irene Longley, are both dead. J. J. Skillings has been one of the most active business men.

There have been a few small mills on Big Jelloway from its early settlement, but the want of water, during the year, has caused some of them to suspend. Emor Barret's grist mill was built about 1833, and is yet in operation. It is run by an overshot wheel 16 feet high. Thomas Wade has a saw mill 2½ miles above it run by an overshot wheel 30 feet high. A set of carding machines have also been run at this stand. The mills of James Blair, Ab. Whitney, and Joseph Hall have gone into dilapidation and decay.

Jacob Roof and his wife Polly, Jacob Darrow and Wm. Prior, Jacob Baugh, Daniel Worley and Richard Deakins, were old settlers.

SUCCESSIVE JUSTICES OF THE PEACE.

Samuel Barkhurst was the first, and Josias Ewing succeeded him in 1826.

1830. James McMillen; re-elected in 1833.

1831. James Blair; re-elected in 1834, '37, '40, '43, '46, '49.

1837. Thomas Wade; re-elected in 1840 and 1844.

1845. John W. Gurberson.

1846. Wm. Soverns; re-elected in 1850.

1850. Joseph Pinkley; re-elected in 1853 and 1857.

1852. Solomon C. Workman.

1854. John Hicks.

1856. J. W. Leonard; re-elected in 1859 and 1862.

CHAPTER XXIX.

JEFFERSON TOWNSHIP.

THE township bearing the honored name of President Jefferson, after having served a tutelage of several years composing a portion of the bailiwick of Brown, is, in 1829, at the March term of the Commissioners, declared a "distinct Township," and an election is ordered for township officers the 1st Monday of April, 1829, at the house of Andrew Lockard. Its metes and bounds had been prescribed on the 9th of March, 1825, but from lack of population an organization was not then effected. The Mohican river passes through this township, furnishing several mill seats. In 1830, it contained 311 inhabitants; in 1840, 994; in 1850, 1,484; and in 1860, 1,458. In this as other eastern townships, the names of a few families predominate. The Greers, the Critchfields, the Sapps, the Hibbitses, the Frosts, the Schultzes, the Bakers, are to be met with on almost every hill. The Critchfields and Sapps we have elsewhere spoken of. The Greers are mainly descendants of that noble old patriarch John Greer, who was a native of the Emerald Isle, and was what is called an Irish patriot. Possessed of a powerful constitution and vigorous intellect, he took a prominent position among the pioneers. He was particularly efficient in the military line, and raised a company for service in the war of 1812. He did much to promote the formation of companies in the eastern townships. He was from 1812 to 1817 Collector of Taxes, in 1830 Representative, and for many years Justice of the Peace, and during his life a very useful citizen. For thirty years some of the Greer name have officiated as Justices in this township. Among its most valued citizens have been Alexander, late County Treasurer, and father of the present Treasurer, Robert, Richard, Silas, Mark, James, "big Jim" and "little Jimmy." Capt. Jack Melton, Aaron Mathene, Andrew Mckee, Ephraim McMillen, Jacob Shiner and George Greer, were also old settlers.

Jacob Colopy has resided in this township since 1825. He is a son of Timothy, a native of Ireland, who emigrated from Virginia in 1813. Jacob married a daughter of George Sapp, in 1825. They have eight children—five now living in the eastern part of Knox. John Hibbets, Joseph Critchfield, Josiah Trimbly, Matthew Davidson, Charles Miller were also much respected.

In this township there are two post offices—Greersville and Nonpareil. Greersville was established about 1848, and the post masters have been Robert Greer and Alexander Greer. Nonpareil is at Mt. Holly, and was established in 1849. Its post masters have been Robert Long, A. Gardner, John Critchfield and A. Gardner.

In early times there were many insects and reptiles of great annoyance to the early settlers. Among other evidences of the fact is the following comical affair related by a citizen of this township: Old John Daily and Alex. Darling got up a bet of a quart of whisky about the ability of a man to stand black ants, ticks and all else, save gallinippers, without flinching. Daily, accordingly, to show it could be done, stripped off his clothes and laid down on his face in the sand, where the ants were thick, and Darling was to keep the gallinippers off. After laying there several minutes Darling let three or four gallinippers on his bare back, but Daily did not flinch for them—then determined to win his bet he whispered to one of the spectators to bring him a coal of fire, which was got and put on him, but Daily let the live coal roast his flesh for fifteen minutes without ever flinching, and with his muscles firm bore it together with the ants and gallinippers until the half hour was up, and won the quart of whisky.

JUSTICES OF THE PEACE.

1825. Jas. Henderson.	1855. Robert Greer.
1829. " "	1838. Josiah Frost.
1829. John Greer.	1854. " "
1832. " "	1857. " "
1835. James Greer.	1837. James Witherow.
1838. Joseph Sapp.	1840. " "
1840. James Greer.	1843. " "
1842. Alex. Greer.	1846. " "
1845. " "	1857. James Greer.
1848. " "	1858. Charles Miller.
1851. " "	1860. James Greer.
1849. Robert Greer.	1861. Charles Miller.
1852. " "	

CHAPTER XXX.

MONROE TOWNSHIP.

THIS township was created March 9th, 1825, and favored with the name of President Monroe. The surface of the country is broken; it is well watered and thickly timbered; and its citizens have generally been noted for their unflinching democracy and their strict attention to home affairs. The population in 1830 was 437, and the acres listed for taxation 13,455. In 1840, it contained 1,258 inhabitants; in 1850, 1,324; and in 1860, 1,084.

The principal place of business is Monroe Mills, where Davis and the Boyntons for many years sold goods, bought produce, and had a post-office established in 1849. Schenck's Creek, passing through the east part, has on it several saw and grist mills. At a very early period James Smith ran a mill upon it; and Jacob Davis, another very useful citizen, erected and operated until his death a good mill, which is yet carried on. This stream took its name from Gen. W. C. Schenck, who owned the lands subsequently improved by Captain Coleman, David Johnson, the Irelands, and others. In 1817, he sold a large part of his tract to various settlers, who made substantial improvements.

The Colemans were early settlers. Joseph emigrated from Fayette county, Pa., in March, 1806, and lived that year south of Mount Vernon, across the creek, and the next year moved to the place where he died, in 1830, aged 56. Of his children, Ichabod is the only one now in this county; Joe is living in Nebraska, William in Indiana, and Jess. is dead.

The Rev. William Thrift and his family were also among the earliest and best settlers.

Charles Lauderbaugh, of Pennsylvania, in 1828, emigrated to this township, and resided there until his death, in 1854. He had 12 children; now living, John, Henry, Andy and Jesse, Nelly, Mrs. J. Myers, Louisa, Mrs. C. Wolverton, Rachel, Mrs. Wm. King, and Rebecca.

In the list of justices, will be found the names of other respected families; the Dixons, Scotts, Clementses, Becks, Adamses, Irvines, Boyntons, Hutchisons, and Craigs will long be held in remembrance, if not perpetuated by resident descendants in future years. And the calculation would not be complete without enumerating the family of our old friend Bill Dowds, whose standing salutation is, "What's the calculation?" There were also Sam. and Elijah, and their families; the Marshalls and Gilcrests.

Peter Skeen emigrated from Montgomery county, Pa., in 1827; he died in 1855, aged 71. He was an intelligent and industrious citizen.

The Youngs were among the early settlers of this township Isaac Young was born in Fairfield county, Connecticut, in 1760, and served in the Revolutionary war; in 1790 moved to Uniontown, Pa., where he lived for many years, and from thence to Ohio in 1830, and to Monroe in 1836, where he resided until his death, in 1842, at the age of 82 years and 19 days.

Col. H. H. Young, of Fayette county, Pa., was born in 1794; married Rachel Shipley, and moved to Washington county, Pa., and from thence, in 1835, to where he now resides. He is the father of five boys and five girls. Colonel Young, for his ardor in Democracy and Methodism, his hickory pole raisings and marshalship of Democratic processions, will never be forgotten by those who witnessed his zeal in the campaigns of 1836, '40, '44.

Col. John Armstrong, a very estimable gentleman from Jamaica, who died in 1855; Lemuel Holmes, another good man, now living in Iowa; David Hunt, the Berrys, the Barkers and the Millers, for many years resided in this township. The name of Hull is also of long standing.

SUCCESSIVE JUSTICES OF THE PEACE.

1821.	Thos. Dixon.	1856.	Joseph Hutchison.
1824.	" "	1859.	" "
1826.	W. Beck.	"	James Hutchinson.
1831.	Thos. Dixon.	1836.	M. N. Scott.
1834.	" "	1839.	" "
1838.	" "	1843.	" "
1843.	" "	1846.	" "
1840.	Joseph Adams.	1849.	" "
1841.	Jos. Coleman.	1852.	M. N. Scott.
1844.	" "	1846.	R. S. Clements.
1847.	" "	1849.	" "
1850.	" "	1852.	" "
1851.	Isaac Irvine.	1855.	" "
1854.	John Craig.	1858.	" "
1855.	Henry Boynton.	1861.	" "

CHAPTER XXXI.

PIKE TOWNSHIP.

THIS township, established June 7th, 1819, was named after General Pike. The first election was held the 26th of June, at the house of Michael Harter.

The entire voters in 1822 numbered nineteen. Their names we give: John Arnold, Robert Kennedy, Jacob Swails, Thomas Elwell, Wm. Wright, Aaron Wilson, John Scoles, Wm. Smith, Philip Armentrout, Benj. Austin, John Butler, Wm. Spry, Francis Popham, David Holloway, Thomas Scoles, John Gordon, Andrew Scoles, Cyrus McDonald, and George Scoles. In 1820, John Arnold listed the taxable property, and received $5 therefor. Amity was laid out in 1832, and contains about 150 inhabitants, among them wagon makers, Adam Cole, John Scarborough; tanners, John Nyrick, George McClurg; shoemakers, John Cain, George Nyrick; tavern keeper, Newel Dowds. There are two stores. The post-office is called "Democracy." There are three churches: Baptist, Rev. Arnold, Pastor; Methodist, Rev. Ball; and Deciple. The physicians are E. Mast and W. E. Edwards.

In 1840, Pike contained 1,216 inhabitants; in 1850, 1,720; and in 1860, 1,454.

The brothers Bartholomew and John Bartlett, natives of Connecticut, emigrated from Pennsylvania to Knox county in 1808, and were the heads of numerous families of Bartlett in Knox and Morrow. The sons of Bartholomew were William, David, Hugh, and Leonard; and the daughters were Martha, wife of J. C. Irvine, of Mt. Vernon; Polly, wife of Samuel Nye; Betsy, wife of Winn Winship, and Mrs. Jacob Cooper, deceased. Edwin, son of William, lives on the old home place in Morris township; William Bartlett, carpenter in Mt. Vernon, is one of the sons of David; his other son, Simeon, lives in the west. Hugh's children were William F., George, Lafayette, Taylor, and Mary, Mrs. Shurr of Chesterville. Leonard's children were John, George, who married Ellen Cooper, Helen, Preston, Elizabeth, Josephine. John, sr.'s, children were Abner, and Mary, Mrs. John Richards, who is dead. Abner's children are T. M. Bartlett, of Mt. Vernon, Sarah, wife of Robert Maxwell in Morrow county, John D., of Wayne, Abner, Joel, Abel, Maria, wife of John Barber, Mary, Mrs. Fredericks, Loruma, wife of Alvin Casson, all of Morrow county. Of Mrs. Mary Richards' children, but one child—David, at Sparta—lives in this State; the others are in Vermont. When the old settlers came to Knox they settled in Clinton and Morris. The Cains—Elias and James—were early settlers. James now lives in Holmes county; Elias and his brother Robert yet in this township. The Armstrongs, Johnsons and Kirkpatricks are citizens of many years. Conrad

Doub, a native of Frankfort on the Rhine, came to this county in 1832. He is a good farmer; has seven boys living, two of whom are in Co. H, 23d Regt.—Conrad and Lewis. John Mahaffey has since 1833 been a citizen of this township. He came from Washington county, Pa., learnt the blacksmith trade with his brother Joe, in Mt. Vernon, and has for many years carried on business in this township.

SUCCESSIVE JUSTICES OF THE PEACE.

1819. Andrew Scoles.
1820. Wm. Smith.
1822. Bernard Reece.
1823. Wm. Smith.
1825. Bernard Reece.
1825. Wm. Johnson.
1829. Wm. Smith.
1833. " "
1834. John Gordon.
1836. John Cochran.
1839. " "
1843. John Gordon.
1843. Wm. Arnold.
1844. John Ramsey
1847. " "
1849. Eli Dickerson.
1850. C. P. Frederick.
1852. Eli Dickerson.
1855. H. P. Roberts.
1855. J. D. Hammil.
1858. J. D. Hammil.
1859. John Wise.

1819. Robert Silcost.
1825. Wm. McNear.
1823. Aaron Bixby.
1827. Andrew Scoles.
1830. Hugh Kirkpatrick.
1831. F. Popham.
1831. John Cochran, jr.
1834. F. Popham.
1837. John Gordon.
1837. J. Y. Barnhard.
1840. John Gordon.
1842. Emanuel Wagoner.
1846. Amos Dehaven.
1846. W. W. Minteer.
1849. " "
1852. " "
1853. R. C. Sweeney.
1856. " "
1856. David Braddock.
1858. Sam. Kirkpatrick.
1860. R. C. Sweeney.
1861. J. D. Hammil.

CHAPTER XXXII.

HOWARD TOWNSHIP.

IN the general reorganization of March 9th, 1825, this township was formed. The land is generally rolling and well watered by Owl Creek and the Jelloways, which afford considerable water power. The Kinderhook Mills, in the days of Elliott, Warden & Co., did a fine business, and the village of Kinderhook was quite a noted place.

Howard had 590 population in 1830, and 14,586 acres of taxable land. In 1840, the inhabitants numbered 990; in 1850, 1,002; and in 1860, 870.

The Porters emigrated from Maryland in 1816; Thomas J. died in his 83d year. Of his nine children, the living are Henry T., who married Eliza Ann Hedington, Samuel, Michael, Harriet, wife of Hiram Critchfield. Old 'Squire Porter was an honest and intelligent man, who was highly esteemed by all who knew him. For nine years he served his neighbors as a justice, and died universally lamented. Dr. Lewis R. is residing in Clinton township, much respected for his intelligence and worth.

The name of Critchfield has been common in this and the adjoining townships, and will continue so. Nathaniel, William, Joseph, John and Isaac, five brothers, emigrated from the neighborhood of Cumberland, Md., to Owl Creek in 1806. Isaac died shortly after. The others had been soldiers in the Revolutionary War, and drew pensions until their death. Nathaniel married Christina Welker; he died about 1837, and she in July, 1840. They had thirteen children, of whom the following have been generally known, viz: William, Susannah, wife of Jacob Lepley, Joseph, Catharine, wife of Peris Sprague, Jesse, Sally, wife of Jacob Lybarger, Benjamin, Mary, wife of Meshac Casteel, and Isaac, who died. Wm. Critchfield, Sr., died in 1848. His second wife, who was the Widow Barcus, survives. Their children were — Reuben, Samuel, Betsy Thatcher, Drusilla Thomas, Keziah Magers, Sally Critchfield, and James and Benjamin Barcus. Joseph Critchfield married Peggy Sapp; he died in 1843. Of their nine children, we have the following memoranda: Mary was the second wife of Col. John Greer; Elizabeth married Robert Waddle; Catharine, George Lybarger; Phœbe, Wm. Beckwith; Alvin and William are in Indiana; Isaac in Hardin county; John in Mt. Holly; Joseph died in Indiana.

William, son of Nathaniel, married Elizabeth Troutman, of Somerset co., Pa., and begat 13 children. Charles, Reuben, Sam., Hiram, Enoch, who married Maria Dixon; Jesse, Mary Horton; Dr. S. T., Mary Porter, of Allegheny co., Md.; William Jackson is dead; Lucinda married Lewis Lybarger; Matilda married John Cassel; Delilah married Dr. Mast, and Catharine is at home. Hiram and Jesse are dead.

From the loins of these old soldiers have sprung a numerous tribe of athletic and hardy people. The old set were good marksmen, industrious husbandmen, thorough going yeomen, who endured great hardships and perils in the "times that tried men's souls," and left to their hundreds of descendants the light of good example, and a just pride in their well spent lives.

Uriah Tracy, Marvin Tracy, James Logue, Jas. Wade, Paul Welker, Ben. Ellis, Philip, George, jr., and Isaac Dial were of the first settlers. George Lybarger, sr., George, jr., and Andrew, were among the first voters in this township. Ludwick Lybarger and his sons—Sam., George, Lewis, Joseph and Jacob, have long been residents. "Old uncle George" moved west many years ago, and is now dead; he was a kind-hearted man of the pioneer stamp.

The Dawsons and McFarlands, from Washington co., Pa., have resided in this township since 1835, and have been excellent citizens. Henry Eckenrode, a native of Adams co., Pa., settled in this township in 1833, and has helped people it. John Hull has been here since 1820. Here, too, have lived a numerous family of Durbins, the Trolingers, Horns, Whites, Nicholses, Marlows, Millers, Magerses, Berrys, and other most excellent people.

SUCCESSIVE JUSTICES OF THE PEACE.

1822.	Joseph McMahon.	1841.	H. H. McArtor.
1822.	Martin Engle.	1844.	" "
1825.	" "	1847.	" "
1826.	Amos Workman.	1850.	" "
1829.	" "	1853.	" "
1831,	Ben. Hedington.	1846.	Ben. Ellis.
1832.	Thos. J. Porter.	1849.	E. Marshal.
1835.	" "	1852.	J. T. Beum.
1838.	" "	1855.	" "
1832.	William Williams.	1858.	Sam. Cake.
1835.	" "	1859.	A. J. Ellis.
1838.	" "	1858.	Paul Welker.
1840.	Ben. Ellis.	1861.	" "

CHAPTER XXXIII.

MORRIS TOWNSHIP.

On the 2d of March, 1812, upon petition of several citizens this township was laid off, and an order issued for an election to be held at the house of Benjamin Rush for township officers. A majority of the early settlers being natives of Morris county, New Jersey, caused the name of Morris to be selected. The officers of the election, this year, were Wm. Douglass, Daniel Cooper, Wm. Thrift, judges; James Trimble and John Wheeler, clerks. The township was listed by N. C. Boalse, who was paid a $6 county order for his services. At a special meeting of the Associate Judges, March 14, 1812, three justices were allowed to this township at the election ordered by the Commissioners. There were fifty voters. James Trimble was chosen Township Clerk; Scott Durbin and James Miller, Constables; and James Loveridge, Treasurer. At this period, this may be said to have been the foremost township in the county. Clinton was then in its prime, the country around was settled by the very best kind of people; the upper branches of Owl Creek, uniting within its limits, gave them some of its richest bottom lands for cultivation, and the flow of emigration brought much substantial population. At the election of 1816 there were 83 voters. In 1819, Smith Hadley listed the township, and received an $8 order for the same. The foregoing names, together with those in the list of justices, represent many of the most prominent families in this township from its organization. The names of Smith, Cooper, Loveridge, Douglass, Bonar, Coleman, Trimble, Thrift, Wheeler, Durbin, Nye, Ball, Banning and Rush, frequently occur in these pages in connection with events in our past history. Several of the families have not a single representative now in the county. The heads of families have died, and the descendants gone to other parts. The most active of the Clintonians long since left the field. Samuel H. Smith, the head of that settlement, drew around him many mechanics and laborers; he was an energetic, intelligent business man, and has no one of his blood within the county at this time.

S. H. Smith, of Erie co., who we observed a few days since contributed $100 to the war fund of his township, is the only one of his children in Ohio. He is a farmer, and the largest tax-payer in that county, as we have been informed. Ichabod Nye, brother-in-law of Smith, is dead, as also his wife. Henry Smith, the Barneys, Glasses, Enoses, Yeomans, Marshals, Harrison and Dickinson, are also gone. Alexander Enos moved to Richland co., and Wm. C. has gone to parts unknown. Ralph Granger, who sold goods in Clinton in 1815, died long since.

The Coopers, Carey, Daniel and Elias, were brothers. In 1809 Daniel moved from Butler co., Pa., with his family, and was followed shortly after by Carey and Elias. The latter was unmarried. Carey's sons were Charles, Elias, Hugh, John and Lewis, of whom Charles and John alone survive. His two daughters are also dead. Daniel had seven children—Thompson, Wm., George, Henrietta, and Julia, Mrs. John Ray, in this county, Josiah living in Chillicothe, Mo., and Mrs. Sarah Bushfield. Elias Cooper, the old gentleman, is yet living; another Cooper of the early times was "cousin Charley;" they were all natives of New Jersey. Thompson recollects how prosperous Clinton was in 1813, with its four taverns with their inviting signs swinging in the breeze—kept by Ichabod Nye, Alfred Manning, John Barney and Samuel Yeoman. In the war times whisky flowed freely down the throats and business was very brisk. "God's barn" was then the great place of gathering for devotional purposes. The old settlers have a lively recollection of the pious labors of father Scott therein; when, in the summer time, the hogs of the whole village collected together under the floor, which was about two and a half feet from the ground, and would frequently set up such a grunting and squealing as to render inaudible the voice of the good minister. It was a great harbor for fleas, and Capt. Douglass was conspicuous in the meeting with his large feet, bare, endeavoring to catch the marauders who violated the sanctity of the place. He moved to the Wabash country and is dead, as also his son, Aaron; his daughters—Sally, wife of James Rogers; and Phœbe, wife of Richard Ewalt, are living.

Wm. McCartney and Aaron dug the mill race

for Douglass. A sister of Mc. married Enoch Ogle, who kept tavern in Bellville. John Johnson, father of Tom, the old jailor, is dead. Abednego Stevens rests with Shadrach and Meshac, and Amzie Stevens, of Amazonian frame, whose foot was sixteen inches and a quarter, died long, long ago. His skeleton he wished to be preserved as a model, and hence struck a bargain with a doctor by which he was to have the bones for his museum. About 1832, Mr. Bicking and another merchant from Philadelphia, in passing through the country, discovered his foot-prints in the snow, and got out and took the measure of the track, having never seen the like before. Verily he was a monster, and shook the earth with his majestic tread. Grim would have been but a small boy beside him. The children of a future age may exclaim: "There were giants in those days!" William Mitchell was here in 1807. His children were Jacob, Nathaniel, Abigail, Mrs. John H. Mefford; Mary, Mrs. John Young; Hannah, Mrs. Wm. Mefford, Naomi, wife of Lewis Young, deceased, now Mrs. Thos. Evans; Sarah, Mrs. Cyrus Cooper; John, Silas and Wm. All now live but Nathaniel and Sarah. Nathaniel was one of the scouting party at the time of Copus' slaughter, and died in 1813 from disease contracted by exposure in the Indian campaign. William, sr., joined the Baptist Church in 1815, and continued a member until his death, August 12, 1848, in his 83d year. He was very sociable and much esteemed. An old heir-loom of this family is in the possession of Hannah Mefford, being a cup and saucer of peculiar construction, which belonged to her grand-mother, one of the New Jersey matrons of the revolution. The old China set of the last century was used by General Washington when at the old homestead, near Morristown, during the revolutionary war.

James Loveridge and wife, both living, came from Morris co., N. J., in 1805, and Richard in 1812. The latter was an inventive genius; he died several years since. There are many of this name now in Morris. Philip resides on the old farm of Richard. Loveridgeisms are peculiarities of expression in rhyme pertaining to this family. Richard got a patent for a plow in 1828; and an exclusive right to rhyme in conversation has been inherited by this family. Long may the old stock be spared to indulge their propensity for sport in verse. They have been industrious citizens. Another Jersey accession includes the Ball brothers—Hiram, Uzal, Cyrus and Timothy. Their father divided equally 1,000 acres of the best Owl Creek bottom land among them, and for a half century it has been held and cultivated by the Balls. The Ebersole family is another one of the old stock. Some of the descendants, John, Jacob, and others, have made valuable citizens. An incident of this township worthy of record occurred in the time when it was customary to warn out of townships any new comer who was likely to become a township charge. One of these settlers, by the name of Pope, having located within the limits, Silas Ball was ordered to warn him out. He remonstrated against doing so, saying, "God made man, and he has a right to a place on earth, and if

Pope is warned out of Morris he may be warned out of any other township he goes into, and it is contrary to God's will that he should have no abiding place." The warrant was fixed out and handed to him to serve, which he took as required, went to Pope's house, and taking it in his hand was about to read it, when his feelings overcame him, and he exclaimed, "Pope, I warn you off the face of God's earth!" and turned around and went back with the writ. He was asked if he served it by reading, or by copy; he replied, "neither," and gave the words he employed. The result was that Pope remained, and Ball's better nature triumphed. He was a staunch Universalist, and a kind-hearted citizen.

Among the names of long standing is that of Bonar. In 1812, Barnet and Matthew, brothers, emigrated from Washington county, Pa.; about the same time came a cousin of theirs, named Matthew, and a brother-in-law, Dr. John Byers. The latter-named Matthew moved some years ago to Illinois, where he was living at last accounts. The brother of Barnet was a bachelor, and died about 1815. Barnet died in May, 1844, aged 84, and his wife in 1858, aged 89. They had the following children: David, who died about 1816; Matthew, living in Richland county; John, who died in 1859; William, at the old homestead on Granny's Creek; Ann, wife of Gavin Mitchell, of Richland county, died in 1835, leaving a considerable family; Martha, wife of Adam Rinehart, living in this township; Sarah, wife of E. P. Young, died about 1840; Isabel, who died about 1828;

Margaret, married A. Greenlee, and died about 1850. John was a hard-working, intelligent farmer, who was highly esteemed, and died in his 54th year, from a cancer. His wife was Lucinda, daughter of Charles Cooper. She had one son—Josiah, who married a daughter of Charles Swan—and two daughters; Bell married Thomas Swan, also in Morris, and Catharine is the wife of H. Leonard, of Wayne. William Bonar married A. L. Case, and has four children living: David; Elizabeth, wife of Rev. J. W. White, of Marion, Whitesides county, Illinois; Sarah Jane, and Caroline. Isabel died in 1860. William Bonar's name will be found among the Senators from this district. He is the only son of the old pioneer now within our county limits.

Among the early incidents of this section is the following curious hunting exploit. Deer were very abundant then on Granny's Creek, and one day Barnet shot a large doe, and as it fell, and life's current was ebbing away, he discovered that she was in the pains of parturition, when he ripped her open with his knife, and took from her two fawns, one of which he gave to Alex. Johnson, and the other he kept. They both lived for some time. His own, having lost its eyes by exposure to fire, first died; but the other grew up a large and healthy tame deer, and was an object of peculiar interest to the neighborhood, on account of its singular birth.

Samuel H. Smith was always spry and active. During the time of his mercantile operations he received a good deal of money, and on one occasion he threw a shot-bag full of specie on the counter, and said that any one who could run away from him with that bag, might have it. Taking him at his word, Henry Smith, who was a sprightly young man, grabbed it and ran, pursued by Sam., and, after coursing down the road some distance, finding the old gentleman gaining on him, he broke for the fence, and climbed over it into the field; but Sam. caught him, and he gave up the bag amid the shouts and cheers of Capt. Nye's horse company, who were spectators of the ludicrous scene.

The Duhamels, Amos and Henry, in 1824, emigrated from Frederick, Md. Henry now lives near Maumee City; Amos in Franklin, Ill., with his third wife. By his former wives he had eleven children; number by the present not known. Of these we have the following account: Peter C. resides in Morris township; Emily, wife of Geo. W. Litt, in Pike township; Frances Jane, wife of James Logsden, is in Iowa; Louisa Ann, wife of David Spickler, in Allen county. Peter C. learned the carpenter trade with Robert Spears, Belville, and works at it. The Cosners were very industrious citizens. Old "Uncle Philip" was noted as being one of the most successful tobacco-growers. Peter Rush is another of the old stock of farmers. The Winterbothams were a highly intelligent family, none of whom are now in Knox. Of the number of children is Mrs. Ann S. Stephens, the accomplished authoress, residing in New York; John H., an energetic business man, in Fort Madison, Iowa; Robert, in Columbus; Samuel, in Iowa; and William, in Wisconsin. Adam Rinehart, another valued citizen, with his family, resides here; also the Cassels, Swans, Pearres, John Lamb, and Henry Johnson. Benjamin Rush, of Morris county, N. J., with his wife, Margaret Logan, also of said county, emigrated with their children, Job, Andrew M., Mary, Johannah and Margaret, to this township, from Morris township, Washington county, Pa. The two latter are dead; other children, born in this township, were Eunice, Sarah Ann and Lucinda. Benjamin died in March, 1849, in his 80th year, and the old lady in October, 1858, in her 85th year. They were among the best citizens. Richard Ayres, John Erwin, and Mrs. Galloway, were also early settlers. Of these, the only remaining trace in this county, is Erwin's daughter, Mrs. Mary McFarland. John Wheeler, a carpenter, married a daughter of Mrs. Galloway, and moved to Sandusky, taking with him Mrs. Galloway and her son. John Sawyer, first blacksmith at Clinton, and a good horse-shoer, emigrated to Indiana, and died. His only descendant in this county is Mrs. W. O. Johnson. In 1830, the population of Morris was 812, and 13,066 acres of land were listed for taxation. In 1840, there were 1,079 inhabitants; in 1850, 1,028; and in 1860, 1,013.

Of the fifty men who voted at the first election in Morris, James Loveridge is the only one living in this county.

The Clinton post-office was the first in the county. Its various postmasters were Samuel H. Smith, Richard Fishback, Ichabod Marshal and S. H. Smith. The last known of it, Andrew Clark was acting as deputy postmaster, in 1819.

Smith's house was the first one erected in the village. Samuel Ayres and Amoriah Watson got out the timber, Loveridge and Douglass helped to raise it. They all boarded with Loveridge during the work. Douglass had Wm. McLoud put up the first stone house in the county. John Miller, the first dresser of buck-skin for breeches, hunting shirts, etc., married Patsey Zerrick; she is living on the old farm with her sister Edna, the only representatives of the old Virginian Daniel, who died in 1851, aged 86.

SUCCESSIVE JUSTICES OF THE PEACE.

1812. John Trimble, Benjamin Barney, Joseph Coleman.
1816. Wm. Doulass; re-elected in 1819.
1816. Jos. Coleman; re-elected in 1819.
1819. James Dickson.
1820. Alfred Manning.
1822. Carey Cooper.
1823. Uzal Ball; re-elected in 1826.
1823. John Trimble; re-elected in 1826.
1830. James Adams; re-elected in 1833 and in 1836.
1831. B. H. Taylor.
1832. Uzal Ball.
1835. B. H. Taylor; re-elected in 1838 and 1841.
1836. Thompson Cooper; re-elected in 1839, '42, '45.
1837. George Irwin; re-elected in 1840.
1840. John Durbin.
1844. Alex. M'Grew; re-elected in 1847.
1847. B. H. Taylor.
1848. John H. Winterbotham;
1848. Wm. Bonar.
1850. Benj. B. Brown.
1851. Thompson Cooper.
1852. John Dwyer.
1853. Uzal Ball; re-elected in 1856.
1854. John McIntyre.
1855. B. F. Smith.
1856. Allen Scott.
1857. John McIntyre.
1859. J. L. Jackson.
1861. John McIntyre.
1862. J. L. Jackson.

CHAPTER XXXIV.

WAYNE TOWNSHIP.

ONE of the first townships was named for the distinguished, brave General Wayne, more generally known by the sobriquet "Mad Anthony." In the general reorganization it was reduced to its present limits. The general appearance of the surface of the country is beautiful. It is well watered, well timbered, healthy, and possessed of uncommon attractions for a home. In 1830, it listed 16,258 acres of land for taxation, and contained 1,047 inhabitants; in 1850, 1,864; and in 1860, 1,789. We have given the officers and voters at the first election. In 1811, the Judges were Joseph Denman, Daniel Ayres, James Trimble; Clerks, John Trimble and Wm. Johnson. In 1812, Henry Roberts listed the township. John Kerr, Samuel Wilson and Daniel Beers were then Judges; Willis Speakman and Joseph Townsend, Clerks. In the list of Justices and names heretofore given will be found most of the early settlers who exerted an influence upon the society of this section. It can not be expected that we shall enumerate all the good citizens of different periods; the limits prescribed for our work preclude such an idea. The lands upon the South Fork and East Fork of Owl Creek are unsurpassed in fertility, and the water power thereon has been so improved as to give the producers every facility for acquiring a competency.

FREDERICKTOWN, the principal mart of business for the farmers of the north western portion of Knox, was laid out in 1807, by John Kerr, with its streets—"First or Donation," "Second st.," "Third or Sandusky st.," "Fourth st.," "Vine alley," "Chambers st.," "State road and Main st.," and "Strawberry alley." The original tract upon which it is situated belonged to Mr. Sullivant, of Franklinton, who, with commendable liberality, gave John Kerr his choice of 50 out of 4,000 acres, including a mill seat, if he would settle upon and build a mill there. Accordingly, in the fall of 1807, he constructed a dam, raised a little log house and set one run of stone to grinding, or "cracking corn." On this 50 acres the town was laid out, and Kerr then bought 450 acres around it. W. Y. Farquhar was the surveyor, and the name of Frederick in honor of the old home, in Maryland, was given to this town in the wilderness. W. Y. Farquhar erected and occupied the first cabin in Fredericktown; it was a little stake and rider pen 18 feet square.

The next family to pitch their habitation within the plat, was that of Mrs. Ayres, and her sons, David and Abner, at once became leading men. John Milligan and Jeduthan Dodd, from Ten Mile, Pa., came shortly after, with their connections, John and Jacob Cook and Jacob Haldeman. In 1809, Rachel Richardson bought out the little improvement of John Cook, and settled there with her family, consisting of William, Isaac N., Polly and Nancy, who subsequently married Samuel Watson and John Wright. Charles McGowan, a droll old Irishman, took a lease near by, and Thomas Durbin, Samuel Wilson and Thomas Townsend, Quakers, and John Walker, who subsequently married a Shurr, came also. In 1812, within the town were nine log cabins and one frame building; dwellings, shops, huts all told. Willis Speakman, Rachel Richardson, John Garrison, John Vennum, and the Ayres' families, at one time occupied all these.

Mr. Garrison opened the first store in 1812, and then dwelt in the only frame; it was situated where the Methodist Church now stands. He is the only one of the then settlers within the village now living, and has led a migratory life. He is a native of New Jersey; married near Philadelphia; moved to New York; thence to Knox county, where he sold goods for several years; thence to Mansfield; from there to Detroit; back again to Knox; off again to Chicago, Ill.; and now resides at Cedar Falls, Iowa. He has been merchandising at each point, and in his 91st year enjoys good health. Three of his children are in Iowa, one in Detroit, and another, Mrs. Richard Roberts, in this county. This year he visited this county, and saw his great-great-grandchild and many other descendants in Berlin and Wayne.

Nicholas McCarty was the second merchant. He moved from Mount Vernon to this place. In July, 1817, N. McC. & Co. closed up their mercantile business and left their notes and accounts with

Abner Ayres, Esq., for settlement, and also a quantity of lake fish. The mother of Mr. McCarty died at Fredericktown; he moved to Indiana, and for many years drove a prosperous trade at the State capital. In 1853, he returned to Frederick on a mission of filial affection, and erected a monument at his mother's grave. In 1855, he paid the debt of nature, leaving a large family in prosperous circumstances. During his life he was a zealous Whig, and represented the capital district in the Senate of Indiana, and was also the candidate of his party for Governor of the State. He had the respect and confidence of all, and well deserved the title he bore,—"Honest Nic. McCarty."

James Rigby, who so long and faithfully followed merchandising here, is yet living in the enjoyment of good health, surrounded by his children and friends, one of the oldest inhabitants. George Girty was another merchant, who left this section about 1815 for other parts. Joshua Vennum, the first house-joiner, built the first frame house in the village. None of his name survive in this county.

Mrs. Wolf kept the first boarding-house. She is dead long since. Her oldest son, Peter, lived on a farm near the Burkholder flat, which he sold to Henry B. Carter, who was a brother to Jacob Cook's wife, and moved to Knox County in 1810. Samuel Wolf was a sterling man—lived in Richland, and served as Sheriff. When the county went wild for Jackson he was an Adams man, and consequently "done for politically." Her daughters have done well. Artemissa married lawyer May, of Mansfield; Eliza, as elsewhere related, Mr.

Drennan, and Mary married and lived in the neighborhood of Lancaster. The first tavern was opened by Abner Ayres, and with a slight intermission during the war, when, for good and sufficient reasons, his brother Daniel took it; the same hotel was kept up for more than forty years. "Uncle Abner" was not any "great shakes" in the way of dancing attendance on guests, but "Aunt Amy" did know how to have the culinary department carried on; and, we do affirm, that for making good brandy mince pies, and brandy peaches, she was unsurpassed by any of womankind since Eve eat the forbidden fruit. She knew just when, where, and how to apply the spirit to make it most palatable, as all of the generation, who feasted there during sleighing excursions, well know. They have both departed to a better land, leaving the record of a life spent in contributing to the happiness of their fellow-creatures. Abner served as Captain in the war of 1812, as a Justice of the Peace fifteen years, and Associate Judge seven years, a County Commissioner three years, and Postmaster near forty years. He was as quiet, unassuming and well disposed man as ever wore shoe-leather.

The first preaching was in the little school-house, heretofore spoken of as a Fort, etc. In it ministers of various denominations held forth at stated times. About 1820 the Presbyterians undertook to build a church, but, having started out on too large a scale, they were compelled to succumb, and the building, in its unfinished state, a mere shell, was sold to Absalom Thrift, who converted it into a ware-house, and it is to this day used as a livery stable. Some time after, the Universalists, who have ever been quite numerous in this locality, erected a spacious frame church, which they have since occupied, until for a few years past the supply from some cause has ceased. The Presbyterians made another effort, and built the present excellent edifice; and the Methodists and Baptists have also fine churches. The population is of a decidedly "go to meeting" character; they have also been noted for their zealous efforts in behalf of Temperance, and have kept up various organizations of a reform class for many years.

The first blacksmith was Thomas Ayres, who went to work in 1808, and continued for many years. The first school was kept by Wm. Y. Farquhar; the first shoe-shop by Osgood Dustin. The first hatter was Celestial Le Blond, a little frisky Frenchman, whose vote, in 1811, is entered as "Celestial Light" on the poll-books. He was the son of a wealthy French gentleman, and had to flee from his native land in consequence of having killed an antagonist in a duel. He frequently received from his father remittances of $500, or so, but made very foolish bargains. With money once sent he bought a mill-seat, set about erecting a mill where Shalers now is, and "broke flat" by the time he got a saw-mill up. The premises were then sold to Christopher Brollier, and by him to David Shaler, an energetic millwright. Shortly after this Celestial received another remittance and moved to Bellville. In 1838 he went to France, obtained a considerable sum of money, and returned with a large stock of goods. He died at

Bellville leaving a very respectable family. An old man named McCoy, a sort of cobbler, tried his hand at making cloth shoes for the women at an early day. The men then generally wore moccasins. A singular freak of another creature, in 1809, has been related to us. His name was Ebenezar Taylor, and he undertook to do work in the shoe line, but before he got fairly started an itinerant preacher came along, and Ebnezar was so taken with his discourse that he followed him off, leaving his kit of tools, and an estray animal, which he had taken up and advertised, and has never been heard of since. Speaking of shoemakers reminds us of a somewhat noted man in these parts, Jedediah Peck, who attempted to get up a patent way of making boots, having last and tree all together, but found that it was easier to make them on than to get the boot off the tree, which, after vain attempts, he concluded to fasten to the house and hitch a mule to pull it off. His house was built around a walnut tree, and it was considerable of a curiosity to travelers to see a tree growing out of the top of a house. Jedediah and his wife died without issue, and his two pretty nieces, who dwelt with him, are gone also.

In 1815, Capt. John Williams, of Frederick, Md., bought out John Kerrs' mill property, and at the same time started a store in the village. He brought out $40,000 in money, and dissipated through the country. He was a man of talent, clever and sociable, and is spoken well of by all old settlers. He came to this county in 1814 with his family. His children are much scattered.

William lives in Peoria, Illinois; Thomas in Henry county, in that State, as also Rachel, wife of Col. Prather, in the same county. Eliza, wife of Milton Bevans, in Fulton county, Illinois. Pendy died in Illinois, Abraham in this county, and Gist W. in Missouri, in 1852. His son States, now lives in Morris. But two of Capt. John William's family are to-day living in this county, Emaline, wife of Frank Wilkins, of Liberty, and Dan., who is living with States, his nephew, in Morris. Dan. was born in Frederick, Md., October 6th, 1792. His four sons are doing well. Clark and Charles reside in West Newton, Allen county, John and Milton B. in Berlin. Clark married Ellen Lane, and Charles her sister Jane. Milton married Elizabeth, daughter of Richard Roberts. The post office kept from its establishment by Abner Ayres, until in 1850, B. J. Lewis succeeded him; in May, 1852, Thomas A. Reed vice Lewis, resigned; L. S. McCoy followed, and his successor was Geo. Ball.

In 1840, Fredericktown contained 500 inhabitants; in 1850, 712; and in 1860, 790, of whom 16 were negroes. The place, some twelve years since, put on city airs, and with Geo. W. Woodcock as mayor, and T. A. Reed, Recorder, carried on a right sharp crusade against the "doggeries." The warfare was subsequently taken up by the Common Pleas Courts, and for a time better "order reigned in Warsaw. Of late years, however, we have been informed that there has been "something rotten in Denmark," and the spirits have assumed at times a very bold and threatening appearance. Taken altogether, however, Frederick may be said, during its existence, to have been a model town in the line of "law and order." In 1816, the entire township cast but 81 votes.

The 4th of July, 1817, was duly commemorated at *Anson Brown's*, in Fredericktown. Daniel Beers was chosen Moderator, and Anson Brown, Clerk. The Committee of Arrangements consisted of Christian Holderman, Job Allen, Munson Pond, Joseph Talmage, Jacob Young and Henry Markley. Munson Pond was Officer of the Day. Job Allen commanded the volunteer company; Jabez Beers was Reader; Truman Strong, Orator. Benjamin Jackson, Anson Brown and Benjamin Jackson, jr., conducted the Singing. The Rev. John Cook and James Scott were present—and last, but not least, Alvin Bateman was *Toast Master*. A good dinner was eaten, and all felt glorious. The McCutchens, Strubles, Cochrans, Cravens, Sagerses, Beerses, Leonards, Thrifts, Harters, Strongs and Corbins, were among the early settlers. Of the Cochrans, William and Samuel were young men of good mind. The former is dead, and the latter, a preacher of celebrity, in N. Y.; Josiah M. is quartermaster in 43d Reg't., O. V. Jabez Beers was one of the old settlers, and his son, Joseph, lived in Frederick at an early day.

Dr. John Byers located here in 1812. He moved west about 1835, and is now living in Hardin co. His three sons emigrated to Arkansas; Thomas and John are both dead—William yet lives at Batesville, Ark. The boys acquired considerable distinction as Attorneys. The old gentleman was one of the earliest practitioners of medicine in this township. Dr. David Wadsworth, another physician, died many years ago. His son, T. B., died a soldier in the Mexican war; and his daughter, Eliza Ellen, Mrs. Struble, is the sole survivor of the family. The Bryants have been quite numerous in Wayne, and among them James has been prominent; he was a very strict man, of the steady and straight "Sunday go to meeting" kind, and as his neighbors to the west did not walk in his ways, he called their settlement "Sodom," a name it has ever since borne notwithstanding that it has had in it many first rate citizens. Nicknames, once given and received, are hard to be obliterated.

An old settler upon Granny's Creek is Truman Ransoin, who with his family located, in 1824, where he has ever since resided. Mr. Ransom was a native of Connecticut, and, with his father's family, moved to this State in 1812, and settled on the Muskingum, near its mouth. He there married Miss Temperance, daughter of Thomas Lord, whose grandmother was a daughter of Col. Oliver, one of the officers in command at the time the Marietta settlement was attacked by the Indians. Her father was Judge of the Court of Washington county, and a prominent member of the "Ohio Company." Of Mr. R.'s seven children, one is dead; Edwin and Albert are living in Missouri; Thomas in Liberty; Bryan, William Wallace and Robert Bruce in Wayne. Mr. R. has been a hard working man, and has met with various streaks of ill luck; his losses have been heavy, by fire and water, and his escape from the jaws of death has been almost miraculous. His dwelling-house, with much furniture, was burnt up in the spring of 1852 —to his damage some $2000. In attempting to cross Owl Creek with a wagon and four-horse team he lost all, amounting probably to $800, and did well to get off with his "own skin whole." Having a small mill site on Granny's Creek, he erected, in 1828, a saw-mill, that is yet in operation.

In the Granny's Creek school-house a Temperance Society was gotten up many years ago, and also a Sabbath-School, which has been well attended. Regular preaching has been had also since 1830, by the Methodist, Episcopal, Presbyterian and other denominations.

But two men are now living in the neighborhood of Frederick who were young men grown in 1812 —Richard Roberts, of Berlin, and Jacob Mitchell. The first of these helped cut the first road out from Mt. Vernon to Frederick, under the supervisorship of Joe Walker; and the second rode express for General Harrison in the war of 1812. Then they were both boys full of mettle and spirit, and their fathers were among the old men of the settlement; and now their fathers are dead, and they in turn are old men—heads of families—grandfathers—yes, great grandparents—and a new generation is upon the stage of action. What changes they have witnessed in their lifetime, little as we may be disposed to think things change before our vision in this fast age!

SUCCESSIVE JUSTICES OF THE PEACE.

1808. Wm. Y. Farquhar.	1809. Daniel Ayres.
1812. Abner Ayres.	1816. Abner Ayres.
1815. W. W. Farquhar.	1819. " "
1818. " "	1822. " "
1817. Daniel Beers.	1825. " "
1821. Anson Brown.	1831. George H. Bull.
1826. David. Wadsworth.	1834. " "
1826. Byram Leonard.	1837. " "
1829. " "	1840. " "
1830. Michael Sockman.	1837. Byram Leonard.
1830. John Allen.	1840. John Lewis.
1836. Samuel Bryant.	1843. A. Greenlee.
1839. " "	1846. G. W. Woodcock.
1842. " "	1849. " "
1845. " "	1852. " "
1848. " "	1855. " "
1846. Peter Ink.	1855. W. G. Strong.
1849. J. B. Roberts.	1856. T. V. Parke.
1851. Mitchel Lewis.	1858. Henry Phillips.
1852. Geo. T. Potter.	1859. D. S. Beers.
1855. " "	1860. W. D. Bonner.
1857. A. Greenlee.	1862. D. S. Beers.
1860. " "	1862. Wm. Wyker.

CHAPTER XXXV.

LIBERTY TOWNSHIP.

THIS township, as at present bounded, was created March 9, 1825, and, in a spirit of freedom, styled Liberty. In 1830, it contained 553 inhabitants; in 1840, 1,205; in 1850, 1,320; and in 1860, 1,251. Mt. Liberty contains about 150 inhabitants. It occupies an elevated position, and being situated upon the State road to the capital, and in the heart of a productive country on Dry Creek, it has been a place of considerable business. It was surveyed by T. G. Plumer, and laid out by Samuel Thatcher and George Beardsheare, Oct. 8, 1835. It has two stores, kept by E. D. Bryant and Judson Hildreth; a grocery, by Daniel Veatch; a tavern, by John Thompson; two cabinet shops, by S. Wilson, and by J. W. Jackson and C. K. Lineweaver; two mantuamakers, Miss Samantha Severe and Miss Mary Veatch; the carpenters are John Inscho, Arthur Pratt, Joseph Crosby; shoemakers, Jas. Cleghorn, Wm. Cleghorn, Philip Crable; wagonmakers, J. A. Mostetler, David and George Mosteller, and Daniel Burkholder; two mills are run by Youngblood and Weller, and Peter Shafer. There are two churches, Methodist and Disciple. The Higginses, Coyles, Humphreys, Severes, Careys, Hollisters, Magoons and Gearharts are among the earliest in this section, and their descendants are quite numerous. The most extensive families are the Brickers, Lewises, Ewalts and Rineharts. Of the old stock we shall give a brief account; as to the new, their name is "legion," and it would be too prolix for the general reader did we attempt to sketch them.

Lewis Bricker, Sr., of Greene county, Pa., had a very large family, and determined to distribute them in the western country, where lands were cheap and he could provide them with farms. Accordingly he bought 1,600 acres of land in this new country, and started the elder members of his family to it in the spring of 1810. Of the number were Peter Bricker, and George Lewis, his brother-in-law. They came out to this wilderness region, camped one night, and the next morning hitched in their teams, and by noon were on their way back. They reported the country wild, and they did not believe it ever would be settled. They saw many Indians, and heard the owls too-whooing and the wolves howling all night; and, unaccustomed to these things, they agreed with their wives to let the land go to the devil before they would risk their lives and their children in the Owl Creek regions, which they believed to be the next thing to, if not quite, the infernal regions. Their father, accustomed to frontier life, and knowing also the value of lands in this country, determined in the fall to make another effort at a settlement. Accordingly he sent another delegation of his tribe, and continued the work until he got into this township the following children: Peter, George, John, Jacob, David, Solomon, Lewis, Catharine, Rachel and Mrs. George Lewis, who have in their own time peopled the wilderness region, felled the forest trees and cultivated the ground, multiplying the original by "the double rule of three." Peter Bricker had a dozen children, and George Lewis sixteen; George Bricker, eight; John Bricker, who came about a year later, six; Jacob, who came about 1813, five; David came about 1817, and had six; Solomon came out the same year, and added eleven children; Lewis came in 1819, he had six; Catharine married John Conkle about 1827, and had six children; Rachel married John Pruner, and had seven. All of the original Brickers remarried in Liberty, except David, who is in Morgan township.

George Lewis is dead. Of his sixteen children, eleven are living, viz.: Jacob, John, George, Isaac, Ben, Peter, Solomon, Sarah, wife of Alex. Craig, Phebe, Susannah Gardner, and Rachel Burkholder.

The children of old George recollect when their father went to Shrimplin's mill with a grist of corn, and left his wife and family alone, with nothing to eat, and the Indians prowled about the premises, and they feared they would not be found alive on his return.

Joseph Shaw, Zach. and Bazil White, John Hobbs, with their families, emigrated from Western Pennsylvania about 1834, and the Tarrs, Coleses, Crafts, and other good families have followed them, and the greater portion of those in the "Wolf Settlement," so styled for Christopher Wolf, Esq., are from the same localities.

Between two of the old settlers there grew up a quarrel in 1815, and a lawsuit ensued before James Smith, J. P. The Reverend James, by practice as well as profession, a peace-maker, proposed that the parties should have a friendly talk, and settle the difficulty without recourse to law. Accordingly they sat down on a log and Solomon Shaffer began in his broken pronunciation—"Now Mr. Lyingbarger"——"sthop," cries George Lybarger, in an angry tone, "my name is not Lyingbarger, but Lybarger, by G——, do you wish to insult me, *Shaf*fer?" "My name is not *Shaf*fer, but Shaf*fer*, don't call me *Shaf*fer, or tammed if I don't knock you down,"—and the parties sprung at each other, when James commanded the peace in the name of the State, and the difficulty between the belligerent old dutchmen had to be settled by the law at last.

SUCCESSIVE JUSTICES OF THE PEACE.

1822.	Frederick Carey.	1844.	Christopher Wolf.
1825.	" "	1850.	" "
1828.	Francis Wilkins.	1853.	" "
1831.	" "	1856.	A. Dalrymple.
1831.	Christopher Wolf.	1846.	John Inscho.
1833.	" "	1849.	" "
1837.	Luther Hill.	1852.	James Severe.
1837.	Joseph Shaw.	1855.	" "
1839.	W. E. Davidson.	1858.	" "
1842.	" "	1858.	J. H. Tarr.
1842.	Wm. Oram.	1861.	" "
1842.	Joseph Shaw.	1861.	Arthur Pratt.
1847.	Christopher Wolf.		

CHAPTER XXXVI.

HILLIAR TOWNSHIP

WAS laid off from Miller, upon petition of its citizens, August 28, 1818. It is the southwestern township of the county. The first settlement was called "Houck's," and was principally made up of the families of James and Jacob Houck and Joseph Jennings, who erected the first cabins, and graced the principal building, through Mr. Lamson, with the first brick chimney put up in this township. This settlement was about one mile southwest of the present village of Centerburg. When the township was formed the settlers agreed to the name of Hilliar, in compliment to Dr. Richard Hilliar, who was then the largest landholder residing in the limits; he dwelt in a cabin in the southwest corner. It had 16,000 acres of land upon the tax list in 1830. In 1832, there were but 40 voters. In 1840, the population was 1,012; in 1850, 1,141; and in 1860, 1,088. Centerburg, its principal mart of business, is on the old stage route from all the "north countrie" to the State Capital. It is 13 miles from Mt. Vernon. We have heard it said that it received its name from the fact that Harvey Jones presumed it to be the exact geographical center of Ohio; and many long years ago, when politicians and legislators threatened to move the Capital, some of the oldest inhabitants there believed it might become the Capital of the Buckeye State. If such a thing was hinted at by members who occasionally had the good luck in cold weather and muddy roads to call on Harvey Jones, enjoy his feast of fat things, and rest in his soft and downy beds, it is no wonder that by contrast with the then Columbus fare they "smiled" at the idea, and took another encouraging horn upon the strength of it with "mine host." As early as 1820 travel from Northern Ohio to the Capital through or by this route dates. Business may be said to have started with Mr. Jones, who was the most enterprising man at Centerburg from 1834 until 1848. He was a corpulent, jovial, kind-hearted man, who held out by unmistakable sign that he had good fare, and enjoyed the good things of this world.

In the early days the people were disposed to "pull together" at elections. It was their custom to meet when the day of voting came round, and canvass in a friendly manner the merits of candidates, and to make their voice felt by voting "plumpers." The electors would set down upon logs before any ballots were cast, and read over the names upon the tickets, and settle all conflicting opinions by voting unanimously for the same men. In this way they made, as an old one of their number said, the candidates who were defeated "to howl," and caused aspirants to look with fear and trembling for the returns from Hilliar. In 1818, the entire vote was 17, unanimous for Ethan A. Brown for Governor; Benj. Martin, Congress; John Spencer, State Senator; W. W. Farquhar,

Representative. In October, 1824, there was one stubborn man who would vote for Allen Trimble for Governor; the other 14 votes were cast for Morrow. The first place of public entertainment kept in this part of Knox county was by Joseph Jennings.

Great difficulty was experienced by the early settlers in getting to and from mill. We find as early as April 26, 1810, Jacob and James Houck, Joseph Jennings, John and Josias Simpson, Henry Matthews, John Karr, John Hinton and others, met at doctor Hilliar's farm and united in petitioning for a road to Douglass' mill. The prayer was granted, and Wm. Gass, Charles Cooper and Isaac Bonnet were appointed viewers. They met at Clinton at the time named, but refused to proceed to view what, in their opinion, was an unnecessary road. Nothing daunted, the few petitioners added two or three more names to their request and sent up another petition on the 17th of September, and Jabez Beers, Henry Roberts and William Mitchell, were appointed viewers, and Ichabod Marshal, surveyor. The viewers met and the surveyor declining to act, S. H. Smith accompanied them as surveyor, and returned a report and plat of the road, 16 miles in length—the surveyor reporting "it can be a tolerable good road, is very good ground, but the viewers say that at this time it would be too burthensome to the county to open said road." "Ordered, therefore, that the same cannot be granted."

The citizens then began petitioning for a new

township, which they succeeded in getting in August, 1818, and the first election was held at the house of Thomas Merril. The Judges of that election were Joe Jennings, Jas. Houck, Jas. Pell; Clerks, John Borden, Wm. Reynolds. In 1819, Jacob Houck listed Hilliar, and was paid a $4 county order therefor. The same duty he performed, for like pay, in 1820. The Judges of election, October, 1820, were Joseph Jennings, James Severe, Wm. Reynolds; Clerks, John Borden, John Davis. Henry Matthews, Benj. F. Hilliar, John Severe, James Pell and John Pell were other early voters. The Messmores, Mahannahs, Hollisters and Bottomfields were other settlers of a later period. John Thomas projected a town in 1834, but it never made headway. Rich Hill is a new business point that is thriving considerably.

JUSTICES OF THE PEACE.

May 10, 1819, the Court of Common Pleas allowed Hilliar one Justice, and in July, Jacob Houck was elected.

1822.	Wm. Reynolds.	1827.	John Borden.
1824.	Jacob Houck.	1830.	" "
1835.	Harvey Jones.	1833.	" "
1838.	" "	1836.	Daniel Nofsinger.
1839.	Ferdinand McLene.	1841.	Gideon Sutton.
1842.	" "	1844.	" "
1845.	Daniel Wolf.	1847.	N. Borden.
1848.	" "	1850.	" "
1851.	David F. Halsey.	1851.	E. Nichols.
1854.	D. S. Lyon.	1854.	" "
1857.	T. M. Owen.	1857.	" "
1860.	Simon Shaffer.	1860.	" "

CHAPTER XXXVII.

MILFORD TOWNSHIP.

THIS township was created in 1823, March 3d, out of territory taken from Miller. The land is generally level and soil fertile. The first election was held the first Monday of April, 1823, at the school-house near the center.

It received its name in the following manner: The settlers met together and various names were presented; among the number Judson Lamson proposed that it should be called Milford, taking the idea from his native town New Milford, Connecticut. Some objection was offered to every other name but this, and in consideration of the fact that Mr. Lamson was one of the oldest settlers, and also its being a New England name—those present being all from "Down East"—it was adopted.

The settlers at that time were Uzziel Stephens, from Vermont; Gardner Bishop, Stephen Hawkins, John Jeffries, Jesse Smith, Harris Hawkins, from Rhode Island; Wm. Beardslee and John Beardslee from New Haven, Ct.; Judson Lamson from New Milford, Ct.; Aaron Hill from Massachusetts.

The original stock now living are upon the lands selected by them at first, and the children and families of the departed, as a general thing, reside upon the old home tracts.

They were industrious, temperate and orderly citizens, and their families have followed in their footsteps closely, as is customary in the land of steady habits. There was no store or trading establishment in this township; the citizens transacted their entire business at the county seat. James Smith preached the first sermon, and the ministerial duties since have been principally discharged by the Christian Church.

Wolves were very plenty and impudent in this township at an early day. One of the incidents of those times was as follows: When Platt G. Beardsley was a boy, and out cow hunting, he lost his way and came upon a considerable sized swamp which at first he took to be a clearing; as soon as he came by its side a gang of wolves set up their infernal howling, he took to his heels badly scared, and ran along Sycamore creek, the wolves following close at his heels; as he neared home the dogs rushed out and attacked the wolves, when one of the dogs was torn in pieces by the wolves, and Platt made his escape into the house.

By the census of 1830, 498 inhabitants were then reported within its limits, and 13,472 acres of land returned for taxation. In 1840, the population was 1,157; in 1850, 1,349; in 1860, 1,084.

The two prominent points are styled the "Five Corners" and "Lock"—the latter is a post-office, at the county line, where there is some business transacted by the citizens of Knox and Licking.

Judson Lamson was born July 14, 1779. In

1817 he settled where he now resides. By trade a brickmason, after preparing quarters for his family, he went to Mt. Vernon to purchase some supplies, and, on entering a store kept by "Uncle Jimmy Smith" to buy a few articles, he heard him regretting that he had no mason at hand to lay up a piece of his stone wall that had fallen down; when Mr. Lamson told him that he could do it for him, and the bargain was struck, and he went right at the job and completed it to Mr. Smith's satisfaction. Daniel S. Norton shortly after met him on the street and informed him that he held his note, given to Dr. Lee for medical service in attendance on his daughter, who had been sick from his entering the country. The note was for $10; and Mr. L. told him that he had no money to pay him, and did not know when he would have so much, as money was a scarce article in those times. Mr. Norton at once replied, I do not want your money, but your work, if the note is right—accordingly took his second job of work in underpinning the house where N. then resided, on the lot where Judge Hurd now lives, on Main street. While working there old John Warden, who lived opposite, came across and said, "you beat all men to work I have ever known, you do two days work in one." And the remark was literally true. He subsequently worked on the brick building, where Daniel S. Norton formerly resided, on High street, near the railroad depot, now the "Buckeye house," and did almost all his other work at the mills, quarrying stone, etc. Mr. L., and his son Levi J., have contributed greatly to the improvement of

Mt. Vernon and the surrounding country. Among the buildings erected, under his superintendence, we may mention the Pyle block, Browning & Miller's block, Norton block, on Main street, the residence of C. Delano, Esq., and many other of the best structures in town and county. Mr. L. also worked at his trade in various parts of this county and Licking county. He has also been a successful farmer, and now, at a good old age, enjoys a competency and the respect of his fellow-men. His son, Levi. J., and his daughter, Mrs. W. A. Disney, reside near him, and other descendants in the west.

The McKowns were among the settlers at the time of organization, and worthy of notice at our hands. The old patriarch, James McKown, was a soldier of the Revolutionary war, and wounded at the battle of Brandywine. In 1820, with a portion of his family, he moved to this county from Virginia, and died in 1850 at the good old age of 98. His wife survived until 1852, when she died, aged 103 years. We recollect well the zeal of the old soldier in behalf of General Harrison for the Presidency. He was master of ceremonies at the great Barbecue of 1840, when the big ox was roasted whole. Of his children we make this record:—Gilbert McKown moved from Milford to Virginia; James moved to Illinois, where he has since died; Phoebe, wife of Joseph Tegarden, lives in Linn county, Mo.; Samuel came to this county in 1820, and settled where he died, in his 70th year, in 1861. Nine children are living, to wit: Rev. Samuel S., of the Christian Church, now in Northern Ohio;

Isaac, John, Hosmer, and Gilbert E.; Minerva, Mrs. Ira Gearhart, Cynthia, Mrs. David Gotshall, Emaline L., Mrs. John Gotshall, and Miss Margaret, all of this county. Gilbert E. is a resident dentist, Mt. Vernon. John Jeffries had six children; of this number those who survive are, Mary Ann, wife of Smith Bishop; Laura, widow of David Hill; Almira, wife of Johnston King, and Olney Jeffries, of Mt. Vernon. Preserve Smith and Dr. Hayes have been residents for many years.

The brothers Beardslee, William and John, natives of Stratford, and the Hawkinses, Harris and Stephen, natives of Rhode Island, may be classed among the early settlers who contributed to the advancement of Milford. The Beardslees are descendants of the Rev. John Beardslee, of Stratford, on Avon, Shakespear's home. William Beardslee married Eunice Gardner, of Hancock, Berkshire co., Mass., and emigrated west. They moved to Ohio, and we find William a resident of Granville in 1814: subsequently of Homer, and from thence, in 1818, he cut the road with his own hands for three miles to get to his land, where he afterwards resided. The road to this day is known as the Beardslee road. Their sons now living are Col. Platt G., of Milford, Job H. G., of Union county, Dr. Wm. B., and John Binns, of Mount Vernon. The daughters living are Catharine, widow of Erastus Rouse, deceased, Betsy, wife of George L. Benedict, Adaline, wife of Lieut. Nathan Bostwick, all of this county. Mary, who married Arnold Hildreth, is dead. William Beardslee, sr., at the advanced age of 79, and his wife, aged 76 years, are living in this county, surrounded by children and grand children to the number of 70. John Beardslee married Mary Fitch, of New Haven, Ct., and emigrated to Knox. Their children are Geo. F., of Milford, Dr. Charles, editor of the *Herald*, Oskaloosa, Iowa, Henry, Galesburg, Ill., Elizabeth, wife of Nathaniel McDaniel, Mary and Melissa. The original Hawkinses were Harris and Stephen. The former had the following children: Ephraim, Harris and Daniel, all living at and about the old homestead, and Charles in Illinois. Margaret, twin sister of Harris, married Almon Mitchel. Martha married Mr. Rice, and Clarissa died. Stephen Hawkins is dead. His first wife, who was a Belknap, is also dead, and of their children the following have died: Col. Emor B., Joseph, Stephen and Laura. Their son William married Miss Reach. They are now living in Milford, and Sally Ann and Mary, two girls, the latter by second marriage, survive.

SUCCESSIVE JUSTICES OF THE PEACE.

1823. Nath'l Stoughton.
1823. John Stephens.
1826. John Jeffries.
1829. " "
1832. " "
1835. Smith Bishop.
1836. Platt G. Beardsley.
1839. " "
1848. James Conden.
1848. Wm. Orme.
1851. " "
1854. John Stephens.
1857. " "
1860. Geo. F. Beardslee.
1826. Nath'l Stoughton.
1829. " "
1830. Sylvanus Mitchell.
1833. " "
1838. David L. Hill.
1841. " "
1842. Joseph Montagna.
1845. Emor B. Hawkins.
1849. Smith Bishop.
1852. John Litzenburg.
1855. Silas Jaggers.
1858. David Pattison.
1861. " "

CHAPTER XXXVIII.

MILLER TOWNSHIP

THE first time this name occurs on the Journals reads thus:—"Miller Township special election, 1816, June 4th, judges Jonathan Hunt, jr., Wm. Bare, Lemuel Chapman; clerks, James Miller, John Mott." Thus Miller appears to have sprung suddenly into existence as a township, without any of the preliminary symptoms, or pains and pangs of parturition. One thing we do know, and that is this, the township was named after one of its earliest settlers, James Miller, Esq., a very worthy gentleman, who possessed to an extraordinary degree the respect and confidence of his compeers. He was a small man, with a strong mind and excellent sense; a native of Vermont, and in company with Turner, a deist, who was a quick, clever old man, and wrote poetry, and went about repeating it, made the first settlement. John Olney, and Emor Harris, Cyrus Gates and James Sealts were also early settlers. They were mostly from Vermont and Rhode Island. In early times this was called the "Beech Settlement."

Its population in 1830, was 548; in 1840, 977; in 1850, 1,064; in 1860, 996.

One of the first houses was a small log cabin, in the south-east corner, put up by Vance, whose sons

John and Jacob, with their families, are living in the township. Cornelius Thompson of Hardy co., Va., settled in this township in 1810. His son now lives near the old home, in his 52d year; his daughter, Mrs. Scott is at Pataskala, Licking co. The Hildreth name has long been associated with this township. The old stock came from Marlboro, Ct. Wm. Hildreth emigrated to Zanesville, in 1812, and here in 1828; he died, and his children living are John M., in Mt. Vernon ; Wm. at Scott's Corners, Union co.; Arnold and Epaphro in Miller township.

In 1816, at the October election, 33 votes were polled: for Worthington, 32; Ethan A. Brown, 1. The judges of election and clerks in 1816 and 1817 were Rufus Ward, Wm. Campbell, Jonathan Hunt, Jr., Timothy Colopy and John H. Simonds. In 1818, the same officers, except Campbell, whose place was supplied by Titus Hill; and these constituted the board of election of 1819. In 1820, Rufus Ward, James Miller and Wm. Beardslee were judges, and Timothy Colopy and Enoch F. Kinney clerks. In 1821, the same, except Miller, whose place was supplied by Phineas Squire.

The old veteran, Rufus Ward, is worthy of special notice as a faithful soldier, who participated in the battle of White Plains, the capture of Burgoyne, and various other battles of the Revolution. He was born at Boston, Mass., in 1758, married Elizabeth Barnes, of Southington, Conn., and emigrated from Vermont in February, 1814, to the place where he died September 8, 1834, in his 76th year. His widow died June 19, 1849, aged 85, and was a U.S.

pensioner for many years. Seven children survive, viz.: Mrs. Mary Hinds, in Indiana; Mrs. Elizabeth Rowley, widow of Samuel; Mrs. Abigail Gabriel, wife of John Gabriel, of Columbus; Jonas, collector, at Piqua; Rufus, farmer, of Miller; Dr. Truman, druggist, at Mt. Vernon; and Levi, merchant, at Bellville. Emma, wife of Alpheus Chapman, is dead, as also her husband.

Col. Royal D. Simons emigrated from Connecticut in 1816. He was a man of education and talent, possessed of a very social disposition, and served the people as Assessor and Representative for several terms. His children living are Louisa, wife of J. W. Lybrand, and Caroline, wife of C. P. Young, both residing at Richland Center, Wisconsin. Mrs. Lybrand's only child living (George D.) is at the same place.

Timothy Colopy, a warm-hearted Irishman, had lived in Maryland and Virginia until 1813, when he settled in this township. He died in Mt. Vernon in his 68th year, and his widow died about 1852, aged 72 years. His surviving children are Jacob, Mary, Mrs. Levi Sapp, Sarah, Mrs. F. J. Zimmerman, and Matilda, wife of H. Conley, in Iowa. Timothy was a devout Catholic and a zealous Democrat, liberal and generous, public-spirited and benevolent. He was an excellent Justice of the Peace, and a much-esteemed citizen.

Col. Emor Harris emigrated from Rhode Island in 1817; died in 1850, aged 58. His wife, Sarah Sweet, whom he married in Rhode Island, is living in her 65th year. They had eight children; five survive, viz.: Caroline, wife of R. C. Walker, in

Delaware county; Mrs. Mary Miller; Emor Brown, also a native of this township; and Henry and Sarah, upon the old home place.

Philip Dennis, of Maryland, for many years resided in this township with his accomplished wife, Ann Dennis, who deceased in 1854. They were among the most intelligent and best citizens.

"The Four Corners" was the name by which the principal settlement went. A post-office was established at this point, February 15, 1839, called "Hildreth's," and Miner Hildreth was appointed postmaster. After Hildreth resigned, the name was changed to "Brandon," and H. C. Lockwood was appointed. In the spring of 1851, H. removed to Danville, where he is engaged in the mercantile business. Brandon is six miles from Mt. Vernon, and four from Homer. It has two churches, two stores, two blacksmith and wagon shops, one steam sawmill, one tavern. The denominational preaching is Methodist Episcopal, Baptist and Christian. Revs. John Mitchell and Moffett, Methodist, Rev. M. Herod, Christian, Rev. J. G. Tunison, Baptist, are the regular ministers.

CONSECUTIVE JUSTICES OF THE PEACE.

1816. John Mott, jr., and re-elected in 1819, 1822 and 1825.
1816. John J. Tulloss, " " " "
1820. James Miller, and again elected 1825.
1825. Royal D. Simons. 1828. John Morey.
1831. Tim. Colopy. 1832. Nathaniel Losh.
1831. Emor Harris, re-elected 1834, 1837, 1840, 1843, 1846 and 1849.
1836. E. S. S. Rouse, re-elected 1839 and 1842.
1845. James Ozborn, re-elected 1848.
1850. Erastus Rouse, re-elected 1853 and 1856.
1851. W. B. Beardslee.
1850. Rufus Ward, re-elected 1853, 1856, 1859 and 1862.
1858. Jesse Babbs, re-elected 1861.

CHAPTER XXXIX.

MORGAN TOWNSHIP.

In the first division of the county one of the four townships was called Morgan, in honor of the brave native of New Jersey, Daniel Morgan, the distinguished General in our Revolutionary war, who was a member of Congress from 1795 to 1799, and died July 6, 1802; and in the general reorganization of townships in March, 1825, it was reduced to its present limits. Under the old dispensation we find the total number of voters at the October election, 1809, to have been 13. In October, 1813, Moses Merrit, Jacob Hanger, Abraham Carnes were Judges; John Dunlap and John Boyle, Clerks. The number of voters had increased to 27, and among them were Jonathan Agnew, Ben. Leonard, Wm. Beam, Wm. Knight, Geo. Cooper, Philip Melker, Jacob Smith, and Smith Hadley. Other early settlers, besides the above named, were John Losh, Philip Smith, Thompson and Michael Mills, Abner and David Brown, Joseph and John Harris, John and Adam Fox, John Vance, sr., and John, jr., Jacob Rabb, Azariah Davis, Titus Rigby, Cornelius Callighan, and the Harrods. The only ones of this old set now known to be living are Smith Hadley, Levi, Wm. and Sam. Harrod, and Philip Smith. Hadley is in Centerburg, Levi and

Sam. Harrod in Clay, and Wm. Harrod in Indiana, where he moved some fourteen years ago. Philip Smith lives on Big Run, where he first located. His sons James and Wm. are in Clay, his daughter, Mrs. Henry McLain, is in this township, and Rebecca, wife of George Swank, lives in Union county. John J. Tulloss, a Captain in the war of 1812, emigrated from Fauquier co., Va., in 1807. He was a brick maker, school teacher, and farmer, first in Licking and afterwards in Knox; his widow is living, aged 76, with her children.

In 1816, at the October election, there were 35 voters. Among these was Caleb Pumphry, who died in 1817. There is not one of this family now living in the county. They were very kind and hospitable, zealous Methodists, and as their house was a sort of head-quarters for itinerants, the fame of Pumphry's tavern, as it was called, was quite extensive. Bernard Reece was another old settler; and another was Wm. Green, of Maryland, who moved into Morgan from Licking co., in 1816; he died in 1856. Of his 10 children the only ones living are Daniel of Harrison, Hugh of Chesterville, Mrs. B. McClurg and Mrs. J. Kegg in Indiana. Another father of 10 was Bennet Thompson, of Va., whose only child now in Knox is James, who was born in this township in 1827, married Mahala, daughter of Jesse Larue, in 1850, and has six children, of whom George Washington and Thomas Jefferson, now five years old, are twins.

John F. McLain emigrated from Seneca co., Pa., in 1828, and was for many years a prominent citizen. He was a large operator in stock and farming, and about 1836–8, was interested in a store in Mt. Vernon; he died in 1858, in his 61st year. His sons, Charles S. and Abijah, are in Morgan, and Wm. in Wyandot co. His daughters, Mrs. Sarah Welsh and Mrs. Amelia Hufty are in Crawford co.; Mary, wife of Morgan Booze and Cassandra, Levi Sellers are in this township. C. S. married Miss Berryhill; Henry Miss Smith, and Abijah, Miss Hook.

Simon Litzenburg emigrated from Washington county, Pa., to this township in 1829, bought part of the celebrated prairie farm, and has lived upon it ever since. He is now in his 79th year. Henry Barnes married one of his daughters, and Dr. M. H. Litzenburg, of Cheviot, is one of his sons.

The West brothers and the Ewarts are deserving of notice. The former were natives of Brooke county, Va. Samuel, in 1830, emigrated from Washington county, Pa., and is now in his 77th year. His wife, Mary Clear, was also a native of Virginia, and is yet living. Of their eight children, four are living—Alexander Clear at the old homestead; William H., of Logan county; Thomas in Morrow county; and Samuel, a Baptist preacher, in South English, Iowa. Amos West, Sr. is living, in his 72d year; has had 11 children, of whom those living are: Enos, in Tazewell county, Ills.; William in Morgan; Joe in Pleasant; John in Le Roy, Ills.; Amos in Buchanan county, Iowa; Margaret in Morgan; Ann Eliza, wife of John Penick; and Elizabeth Woodruff. These are descendants of Jonathan West, one of the first born in Brooke county, Va.

The Ewarts are from Greene county, Pa., and natives of Ireland—Robert and John, and their sisters, Mrs. Haver and Mrs. Ewart. John died in 1858. Haver emigrated from Greene county, Pa. They are intelligent and industrious people.

Jesse Mattocks, a native of Erie co., Pa., who married Elizabeth Johnson, and has had six children, is worthy of note for two reasons, first, he has served 13 years as constable, and second, he furnished the country round with their baskets for gathering corn, for many years, and therein has been a benefactor.

In 1830, the inhabitants numbered 653, and 16,582 acres were upon the tax list; in 1840, there were 912 inhabitants; in 1850, 823; in 1860, 688

CONSECUTIVE JUSTICES OF THE PEACE.

1810. John Harrod.
1815. John Green.
1817. Peter Veatch.
1818. Jacob Hanger.
1819. John Wheeler.
1820. Thomas Smith.
1821. Peter Veatch.
1822. John Wheeler.
1825. " "
1830. Ziba Leonard.
1821. Jacob Hanger.
1824. " "
1827. " "
1831. " "
1830. Jacob Sperry.
1833. " "
1836. " "
1839. Jacob Sperry.
1833. James H. Smith.
1836. John Clutter.
1839. " "
1842. " "
1845. " "
1842. Jacob Bell.
1845. " "
1848. C. S. McLain.
1851. " "
1854. " "
1855. John Miller.
1857. Henry Barnes.
1858. A. H. Thornhill.
1860. Carey Bell.
1860. James Campbell.

CHAPTER XL.

PLEASANT TOWNSHIP

MARCH 9, 1825, this township was created, and named on account of its delightful views. Its settlement was much retarded by large landholders. In 1830, it had 918 inhabitants; in 1840, 1,888; in 1850, 909; and in 1860, 828. Among its earliest and best settlers were the Melkers, Grahams, Veatches, Laymans, Herrods, Hunts, Patricks, Bechtels, Buckinghams, Walkers, Stinemetses, Schnebleys, Beatys, Lettses, Crawfords, Crouses, Colvilles, Morrisons, Swans, Rohrers, Dunns, and their connections. The settlers have been principally from Western Pennsylvania, Virginia, and Maryland. Several good mill seats within this township have been improved and occupied by John Kerr, Elisha Gibbs, the Morrisons, Nortons, Hadley and Miller; and several distilleries have in the past been propelled successfully. The principal business has been farming and stock raising, at which many have grown rich.

SUCCESSIVE JUSTICES OF THE PEACE.

1825.	David Ash.	1845.	Robert Graham.
1825.	Frederick Rohrer.	1848.	" "
1828.	" "	1851.	" "
1831.	" "	1854.	" "
1832.	James Parks.	1861.	Henry McLain.
1832.	Silas Brown.	1839.	Jas. D. Porter.
1835.	" "	1842.	" "
1837.	Alvin Foote.	1845.	Richard Hunt
1858.	Henry McLain.	1848.	" "
1827.	Harvey Brown.	1851.	" "
1835.	Robert Graham.	1854.	John Colville.
1839.	" "	1857.	J. V. Parks.
1842.	" "	1860.	" "

CHAPTER XLI.

CLAY TOWNSHIP.

On the 9th of March, 1825, this township was created, and honored with the name of the great American commoner, Henry Clay. The surface of the country is uneven, the soil is generally very fertile, and the tillers of it have ever been among our foremost for industry and intelligence. In 1830, the population was 1,300, and upwards of 15,000 acres were returned for taxation. In 1840, the inhabitants counted 1,304; in 1850, 1,240; in 1860, there were 1,098 white and 10 colored persons. There were six industrial establishments, producing to the value of $10,830. Among the old settlers were Ziba Leonard, I. D. Johnson, the Elliotts, the Greens, the Barneses, Vances, Pollock, Paul, Harrods, Larrisons. Insley D. Johnson, from about 1823 until 1837, was in business, and during the latter part of his mercantile existence was one of the heaviest operators in produce in Central Ohio. David Lawman, of Rockingham co., Va., came here in 1833; he is engaged in farming and milling. The Boggs family have been among the good citizens of this township for many years. The oldest was William, a native of Virginia. His son William, the first white child born in Belmont, died in Richland co., about 1835. William, sr., died about 1854, aged 98 years, and

Elizabeth his wife died in 1861, aged 93 years. Their children, John and Ezekiel, born in Belmont, have been long known to our citizens. Ezekiel served as Representative, and died in 1853. His wife is living in Clay. John Boggs married a daughter of one of the old settlers, Catharine Stephenson. Mary married Wallace McWilliams, and lives in Kansas.

Martinsburg has ever possessed a very patriotic population. At the celebration of July 4, 1861, addresses were made by Henry Hervey and A. J. Lyon, and a good dinner eaten. An accident occurred to mar the pleasures. John Clark had two of his fingers shot off by discharge of a small cannon. Martinsburg contains 300 inhabitants. It was part styled Hanover, and the other part Williamsburg, and the present name is a compromise. The following are the artisans and business men: Philo Higgins, blacksmith; E. Hardiman, tailor; wagon maker, Wm. Henderson; saddlers, M. L. Dayton, J. M. Bowland; shoemakers, S. Kidwell, S. Hollabaugh, S. D. Rouse, M. Chandler, A. Lyon; Wm. Penick carries on a tanyard; A. & R. Barnes and Thomas Rodgers are the merchants; M. L. Dayton sells groceries; D. Booze keeps the tavern. The physicians are D. H. Ralston, Peter Pickard, and S. B. Dodd. There are five churches: Presbyterian, Rev. H. Hervey; Methodist, Rev. A. J. Lyon; Free Presbyterian, Rev. J. Whitam; Baptist, Rev. G. Tunison; Associate Reformed, Rev. G. Torrance. Its schools are good, and the Rev. Henry Hervey deserves special commendation for his long and faithful service in the cause of christianity and education. For over 35 years he has devoted himself zealously to the work in this place. J. M. Coulter is Principal of the Academy; A. S. Kerr and Miss Susan Jennings are also teachers. The only men now living in the village who were here in 1822 are W. McCreary, C. Barkalow, and W. McWilliams. The post-office was established by the name of Hanover in 1820, and changed afterwards to Martinsburg. The postmasters have been I. D. Johnson (S. P. Warden, deputy), Jacob Pearson, Wesley Spratt, J. H. Pierson, W. McCreary, Johnson, W. McWilliams, and W. McCreary.

Since the foregoing was written, the patriotism of Clay and Morgan has been verified, by the spontaneous uprising of the hardy sons to defend the soil of Ohio from invasion, when, under Captain Norton, and Lieutenants Bell and Mercer, they responded to Governor Tod's call; and, assisted by Capt. Baugh and Lieutenants Mefford and Church, and Captain Israel's companies, *they saved Cincinnati from the devouring Secessionists.*

SUCCESSIVE JUSTICES OF THE PEACE.

1827.	James Elliott.	1831.	W. McCreary.
1830.	" "	1834.	" "
1833.	W. Spratt.	1837.	" "
1839.	James Paul.	1840.	" "
1842.	" "	1843.	" "
1845.	Wallace McWilliams.	1846.	" "
1846.	John Boggs.	1855.	Mercer McFadden,
1848.	Wallace McWilliams.	1857.	W. McWilliams.
1849.	John Boggs.	1858.	Isaac Bell.
1851.	W. McWilliams.	1860.	W. McWilliams.
1852.	John Boggs.	1860.	James Elliott.
1854.	W. McWilliams.		

CHAPTER XLII.

JACKSON TOWNSHIP.

In honor of General Andrew Jackson, the Commissioners, on the 4th of September, 1815, erected this township. John Mills, Jacob Lepley, and Joseph Kerr were the first judges of election, and James Thomas and David Melick the clerks.

In 1816, there were 35 voters. Jacob Lepley was the first lister, and Abraham Carpenter first appraiser. This, the south-eastern township of the county, is watered by the Wakatomika; the ground is generally rolling, but quite productive. In 1830 the inhabitants numbered 626; in 1840, 994; in 1850, 1,080; in 1860, 960. The only town and post-office is Bladensburg; it contains 200 inhabitants.

Washington Houck kept the first tavern, in 1833, and continued it, with short intermission, till the present date. Thomas Axtell kept the second house of entertainment, about 1838; he was a good citizen, and emigrated to Indiana. James Loveridge for a short time kept tavern; and John Hannah now keeps the hotel.

The first goods sold in this town were by John Wheeler, who was for many years engaged in merchandising at Bladensburg. He took great delight in the militia trainings, being a captain; in the Christian church, being an elder; in the Whig party, being a committee-man. In all respects, long was John Wheeler a good citizen; he now lives, at an advanced age, in Iowa. The second store was carried on by W. Houck, who for twelve years sold goods. T. Axtell, Peter Berry, James Loveridge, Alphonso Byam, T. & C. L. Marquand, have also sold goods there. The present merchants are, Mark Hammond and Samuel Richard.

The first Disciple Church in the State was gotten up by John Wheeler, W. Houck, Elijah Harris, and their wives, about 1833. They have a neat Church edifice, of which the Rev. Van Voris is minister. The Presbyterians have also a church building, in which Rev. —— Brough officiates. The Cumberland Presbyterian Church was the first house of worship built in the township. Thos. Axtell was the most active in getting up the church. James Elliott was mainly instrumental in building the O. S. Presbyterian meeting-house. The Methodists worship in the Presbyterian Church.

The present mechanics are, John Upfold, tailor; Thomas Hilman, wagon-maker; Lew. Husser and Wilson Hartupee, blacksmiths; the Baltzells, Andrew, John and Joseph, and James Ross, shoemakers; Lemuel Hall, carpenter; Richard Mavis, cabinet-maker. A good school is kept up in the village, of which Mr. Campbell is teacher.

A grist-mill is in the town, formerly carried on by Houck, now by James Gaub. Within a half mile, another mill is carried on by Mr. Schooler.

About 1852, James Harris started a pottery, which is now owned by James Green. The clay is excellent, and some very good ware has been turned out at this manufactory, which is sold in adjoining towns.

Among the old citizens whose names should appear in this sketch, are Adam Earlywine, Jacob Stricker, George and James Melick, William and Robert Wilson, Daniel Blue, John Hammel, Wm. Braddock, the Hills, the Horns, the McCammets, the Halls, the Dennys and Stephensons.

Washington Houck, of Huntington county, Pa., moved to Knox county, Clay township, in 1805, where he resided until 1833, when he moved to Jackson.

Joseph Scott, Wm. Rawdon, David and Daniel Stricker, Daniel Mossholder, Peter Miller, Philip Dennis, George Holt and Christian Baughman, have been citizens of long standing.

Col. James Elliott, long a resident of Clay, who has officiated as Justice and Representative, now resides in Bladensburg.

JUSTICES OF THE PEACE.

April 15, 1815, two Justices were allowed this township, to be chosen at the house of Joseph Kerr.

January 13, 1816, Jacob Lepley and David Melick were elected, and Lepley was re-elected in 1819 and in 1822.

1820. Thomas Hall.	1838. W. K. Corbin.
1823. " "	1836. S. C. Porterfield.
1824. David Melick.	1847. James Myers.
1827. " "	" A. C. Scott.
1829. John Stephenson.	1850. W. H. Blue.
" R. C. Davis.	" James Myers.
1832. " "	1853. Daniel Gault.
1835. " "	" W. K. Corbin.
1838. " "	1856. J. S. McCammen.
1831. A. Darling.	1859. " "
1832. W. K. Corbin.	1857. James Blunt.
1835. " "	1860. Wm. Darling.

CHAPTER XLIII.

BUTLER TOWNSHIP.

THIS township was created in March, 1825, and named after Richard Butler, Major-General of the U. S. A., killed by the Indians in the great battle between them and Gen. St. Clair, Nov. 4, 1791. He was one of the bravest of the brave, and as he lay upon the ground helpless and bleeding from wounds received in the battle, the savages scalped and tomahawked him.

We have been at considerable pains to find out the origin of the name, and were led for some time to believe that it was given in compliment to the sturdy old settlers, the Butlers, but have become satisfied from our investigation that the object was to perpetuate with the names of Gens. Knox, Harrison, Jackson, Pike, the fame of the ill-fated brave Richard Butler. The land is generally rough and broken, and the population has usually been smaller than in any other township. The wild and picturesque scenery, giving an air of romance to much of the country, we must believe contributes to the health of the people, if we take Joe Stotts, Ben. Butler, Nich. Riley, Geo. Sturgeon, Abe Darling, and others of the oldest settlers now living, as evidence. The Lepleys, Jacob, George and Joseph, the Shrimplins, Abraham and William, the Campbells, the Morningstars, the Horns, the Hammills, the Carpenters, the Burkholders, the Cogginses, the McLarnens, the Darlings, the Wolfs, the Melicks, the Gambles, have been long residents of this township. John Busenburg, Philip Ely, Benj. Hugh, John Jones, Sam. Cermerer, Jesse Ashcroft, W. Beaty, Job Lewis, Elijah Farquhar, Wm. Seamen and Ephraim Thornberg also lived in it many years ago. Orange Hollister for many years was one of the most active and useful citizens, spending many thousand dollars among the people erecting mills and machinery for their benefit; he is now living in Iowa, and Ben. Butler is operating the mills. Robert Giffin was another useful man in the milling line, and his death was much of a loss. John R. Gamble was much noted for his business qualifications. Nicholas Riley emigrated from Washington co., Pa., in 1805, to Coshocton co., and in 1807 to Knox; he is in his 82d year. We have the following account of his offspring: William lives in Illinois; Harriet, wife of Abráham Darling, is in Wayne; Eliza, wife of Isaac Wood, Rachel, wife of John Welker, jr., Susan, wife of Geo. Spurgeon, and Almira, wife of Amos Wolf, all live in Illinois; Abraham is dead; George, Nicholas and Hannah live in Butler; and Mary, Mrs. Wm. Parks, lives in Hancock county.

In 1830, the population was 419; in 1840, 647; in 1850, 763; and in 1860, 727. About 1817, a post-office called Owl Creek was kept by Abraham Darling as postmaster, but the Judge, some fifteen years ago, became tired of and gave it up. Many years since there was a store kept in this township, and a post-office was established thereat called "Hollister's," but it has been discontinued.

Uncle Bob and Aunt Hetty Giffin were noted characters. They selected the most romantic spot on Owl Creek for their residence, and amid the rough, rugged and wild scenery known in olden time as "the rocks"—of later days as "the caves"—they dwelt and raised a large and respectable family. As early as 1820, they put up Giffin's mills: we say *they*, for everything thereabouts was their joint work, and could not have been created without the two were united in the undertaking. He was quiet, peaceable, with a well-developed mind and an uncommon good judgment. She was violent, resolute and determined, with a strong heart and great physical power. Whatever plans were matured and work determined upon, she put into execution with a warrior spirit.

CONSECUTIVE JUSTICES OF THE PEACE.

In 1820, Joseph Dunlap was a Justice in this "neck of woods," and was again elected in 1824; in 1825, Jacob Lepley; in 1826, Daniel Campbell.

1829. David Campbell.
1831. Horatio G. Cooley.
1834. " "
1837. Wm. Coggins.
1841. David Barnhard.
1844. " "
1848. James Frisby.
1849. C. Musser.
1852. " "
1858. C. C. Gamble.
1860. Wm. Killer.
1861. Joseph Hammill.
1831. Charles Nyhart.
1837. Eli Cummings.
1840. " "
1840. James McLaurin.
1843. Wm. Coggins.
1843. C. Musser.
1846. " "
1851. C. C. Gamble.
1852. C. Tym.
1855. Doty Farmer.
1857. Jas. McCamment.

CHAPTER XLIV.

HARRISON TOWNSHIP.

On the 9th of March, 1825, another township was laid out, and named after General Wm. Henry Harrison.

In 1830, there were 726 inhabitants; in 1840, 833; in 1850, 751; and in 1860, 778.

The earliest settlers were Wendel Melker, Adam Lybarger, the Gorsuches, Peter Wolf, Joseph Horn, Benjamin Horn, Andrew Casto, the Dudgeons, the Biggses, the Schoolers, Philip Melker, Isaac Cohen, Arthur Fawcett, the Welkers. The Dudgeons, among these, deserve more than a passing notice. Three brothers and a sister, at an early day, settled in this wilderness region. In company with their father, they had crossed the Atlantic in 1801. Simon, Moses and Hugh Dudgeon, brothers, were natives of Ireland, who came to this country poor and penniless, and by honest industry acquired a competency. Simon had served six months as a British soldier in the Revolutionary war. He was in his 26th year, of great physical strength, resolute and determined. He landed in the city of New York with only an English shilling in his pocket, which he paid out to a washerwoman for washing his clothes. He worked, as he could get employment, in Vermont, Connecticut and New

York, and lived with his father and brothers, Thomas and Hugh, for eight years, until he accumulated $1000; and with that, in 1810, he started from Delaware county, N. Y., west to hunt a better location, visited Knox county, and bought the tract of land upon which he erected his house and lived until death. He went to Washington county, Pa., married, and returned to his land in 1811. The issue of this marriage was ten children. Nine are now living, to wit: Charles, Moses, David, Simon, May, John, and Andrew in Harrison township; William, Jane, Mrs. Horn, in Auglaize county. Simon, Sr. first bought three quarter sections of land, and added to it by purchase till, at his death, he had 712 acres. He was very industrious and domestic in his habits.

Paul Welker, one of the oldest settlers in that part of the county, tells, with much humor, the way in which he first became aware of Dudgeon being in the county. He was out hunting one day, and having chased a deer into some underbrush in some frog-ponds, was startled by the sound of an axe cutting wood; he stealthily approached the spot from whence the noise proceeded, expecting to find an Indian, when, greatly to his surprise, he discovered our pioneer chopping trees to make a cabin. He had not heard of this new comer, and could but express his astonishment that he should have chosen a spot back of the big frog-ponds for a house. Forbidding as the place then was, Simon, by dint of labor, there made his living, and left to his children, as its result, an estate of over $25,000, besides some $10,000 advanced to them during his life time. They now own over 1,500 acres of land in that vicinity. Simon died of apoplexy in the street, Mt. Vernon, in his sixty-ninth year. Two of his brothers died of this same disease: Thomas, in Delaware county, N. Y., and Hugh, in Knox county, February 16th, 1861. Moses, another brother, died in this county about thirty years ago. Their sister, Mrs. Young Love, is now living near Fredericktown.

The Lybarger family became quite numerous also. Adam died in April, this year. He had risen from dinner, after eating very hearty, and walked into the yard to get a stick of wood for the fire, when he dropped dead.

Wendel Melker, with his brother Philip, moved into this country from Virginia in 1808. All that survive of the Melker name in Harrison are four children—all mutes.

Silas Ralston, Joseph and Martin Horn, "blathering John" Wolf and John Troutman were other notable settlers of long standing.

Arthur Fawcett was, like the Dudgeons, from the Emerald Isle, and felt the effects of poverty, in early youth. After a time he too makes his way to the "great West," and is found in this county, in 1810, clearing land, upon which he has since resided. He is now in his 77th year, and his wife, Susannah, in her 67th year. They have had ten children—eight now live, viz: Samuel, who married Elizabeth Biggs, daughter of James Hayes. He was born in Harrison township, in 1816, and now lives in Butler. Philip, who married Mary Ellen Vance, lives in Illinois; Elizabeth, wife of

Geo. W. Schooler, in Allen county; Lucinda, wife of Hamilton Marshal, in Allen county; and the following in Harrison township: Anna, wife of Isaac Hays; Mary, Mrs. Ralph Faucett; John, who married Hannah Washburn; Icetas, who married Rebecca Barnett; and Catharine, wife of Joseph Horn.

Andrew Casto moved into Marion county, and died sixteen years ago. None of his blood now live in this county. Isaac Coen, another of the earliest settlers, died, with none here to represent him. Joseph and Benjamin Horn died about the same time, eight years ago. The Biggs brothers—William, Noah and Jeremiah—came to this township about 1811. The Schoolers settled in the neighborhood, where that name is now found, in 1818. John Schooler died in 1853; he was from Beaver county, Pa.: had twelve children—nine now living. Isaac is at Carthage, Jasper county, Mo. George and Rachel, Mrs. Ashbourne, live in Auglaize county, James in Coshocton; William, Joseph, Moses and Samuel are in Harrison. Both the justices of the peace in the township are sons of John Schooler. The people of Knox county twice honored him with a seat in the Legislature; he died some eight years ago, much lamented by a large circle of relatives and friends.

Marvin Tracy held many public positions, and was universally respected for his honesty and integrity. Paul Welker and John Troutman have been hard-working farmers, of good reputation.

Nathaniel Ross emigrated from Greene county, Pa., in 1811, and is yet living, in his sixty-ninth year. His brother, Samuel, came out in 1817, and is now sixty-three years of age. These men have been useful citizens. The first brick house in this township was that of Nathaniel Ross.

The first road laid out was from Mt. Vernon to Coshocton. The proprietors of the town were all from the East, and they then believed light must be sought from that quarter. They did not know there was a Lake Erie, or if they did, they did not seem conscious that the great commerce and trade of this section must be drawn north and south; hence, supposing that travel would be most from east to west, they laid out the town with this view —making its principal street, "High," the widest, and "Market," the present Main Street, much the narrowest.

JUSTICES OF THE PEACE

Within this territory have been the following Justices: 1819, Marvin Tracy, reëlected in 1822 and 1825.

1825. John Schooler.	1836. Asa Freeman.
1829. Israel Dillon.	1839. " "
1831. Ben. Ellis.	1842. " "
1834. " "	1845. " "
1835. Nathaniel Ross.	1847. M. W. Schooler.
1837. Hugh Miller.	1848. Wm. Marlow.
1840. " "	1849. Marvin Tracy.
1843. " "	1852. Jonathan McArtor.
1850. Moses Dudgeon.	1855. " "
1853. " "	1856. M. W. Schooler.
1855. Sam. F. Schooler	1858. Jonathan McArtor.
1862. " "	1859. M. W. Schooler.
1862. Jacob Hays.	

CHAPTER XLV.

UNION TOWNSHIP.

At the session of the Commissioners, March 9, 1825, this old township, notwithstanding its name, was dismembered, and reduced to its present proportions. Among its earliest settlers are many names by this time familiar to the reader: there were the Critchfields, the Lepleys, the Butlers, the Darlings, Wm. and Abraham; the Shrimplins, Abraham, John and Samuel; the Durbins, Ben. and Wm.; the Elwells, the Spurgeons, the Sapps, the Rightmires, the Logues, McMillen, Williams, Titus, Hibbetts, Greer, Stotts, George Davidson, Charles Ryan, Wm. Shaw, John Arnold, and the Welkers. Shortly after came John Konkle, Gasper Richcreek, Jacob Black, David Melick, John Earlywire, Valentine Dial, and George Freshwater. The judges of election, Oct. 10, 1809, were James Rightmire, John Wood, and Thos. Elwell. These were at that time the principal families of the powerful Creek nation; representatives of almost all these are to be met with in this county. In 1811, the officers of election were Wm. Sapp, Thomas Beaty, George Sapp; Daniel Sapp and Jacob Draper.

At the October election, 1810, there were but 23 voters. In 1816 the number had increased to 45.

Having traced out the Critchfields, Darlings, and other families who have contributed abundantly toward the peopling of this county, we cannot pass by the Sapps. Four brothers—Daniel, George, Joseph and William—emigrated from Allegheny county, Md., in 1806, and the Sapps of the present day are descendants of them, and of their uncle George, who came out in 1810; of another Sapp, Adam, who came about 1820; and of yet another, a cousin, known in the neighborhood as "Kentucky George," to distinguish him from the other Georges, who had preceded him. Daniel had a dozen children, of whom Hon. Wm. R., S.W., Dr. Enoch and Dr. Silas have been widely known. Mrs. J. Wauls, of Brown, and Mrs. J. Stover, of Mt. Gilead are only daughters living. George married Catharine Arnold; and of their nine children six are living in the county. Levi is upon the old homestead. He has had eleven children; and of this number is Wm. C., merchant, Mt. Vernon. Joseph's numerous family went to Illinois. William's dozen children are scattered—only two of them are in Knox now. Of Kentucky George's fourteen children we have not space to give an account. James, associated with Wm. J. Morton, in the shoe store in Mt. Vernon, is his grandson. The original roots above named have produced over 200 shoots.

The Rightmires, James and Harrison; the Shrimplins, William, Samuel and Absalom; Solomon Robinson and Gilman Hawn, with their families, well represent the hardy old stock. John Welker, Sr. lives upon the farm he cleared in 1809. His brother-in-law, Jacob Baughman, and his old neighbor, Wm. Robison, yet exchange greetings with him; his brother-in-law, Wm. Lydick, died recently. Many trips these old settlers made, with horse and pack-saddle, to Zanesville for salt and other necessaries. In the war of 1812, John Welker served as a high private, and has received a land-warrant for his services; and that is the highest position he ever sought. He erected the first brick house in this part of the county. A man of sterling worth, he has commanded the respect of his neighbors, while he has reared up a family of fourteen children—only one of whom, Daniel, now resides in this county. The Rev. John, jr., in Illinois, and Judge Martin have acquired considerable reputation for ability.

The towns of Danville, Millwood and Cavallo are in this township. The first is one of the oldest in the county. For the past twenty years it has not improved much. It is the oldest post-office in the eastern part of Knox: its post-masters have been W. R. Sapp, Enoch Sapp. G. H. Davidson, and S. W. Sapp. Cavallo was a great place on paper in the days of the Canal fever. While Isaac Means, S. W. Farquhar, W. V. Richardson, D. S. Fairchild, C. Keller, H. Thomas and others lived there it had much trade. From 1843 to 1848 were its best days; then, almost all the exports and imports of Knox were through this port, four large warehouses were erected, and goods were sold by wholesale; now, the only man living within its limits is Nelson Thatcher, and his neighbor on the old Butler farm is Solomon Gearner. The future will only know of this fast place from this page of our history.

Milwood received its name in consequence of the first mill in this locality having been built in the woods. Elisha Gibbs was the venturesome individual who first carried it on; John Hawn succeeded him, and it has been known since as Welker's mill. The first settlers around the early mill were principally of the Welker family. The village contains about 150 inhabitants, and was laid out by John Hawn. James Britton built the first house in the town plat—a little hewed log cabin, which has been weatherboarded to give it a more modern look. Two of his sons, Lewis and Reuben, are here; James and the rest of his family reside in Iowa. Col. Israel Dillon for many years was a leading business man; he also moved to Iowa. Jacob Garret put in the first tanyard about 1829, and is yet carrying on the business. The Spragues and Carpers of other years are generally in the west. Sam. Welker, the pioneer in keeping "entertainment for man and beast," had the following poetical notice painted over his bar:

"As many a man has trusted to his sorr*y*,
Pay to-day; and I will trust to-morr*y*!"

He kept tavern in the old style; always had plenty to eat and drink of the substantial kind, his table literally groaning under its load; his welcome to guests was a good deal of the order of the old Dutch landlord, who said, "Shust make yourselves perfectly at home: I wish to God you were all at home;" and all felt that they were at liberty to wait upon themselves. Nevertheless, Sam. was a jovial fellow, and his house was a favorite with wayfaring men and those disposed to be joyful. The students of Kenyon occasionally navigated the waters of Owl Creek to Welker's port. Among other trips made there was one in 1833, in a canoe, by R. C. Hurd and Herman Canfield, late Lt. Col. of the 72d Regiment, killed in the battle of Pittsburg; to the memory of our departed friend we will say, that a more honorable and noble youth never lived.

There are three neat church edifices: the Disciple, built in 1858. The building committee consisted of Lewis Critchfield, Albert Ellis, and Wm. Moody; Pastor—Rev. Wm. Moody. The Methodist, built about 1856, through the exertions of Jacob Hammond, who has resided here over thirty years. The Presbyterian, built in 1853. The present Elders are Jesse Wintringer, John P. Smith; Rev. J. Newell, Pastor. This church was mainly established by Rev. John Burns, A.M., a graduate of Kenyon College, was its minister, from 1854 until his death, in April, 1859. The merchants are Christian and Peterman, R. McCloud and Lewis Britton. The postmasters, since 1831, are John Welker, jr., Michael Miller, L. Britton and J. Hammond.

S. Israel, Esq., has put in a substantial dam, improved the old mill, and added carding-machines to the stand. Frank Israel superintends the establishment. Wm. McCloud, a native of Scotland, now in his 66th year, who, in 1816, settled at Clinton, and worked as a stone-cutter until 1840, is here, with his son. Another stone-mason, John Meginnes, resides here; two blacksmiths, D. Saltsman and Josiah Horn; two carpenters, Joseph Butts and Harris Johnson.

The land of this township is generally rolling and hilly, especially in the eastern part where the Mohican courses its way, and upon Owl Creek, which passes through the southern part, affording much valuable water power. In 1830, the population was 851, and 10,867 acres of land were on the tax list. In 1840, the inhabitants counted 1,098; in 1850, 1,192; and in 1860, 1,104.

SUCCESSIVE JUSTICES OF THE PEACE.

1809. George Sapp and Jacob Lepley were elected, and the former re-elected in 1812.

1812. Nicholas Riley. 1817. Robert McMillen.
1819. Daniel Sapp; re-elected in 1822 and 1825.
1819. Jacob Draper. 1826. Ben. Butler.
1829. Charles Waddle. 1832. James Cain.
1832. Daniel Sapp; re-elected in 1835.
1832. Joseph Sapp, " "
1832. Jacob Black, " "
1831. John Welker, Jr., " 1834 and 1837.
1836. Josias Ewing. 1857. John Shaw.
1837. Andrew Black. 1841. Jos. L. Workman.
1840. John Welker, Jr.; re-elected in 1843 and 1846.
1842. George H. Davidson, " 1845, 1848 and 1851.
1849. Michael Miller, " 1852.
1847. Elias Day. 1849. Wm. McLoud.
1844. Sam. McKee. 1855. Jacob Ross.
1854. Wm. Walker; re-elected in 1857 and 1860.
1855. Jacob Hauger. 1857. Washington Hyatt.
1358. Andrew Beach. 1860. Freeman Snow.
1860. J. W. Bradfield. 1862. Nathan Parsons.

CHAPTER XLVI.

COLLEGE TOWNSHIP.

COLLEGE was organized December 21, 1838, and so named in consequence of its being the seat of Kenyon College, and all the land belonging to that institution.

The first election was held at the public house in Gambier kept by M. W. Vore. The officers then elected were: Trustees, O. Lane, J. McMahon, M. W. Vore; Clerk, D. L. Fobes; Constables, O. Welchymer, and N. Head; Overseers of the Poor, J. Kendrick and W. Claytor; Treasurer, M. T. C. Wing; Fence Viewers, T. G. Odiorne, G. C. Johnson, N. Weaver; Supervisors, W. M. Lane and A. K. Fobes. The voters in the early elections numbered from 20 to 30, and almost all of these were connected with the institution as professors, agents, keepers of boarding-houses, or other establishments dependant upon the College for a sustenance.

At the spring election, 1839, J. McMahon, T. G. Odiorne and M. W. Vore were elected Trustees; A. G. Scott, Clerk; and M. T. C. Wing, Treasurer. Mr. Odiorne, the only Trustee living, is now President of an Insurance Company in Cincinnati, and is an efficient business man. M. T. C. Wing was re-elected again and again, until he declined serving in 1842, when G. W. Meyers was chosen Treasurer. Mr. Meyers was one of the earliest settlers of this township; a good practical printer and bookbinder, the first in these two trades on "the hill;" he has contributed much to the preservation of works in the libraries of the Institution.

BEXLEY HALL.

For many years he "ran the machine" of the Acland Press, and now resides at Mt. Vernon. The printing office was the gift of liberal-minded English Protestants to Bishop Chase in 1825, and received its name in honor of Lady Acland, the fair donor who started the subscription. Upon this has been published various literary and religious articles calculated to advance the cause of learning and religion. The students of the College have at several periods projected publications of a literary character; the last, the "Kenyon Collegian," a very creditable magazine, was continued for several years. The first store was called the Bishop's store, from having been commenced by Bishop Chase for the purpose of furnishing work hands with necessary articles, and to supply the boys, so that no excuse could exist for going "to town." This was carried on until in the fall of 1833 an arrangement was made with Mr. White, of New York, by which that business was to be entirely under his control, and M. and G. B. White thereupon located at Gambier. The former remains there, and the latter at this writing is one of the most valued citizens of Mt. Vernon. The Whites are natives of Derby, Ct. The "Bishop's store" was managed for many years by Robert Burnside, until a short time before its discontinuance N. W. Putnam had it in charge. The Whites continued in partnership until 1838, when D. Topping and N. W. Putnam opened a store, and Daniel S. Norton and A. G. Scott established another. Topping & Co., with A. J. Douglass, kept for a few years, when it was closed, and Mr. T. moved to Illinois; Mr. P. is yet living on the hill; Mr. Scott has uninterruptedly resided there, and by his close attention to business, in which for many years has been alone, has acquired a competency. A. B. Norton for several years was engaged in the merchandizing and milling business at Gambier. At this time there are the two stores of A. G. Scott & Co., M. White & Co., and a drug

MILNOR HALL.

and book establishment of Mr. French. Other branches of business have been carried on here; E. Pearce, Witt & Mulford, and G. J. W. Pearce in the boot and shoe line; Russel Clark, Mr. Clements, A. K. Fobes and J. Waugh have carried on the tailoring. Mr. Sharp in early times was the brewer and baker, in a large stone house in the rear of the main College building, now obliterated by time's effacing finger. J. S. Sawer since 1837 has supplied the students and liberal disposed with ice cream and varieties, and many of the boys fed under the Dotheby regime gratefully remember the good cookery and pies of Mrs. Sawer. The hotel and boarding-houses have been kept by Douglass, Vore, Johnson, Bell, Witt, Sims, Riley, and Wright, the latter now holding forth in fine style. The old College mill erected by Bp. Chase many years ago went into decay, and at that seat Daniel S. Norton put up one of the finest mills on the river. The "Kenyon Mills" flour acquired a good reputation. The post-office, upon Bp. Chase's application, established in 1826, has been the greater part of its existence managed by that excellent public officer, M. T. C. Wing. About 1846, partisan violence, through the machinery of a county convention and central committee, brought about the appointment of Benoni Elliott, a student from the District of Columbia. In 1849, M. T. C. Wing was again appointed; in 1853, James Young; in 1857, E. G. Riley; and in 1861, Joseph Leonard. The principal church is Rosse Chapel, bearing the name of its founder, Lady Rosse, eminent for piety and good works. It is a very neat and chaste stone edifice, situated in Harcourt Parish, named for like cause, and in the rear of the church is the beautiful cemetery where rest the dead of Gambier. The parish officers elected Easter Monday, 1862, on the Union ticket, are A. G. Scott, H. L. Smith, Wardens; B. L. Lang, A. Buttles, M. White, J. Leonard, J. S. Sawer, S. T. Bourne, N. W. Putnam,

ROSSE CHAPEL.

E. S. Balcom. Delegates to the Convention, B. L. Lang, A. G. Scott, S. T. Bourne. The M. E. church is a neat frame, erected in 1854 by subscription of liberal citizens. The present minister is

Chilton Craven. The Trustees are D. L. Fobes, J. T. L. Jacobs, F. Clippinger, F. Penhorwood, G. J. W. Pearce. The Cumberland Presbyterians have preaching regularly at their church, one-half mile north of the Public Well. The Rev. Larrimore is the present minister; J. Bennet and T. Minard, trustees. The various College buildings and matters of interest connected with them will appear under the appropriate head. Gambier is a beautiful little village, where those who desire to withdraw from the noise and bustle, the cares and vexations of the active world, can have a safe retreat. A more quiet and secluded spot cannot be found on this continent; of the old residents on the hill, it may with truth be said:

"Along the cool, sequestered *hill* of life,
They kept the noiseless tenor of their way,"

scarcely realizing that the great busy world is all around them. To them we commend Lord Kenyon's motto: "*Magnanimiter crucem sustine.*"

SUCCESSIVE JUSTICES OF THE PEACE.

In 1839 John Powell and C. S. Johnson were elected, but the latter, being a student, upon protest of the Bishop against his acting, resigned, and A. G. Scott was chosen in May, 1840; re-elected in 1843 and in 1845; in 1846, resigned. 1845—G. C. Johnson; re-elected 1848. 1842—A. K. Fobes. 1844—E. M. Gwin; re-elected 1847. 1847—B. Elliott. 1850—N. W. Putnam; re-elected in 1853 and 1856. 1853—D. L. Fobes. 1855—J. H. C. Bonte. 1856—Norman Badger. 1857—John Cunningham; re-elected 1860. 1859—George J. W. Pearce.

CHAPTER XLVII.

CLINTON TOWNSHIP.

James Scott V.D.M.

So often, during the progress of this work, have we had occasion to speak of events occurring within this township, and of its prominent citizens, that we shall not occupy much space in addition to that necessary for its list of justices. It is one of the four townships created at the organization of the county, and, containing the county-seat, has been the central field of operations heretofore quite minutely described. The land is all good; the citizens, generally, moral and industrious. It is well watered by the Ko-ko-sing, Dry Creek and Center Run, and possessed of every article necessary for convenience and health of the inhabitants. The greater part of its wealth and population is within Mt. Vernon, and at this place the business is generally carried on. The township is divided into convenient school and road districts, and the whole is embraced in one election district, which polls usually 1,000 votes. This township, outside the city limits, contained in 1860, 884 whites. The aggregate value of land, as equalized by the State Board, was $543,473.

MOUNT VERNON steadily increased in population and wealth until the present war withdrew a large portion of the citizens from industrial pursuits and caused a general depression, from which the recovery will come with peace. In 1860, there were 61 industrial establishments within the city limits, and the value of products was $704,050. The aggregate population of the five wards was 4,147, of whom 46 were colored persons. The aggregate value of lots and buildings, as equalized by the State Board, was $723,239. We have collected much information, in regard to this place, from its foundation to the present time, which we may hereafter give to the public in a volume. The limits prescribed to this work preclude us now. The citizens have certainly cause to congratulate themselves upon the growth, prosperity and health of the place—upon their many and great advantages, moral, social, educational, religious. The unsurpassed water-power—the superiority of the locality for manufacturing—must cause its continued prosperity. Norton's Mills, the Mount Vernon Iron Works, the Kokosing Foundry, the Woolen Factory, and other manufacturing establishments, and the superiority of Mount Vernon mechanics, have contributed much to the advancement of the city and county. In the not far distant future, this city will be one of the foremost in the interior of Ohio.

The Knox Mutual Insurance Co., incorporated in 1838, went into operation with C. P. Buckingham, H. B. Curtis, G. Browning, J. E. Davidson, C. Delano, E. Miller, I. Hadley, D. S. Norton and Abel Hart, as Directors. Gen. Buckingham was for many years President, and Richard Thomas, Secretary. Present officers: G. W. Hauk, J. Sperry, J. Blake, J. M. Byers, C. Cooper, R. C. Hurd, C. P. Buckingham, W. McClelland, Directors. G. W. Hauk, President, and Wm. Turner, Secretary and Treasurer. The first loss sustained was by the burning of Rev. M. T. C. Wing's dwelling; amount paid, $900.

The Knox Co. Bank, organized in 1847, with Henry B. Curtis, J. W. Russell, C. Delano, J. B. Thomas and Sewall Gray, Directors. Capital stock, $100,000. Henry B. Curtis has been its

President from that time. Its Cashiers—J. C. Ramsey, L. S. Lewis, J. F. Andrews and Hugh Ogilvie.

The Bank of Mt. Vernon was organized April, 1862. Directors: J. W. Russell, Prest.; C. Delano, M. Thompson, W. H. Smith, F. D. Sturges. Mr. Sturges is Cashier, D. W. Lambert, Teller.

CONSECUTIVE JUSTICES OF THE PEACE.

1806. John Mills.
1808. T. B. Patterson.
1809. Matthew Merritt.
1811. Samuel Kratzer.
1811. Silas Brown.
1811. Allen Scott.
1815. James Smith.
1815. Benjamin Barney.
1817. Benjamin Martin.
1817. Stephen Chapman.
1818. John Roberts.
1820. Wm. Y. Farquhar.
1820. Benj. Martin.
1821. John Roberts.
1822. John H. Mefford.
1823. Wm. Y. Farquhar.
1824. John Roberts.
1825. Joseph Brown.
1825. James McGibeny.
1826. John Roberts.
1830. Gideon Mott.
1830. Wm. Bevans.
1831. S. W. Hildreth.
1833. Wm. Bevans.
1833. Thomas Irvine.
1834. S. W. Hildreth.
1836. Johnston Elliott.
1836. Thomas Irvine.
1837. Timothy Colopy.
1839. B. F. Smith.
1839. Robert F. Hickman.
1840. Wm. Welsh.
1842. B. F. Smith.
1842. R. F. Hickman.
1842. E. W. Cotton.
1843. Wm. H. Cochran.
1845. Benjamin McCracken.
1845. E. W. Cotton.
1846. Nath. McGiffin.
1846. W. H. Cochran.
1846. Truman Ward.
1848. E. W. Cotton.
1849. W. H. Cochran.
1850. Joseph S. Davis.
1851. Emmet W. Cotton.
1852. W. H. Cochran.
1853. Joseph S. Davis.
1854. Thompson Cooper.
1855. Samuel O. Beach.
1855. W. H. Cochran.
1858. Thompson Cooper.
1858. Thos. V. Parke.
1858. W. H. Cochran.
1860. C. C. Baugh.
1860. Thompson Cooper.
1861. Henry Warner.

CHAPTER XLVIII.

INDEPENDENT ORDER OF ODD FELLOWS.

Mt. Vernon Lodge No. 20, was duly instituted on the 21st day of June, 1843, by a dispensation from the R. W. Grand Lodge of Ohio, by D. D. G. Master J. T. Blain, acting under a dispensation from G. M. Thomas Sherlock.

Charter Members.—R. Blake, L. Waite, L. D. Nash, W. Sullivan, and R. Wright. The following officers were duly installed: R. Blake, N. G.; Liberty Waite, V. G.; L. D. Nash, Secretary; W. Sullivan, Treasurer. Initiated at the first meeting: J. K. Miller, D. A. Robertson, and J. R. Wallace.

Celebrations.—The first public celebration was June 22, 1844, D. T. Disney, of Cincinnati, Orator; the second, June 21, 1848, Rev. Mr. Doolittle, of Columbus, Orator; the third, June 19, 1851, Rev. A. T. Mather, Orator.

Officers January 1, 1862.—H. D. Brown, N. G.; Edwin Rogers, V. G.; J. D. Haymes, Secretary; J. W. White, Financial Secretary; R. N. Kindrick, Treasurer. *Trustees.*—Joshua Hyde, W. M. Bunn, H. Phillips.

Representatives to the Grand Lodge of Ohio.—W. M. Bunn, R. C. Kirk, A. C. Elliott, and J. W. White.

Ellicott Lodge No. 267, was instituted at Fredericktown, April 11, 1855, by M. W. G. Master T. J. McLain, assisted by Past Grands W. M. Bunn, J. W. White, J. F. Andrews, R. C. Kirk, J. W. Lybrand, A. C. Elliott, and G. W. Shurr.

Charter Members.—A. Love, T. Mosure, G. Cole, B. F. Mosure, R. Cole, N. B. Rowley, G. W. Condon, J. Z. Griffith, A. Snow, Jr.,

J. B. Roberts, and J. W. Condon. The first officers installed were: G. W. Condon, N. G.; J. Z. Griffith, V. G.; A. Love, Secretary; R. Cole, Treasurer. Initiated at the first meeting: D. S. Headley, C. G. Mount, and R. Ewers. The only *public celebration* was July 4, 1857, P. G. John Lamb, Orator.

Representatives.—P. G. J. Z. Griffith in 1857, and P. G. Issacher Rowley in 1860.

D. D. Grand Masters.—P. G. J. Z. Griffith, 1857; P. G. G. W. Condon, 1860.

Officers, 1862.—J. C. Ebersole, N. G.; D. T. Montague, V. G.; E. J. Breese, Secretary; N. F. Strong, Financial Secretary; W. D. Morrison, Treasurer. *Trustees*—I. Rowley, J. W. Porch, A. Stephens.

Quindaro Lodge No. 316, was duly instituted June 9, 1857, by a dispensation from the R. W. G. Lodge of Ohio, by D. G. Master P. G. A. E. Glenn, acting under a dispensation from G. M. W. C. Chidsey.

Charter Members.—G. B. Arnold, J. M. Byers, A. C. Elliott, J. F. Andrews, J. Lamb, T. P. Frederick, and J. Jennings. Officers installed: J. M. Byers, N. G.; T. P. Frederick, V. G.; G. B. Arnold, Secretary; A. C. Elliott, Financial Secretary; J. F. Andrews, Treasurer. Admitted on card: M. McFarland, A. J. Beach, W. C. Cooper, J. Jennings. Initiated: I. Underwood and L. Monk. The dedication of the new hall, No. 109 Main street, was June 9, 1858. A supper was given to the members of the Order. P. G. Rev. Glancy delivered an address.

Representatives.—P. G. J. F. Andrews, P. G. J. M. Byers.

Officers, 1862.—J. M. Byers, N. G.; E. B. Shinabery, V. G.; H. Graff, Secretary; W. McGaughey, Financial Secretary; J. F. Andrews, Treasurer. *Trustees.*—P. G.'s J. F. Andrews, G. B. Arnold, J. R. Wallace.

Kokosing Encampment No. 38, was instituted at Mt. Vernon, March 29, 1849, by Grand Chief Patriarch Williams, assisted by J. H. Wheeler as Grand

High Priest, H. B. Horton as Grand S. W., J. S. Clark as Grand Scribe.

Charter Members.—J. M. Campbell, S. W. Gribbon, L. G. Prentiss, R. C. Kirk, H. Phillips, A. Ehle, A. P. Mather, U. Stephens. *Officers.*—J. M. Campbell, C. P.; A. P. Mather, H. P.; R. C. Kirk, S. W.; A. Ehle, Scribe; L. G. Prentiss, Treasurer. Initiated at the first meeting: W. M. Bunn, J. A. Shannon, T. T. Tress, J. Cooper, J. Eichelberger, R. B. Wright.

Officers January 1, 1862.—J. W. Porch, C. P.; A. Harnwell, H. P.; E. Shinabery, S. W.; R. N. Kindrick, J. W.; J. W. White, Scribe; J. Hyde, Treasurer. *Trustees.*—J. Hyde, W. M. Bunn, Henry Phillips.

Representatives to the Grand Encampment of Ohio.—Since the adoption of the new constitution, in 1855, the following Patriarchs, viz: W. M. Bunn, J. W. White, J. F. Andrews.

CHAPTER XLIX.

VARIOUS PUBLIC OFFICERS.

SENATORS IN STATE LEGISLATURE.

FROM the Senatorial District of which this land formed a part before the organization of the county, and after its first settlement, we find in the fourth General Assembly, at Chillicothe, Jacob Burton; in the fifth session, Elnathan Scofield. In the sixth session, Jacob Burton appeared and was qualified as Senator from Fairfield, Licking and Knox. In 1809, the Senators from these counties were Elnathan Scofield and Jacob Burton. In 1810, Wm. Trimble and Robert F. Slaughter were the Senators, and they continued as such while the sessions were at Zanesville. In 1812, at Chillicothe, the Senator was Wm. Gavit, and we were in the same district with Richland and Licking for many years. William Gass, Mordecai Bartley, John Spencer, John Shaw and Daniel S. Norton were Senators until the course of political alliance changed, and new connections were formed. The north and south union was severed, and we were associated with the counties to the east until the adoption of the new Constitution in 1851; sometimes, in districting, Knox was put with Holmes, at other times with Coshocton, and then again with both counties. Since that period our associations have been with the west, embracing Morrow, until, in 1861, the district was made to include Wayne, Ashland and Richland. Beside the Senators aforenamed, we have had the following, elected at the periods named, the term of the office being two years, viz.: In 1829, Thomas Rigdon; in 1831, Wm. Gass; in 1832, Byram Leonard; in 1834, Wm. Ravenscroft; in 1836, Peres Sprague; in 1838, James Matthews; in 1840, Byram Leonard; in 1842, John Johnson; in 1844, Jacob Koch; in 1846, Nicholas Spindler; in 1848, Asa G. Dimock; in 1850, L. Van Buskirk. Under the new Constitution we have had—in 1851, L. Van Buskirk; in 1853, John T. Creigh; in 1855, Robert C. Kirk; in 1857, Davis Miles; in 1859, Wm. Bonar; and in 1861, Davis Miles.

REPRESENTATIVES.

1807. Philemon Beecher.
" W. W. Irwin.
1808. E. B. Merwin.
" Patrick Owings.
1809. Alexander Holden.
1810. Jeremiah Munson.
1811. William Gass.
1812. Samuel Kratzer.
1813. William Gass.
1814. Samuel Kratzer.
1815. Alexander Enos.
1816. Jonathan Miller.
1817. Waitstil Hastings.
1818. W. W. Farquhar.
1819. R. D. Simons.
1820. " "
1821. " "
1822. H. Curtis.
1823. R. D. Simons.
1824. Thomas Rigdon.
1825. John Shaw.
1826. Wm. Robison.
1827. Thomas Rigdon.
1828. Charles Colerick.
1829. Byram Leonard.
1830. John Greer.
1831. Charles Colerick.
1832. John Schooler.
1833. " "
1834. Peres Sprague.
1835. " "
1836. Martin Tracy.
" S. W. Hildreth.
1837. Marvin Tracy.
1838. James Elliott.
1839. Byram Leonard.
1840. D. L. McGugin.
1841. C. J. McNulty.
1842. C. J. McNulty.
1843. George Ankeny.
1844. James McFarland.
" George Ankeny.
1845. W. H. Smith.
1846. E. W. Cotton.
" James McFarland.
1847. E. W. Cotton.
1848. L. Van Buskirk.
" Jacob Voorhies.

1849. Ezekiel Boggs.
1850. Eli Glasgo.
" S. F. Gilcrest.
1851. James Witherow.
1853. Jacob Merrin.
1855. George W. True.
1855. B. F. Smith.
1857. Wm. McCreary.
" W. B. Cox.
1859. " "
1861. Wait Whitney.

COMMON PLEAS JUDGES

Who have presided in the districts in which this county has been situated, are William Wilson, of Newark; Alexander Harper, of Zanesville; Ezra Dean, of Wooster; Jacob Parker, of Mansfield; Levi Cox, of Wooster; James Stewart, of Mansfield; Rollin C. Hurd, of Mt. Vernon; Sherman Finch and Thomas C. Jones, of Delaware. Of this number, Judges Hurd, Finch and Jones have been elected by the people; the others were chosen by the Legislature.

CLERKS OF COMMON PLEAS.

Charles Lofland, James Smith, Isaac Hadley, S. W. Farquhar, and A. C. Elliott have served as Clerks. Prior to 1851, they were appointed by the Judges; and since that time, the two last named have been elected by the people. Among the Deputies who have performed longest service, were Henry B. Curtis, E. C. Vore, Horatio S. Miller, F. P. Griffith, A. C. Elliott.

The *Clerks of the Supreme Court* have been Jas. Smith, Alexander Elliott and A. C. Elliott.

ASSOCIATE JUDGES.

1808. John Mills, Wm. W. Farquhar, Wm. Gass.

1810. James Colville, April 30th, in place of Gass, who goes into Richland county.

1813. Jacob Young in place of Farquhar, resigned, Dec. 12th.

1814. Samuel Kratzer, May 9th, in place of Mills.

1815. John Trimble and Abraham Darling.
1818. John H. Mefford in place of Darling.
1819. Stephen Chapman.
1820. Joseph Brown, James McGibeny.
1827. Anthony Banning.
1834. Eli Miller.
" Abner Ayres.
" James Elliott.
1838. William Bevans.
1839. Richard C. Davis.
1841. William Bevans.
" Isaac N. Richardson.
1846. Wm. McCreary.
1848. Jacob B. Brown.
" B. H. Taylor.

By the adoption of the new Constitution, the office was abolished.

COUNTY AUDITORS.

1820. W. Y. Farquhar, the first officer of this description, was appointed at this date, to value the lands for taxation; and when the law creating a distinct bureau passed, having been Clerk of the Board of Commissioners and conversant with its business, he was reappointed annually until 1824, from which time the people have elected for a term of two years.

1824. Alexander Elliott.
1826.
1828. Marvin Tracy.
1830. " "
1832. " "
1834. S. B. Kenton.
1836. " "
1838. " "
1840. " "
1842. K. Winne.
1844. K. Winne.
1846. M. M. Beam.
1848. " "
1850. B. F. Smith.
1852. " "
1854. John Lamb.
1856. " "
1858. S. W. Farquhar.
1860. " "
1862. John D. Thompson.

PROBATE JUDGES.

The New Constitution created this office, and at the first election, in October, 1851, for Probate Judge, to serve three years, commencing February, 1852, Sam'l F. Gilcrest was elected, entered upon the duties of his office February, 1852, and at the expiration of his term was a candidate for re-election, and beaten, 1854, by Joseph S. Davis.

1857. Joseph S. Davis was re-elected.
1860. Thomas V. Parke.

MEMBERS OF CONSTITUTIONAL CONVENTION.

The Convention that framed the present Constitution of Ohio, was held in 1851. Knox and Holmes formed a district, and the Delegates elected were Matthew H. Mitchell and John Sellers, Democrats, over Rollin C. Hurd and John H. Wheeler, Whigs.

MEMBERS OF THE BOARD OF EQUALIZATION.

Daniel S. Norton,
Byram Leonard,
Henry B. Curtis,
James McFarland,
S. T. Cunard.

TREASURERS.

Until 1825 this office was filled by appointment of Commissioners each year, and from that time the people elected for a term of two years. The period at which each Treasurer was chosen, we append:

1808. Henry Haines.
1815. George Downs.
1816. James McGibeny.
1817. Gilman Bryant.
1819. James McGibeny.
1825. W. Y. Farquhar.
1838. S. W. Farquhar.
1841. James Blake.
1847. Jacob W. Lybrand.
1851. J. H. McFarland.
1855. John Beaty.
1859. Alex. Greer.
1861. H. H. Greer.

COUNTY COLLECTORS.

The Commissioners appointed annually the collector of personal tax, and that upon lands of residents. In 1820, the duties of this officer were somewhat changed, and, in 1817, the office was abolished by law, and its business transferred to the County Treasurer.

1808. Silas Brown; amount of bond $658.87.
1809. James Smith.
1812. John Greer.
1817. John Shaw.
1819. Eli Miller.
1820. William Bevans.
1821. Benj. Jackson, Jr.
1822. R. D. Simons.
1823. Joseph Brown.
1824. John Shaw.
1825. Silas Brown.
1827. Jacob M. Banning.

In 1822, a system of cutting under was commenced by competitors for this office, as we find that the State tax was collected this year for 2¾ per cent., and County tax gratis; the next year Brown underbid ¼ per cent.; and Shaw, in 1824, capped the climax by proposing to collect both State and County tax *gratis!*

ASSESSORS.

Assessors have been in our history of two kinds—Township and County. The county were appointed by the Commissioners until, in 1827, the people by law were required to elect such officer; and after 1841 the office for the county was abolished, and the old system of Township Assessors was re-established.

Prior to 1827, the Commissioners appointed, as Assessors, R. D. Simons for 1824 and '5, Marvin Tracy in 1826, and Hill Runyan in 1827, who served from March until the October election, when he was elected for two years. In 1829, John Greer was elected, and, having resigned in October, 1830, Daniel McFarland was elected and continued until, in 1834, Henry B. Carter was chosen, and served two terms. In 1838, Uzal Ball was elected; in 1840, Wait Whitney

COUNTY COMMISSIONERS.

1808. Joseph Walker, John Harrod, John Lewis.

1808. Henry Markley, Matthew Merrit, and Wm. Douglass were elected Oct. 11th; and, by lot, it was declared that Markley continue three years, Merrit two, and Douglass one.

1809. William Douglass.
1810. Robert McMillen.
1811. John Harrod.
1812. Daniel Cooper.
1813. William Mitchell, appointed by Court May 9th, 1814, *vice* Harrod, deceased.
1814. William Mitchell.
1815. Jonathan Miller.
1816. Moses Merrit.
1817. William Mitchell.
" John Warden *vice* Miller.
1818. Allen Scott.
1819. Gilman Bryant.
1820. Abner Ayres.
1821. John Wheeler.
1822. John Kerr.
1823. Abner Ayres.
1824. John Stilley.
1825. Daniel Sapp.
1826. Byram Leonard.
1827. Levi Harrod.
" Gilman Bryant appo'ted.
1828. Peres Sprague, Jabez Beers.
1829. Francis Wilkins; William McCreary for 3 years, Francis Wilkins for 1 year.
1830. David Shaw *vice* Wilkins, deceased.
1831. John Jeffers for 3 years, David Shaw 2 years.
1832. William McCreary.
1833. David Shaw.
1834. Silas Brown.
1835. William McCreary.
1836. David Shaw.
1837. Thomas Wade.
1838. Christopher Wolf.
1839. Thomas Axtell.
1840. Thomas Wade.
1841. Christopher Wolf.
1842. Thomas Axtell, Henry Prather.
1843. Henry Prather.
1844. James Witherow.
1845. Robert Graham.
1846. William Babcock.
1847. James Witherow.
1848. Robert Graham.
1849. Wm. Babcock.
1850. Wait Whitney.
1851. George McWilliams.
1852. Abraham Darling, M. H. Mitchell *vice* Whitney, resigned.
1853. George W. Jackson.
1854. Sewal Gray.
1855. John McElroy.
1856. Jacob Bell, full term.
" W. McClelland, *vice* Gray, resigned.
1857. W. McClelland.
1858. John McElroy.
1859. Jacob Bell.
1860. Wm. McClelland.
1861. J. W. Bradfield.
1862. John S. McCamment.

SHERIFFS.

1808. Silas Brown, appointed by Thos. Kirker, Acting Governor of the State, June 6, till October election, and reappointed by Governor Samuel Huntington, October 11, 1808.

1811. Ichabod Nye.
1813. John Hawn.
1815. John Shaw.
1817. " "

1819. Alexander Elliott.
1820. William Bevans.
1822. " "
1824. Charles Colerick.
1826. " "
1828. John Shaw.
1830. Hugh Neal.
1832. " "
1834. Isaac Hadley.
1836. " "
1838. Wm. Beam.
1840. " "
1842. Absalom Thrift.
1844. " "
1846. David C. Montgomery.
1848. " "
1850. Thomas Wade.
1852. " "
1854. Lewis Strong.
1856. Israel Underwood.
1858. " "
1860. James S. Shaw.
1862. Allen Beach.

The following persons have acted as Deputy Sheriffs at different periods: John Cramer, Isaac Hadley, Resin Yates, Ben. Jackson, Henry Prather, D. C. Zimmerman, Johnson Elliott, Jesse B. Rogers, W. Beam, S. B. Kenton, E. W. Cotton, W. D. Headley, Stiles W. Thrift, D. C. Montgomery, John Beaty, T. P. Morton, James Myers, J. Underwood, T. V. Parke, Josiah Cochran, George W. Steele.

CORONERS.

1808. Jonathan Craig, elected April 4.
" John Merritt, appointed Oct. 11.
1809. John Butler, appointed.
1811. Dr. Timothy Burr.
1813. " "
1815. " "
1817. " "
1818. Dr. Robert D. Moore.
1819. Dr. Waitstil Hastings.
1820. Dr. E. G. Lee.
1822. James McGibeny.
1824. Hill Runyan.
1828. " "
1830. George Low.
1832. W. E. Davidson.
1834. Andrew Vance.
1836. " "
1838. " "
1840. Richard Hunt.
1842. Asa Freeman.
1844. " "
1846. Michael Miller.
1848. " "
1850. Alexander Love.
1852. " "
1854. William Bonar.
1856. Albert Ellis.
1858. " "
1860. John W. Leonard.
1862. M. M. Shaw.

PROSECUTING ATTORNEYS.

The first officer answering to this description was Samuel Kratzer, Esq., who sort o' officiated in behalf of the State when no better qualified person was present. He was not an attorney, but appears to have been allowed fees for his services. Edward Herrick was the main reliance in this branch in the early courts, until 1812, when Samuel Mott was appointed on the 14th of March. In January, 1814, Charles R. Sherman was appointed, and at different terms S. W. Culberson, Wyllis Silliman, Hosmer Curtis, John W. Warden, and other attorneys, were appointed by the court, as business required, until in 1833 the Legislature provided for the Prosecuting Attorney's election biennially by the voters of the county, who have made the following selections:

1833. Benjamin S. Brown.
1835. Columbus Delano.
1837. " "
1839. M. H. Mitchell.
1840. M. A. Sayre.
1842. J. K. Miller.
1844. " "
1846. Lafayette Emmett.
1848. Lafayette Emmett.
1850. Clark Irvine.
1852. William Windom.
1854. W. F. Sapp.
1856. " "
1858. W. C. Cooper.
1860. " "
1862. Frank H. Hurd.

SURVEYORS.

The Court of Common Pleas, until 1831, appointed the Surveyor of the county, and the office was filled by the following persons:

1808. Samuel H. Smith appointed.
1810. John Dunlap appointed June, in place of Smith, resigned.
1815. Wm. Y. Farquhar appointed April 15, and resigned 1827.
1827. Edson Harkness appointed.

The act of the Legislature of March 3d, 1831, having provided for the election of this officer for a term of three years, the first elected by the people was, in

1831. Edson Harkness.
1834. Thomas G. Plummer.
1837. T. C. Hickman.
1840. T. G. Plummer.
1843. T. C. Hickman.
1846. David Gorsuch.

1849. David Gorsuch.	1858. David C. Lewis.
1852. T. C. Hickman.	1861. " "
1855. David C. Lewis.	

COUNTY RECORDER.

The Judges of the Court of Common Pleas appointed this officer until 1829, at the October election, the people chose a Recorder. Under the former system, the term of service was seven years; under the present, three years.

1808. Gilman Bryant, May 2d, until 1815.
1815. Alexander Elliott, May 2d, until 1822.
1822. Henry B. Curtis.

The Legislature of 1828-9 having provided for appointment of Recorders by County Commissioners, where office becomes vacant prior to October, the Commissioners appointed—

1829. John A. Colerick, May 29th, in place of H. B. Curtis, whose term had expired.

1829. Hill Runyan	was elected	in Oct.,	and served until	1838.
1838. David Montgomery	"	"	"	1847.
1847. Elijah Harrod	"	"	"	1857.
1856. Calton C. Baugh	"	"	"	1859.
1859. Elijah Harrod	"	"	and re-elected	1862.

INFIRMARY DIRECTORS.

1842. John Hobbs, J. F. McLain.	1851. Timothy Colopy.
" Wm. Borden.	1852. John McCamment.
1843. W. Borden.	1853. G. W. Jackson.
1844. Abraham Darling.	1854. J. B. McGrew.
1845. C. A. Drake.	1855. Thomas Rogers.
1846. Abraham Darling.	1856. Thomas Larrimore.
" Absalom Buckingham.	1857. E. J. Whitney.
1847. G. W. Jackson.	1858. Thomas Rogers.
1848. Abraham Darling.	1859. Thomas Larrimore.
1849. Christian Musser.	1860. E. J. Whitney.
1850. G. W. Jackson.	1861. Asahel Allen.
	1862. James Scott.

CHAPTER L.

Dan S. Norton

It will be expected that a history of this county will devote more than a passing notice to the memory of that citizen of whom, in July, 1849, the editor of the *Times* said, "We are of opinion that none of the earliest pioneers of our town have ever done so much to promote its growth and prosperity as Mr. Norton. If Mt. Vernon is specially indebted to the enterprise and liberality of any one man, that man is Daniel S. Norton."

The *Democratic Banner* of Nov. 1, 1859, says: "One of our most eminent and highly valued citizens died suddenly, of congestion of the lungs, on Tuesday morning, October 25th, aged 72 years." The following extract from that notice of his death evidences the regard and opinion entertained for his services, and its republication will not be inappropriate:

"He first visited Mt. Vernon in the spring of 1816, and, in the summer of that year, introduced the first complete Carding Machine in this part of the State, and set it up at the mill of William Douglas, now occupied by J. S. Banning. In the summer of 1817, he moved to Mt. Vernon, and in the fall of that year, having secured the admirable mill seat and water power which his sagacious eye had discovered the summer previous, he built the mills, which, improved and enlarged from time to time, as the wants of the county required, he continued to occupy and operate until his death.

"He engaged also in the mercantile business, and carried it on prosperously for many years. He erected a woolen and a cotton factory, and an oil mill, and engaged extensively in agriculture and the raising of cattle and horses, and contributed much to the improvement of the stock of both in the county.

"He was elected to the Senate from Knox and Richland counties, and while in that body took lively interest and an active part in inaugurating and establishing the wise canal policy of the State. He was a member of the committee appointed to welcome De Witt Clinton. At the canal celebration in July, 1825, he first met Bishop Chase, who served as chaplain on that occasion, and during the interview he suggested to the Bishop the eligibility of the grounds which were afterwards chosen for the location of Kenyon College. He contributed liberally to the establishment of that institution, and was always its steadfast friend.

He was always among the foremost in all public enterprises calculated to increase the growth of the town, or improve and develope the resources of the country.

As a man of business, he had no superior. Prompt, energetic and deliberate, he apeared to see the end from the beginning, and his plans, wisely laid, were worked out with a precision which commanded the admiration of all.

A man of social qualities, he was the pride of the society in which he lived. Remarkable for his address and conversational power, his extensive reading, his acute observation and his wonderful memory, he attracted notice wherever he appeared, at home or abroad, and entered no circle which was not entertained and instructed by his presence.

He had a keen perception of merit in the young, and not a few owe the beginning of their prosperous career in business, to his kind and wise patronage. He was ever ready to aid the industrious, and had a lively sympathy for the unfortunate. It was a touching sight to see the poor gather around his bier, and not the least of a good man's reward, to hear them call him blessed."

A brief statement of some of the events of his life, evincing his indomitable spirit, extraordinary business qualifications, great liberality and genuine patriotism, may follow the tribute from another pen. The first American settlers in the Attakapas of Orleans were the Nortons, who for several years endured contentedly the perils and privations in that, then foreign, clime, until sickness and death reduced their number and deprived them of their head; and the management of the affairs of Mrs. Ann Norton, and nine children, devolved entirely upon the young Daniel S., who, possessed of a peculiar business mind and an adventurous spirit, carried on various trading operations in the territory and the Mexican provinces. His papers, carefully preserved, show many ventures that few would have the nerve to undertake; and yet success invariably crowned his efforts. Some of his practical operations are worthy of notice. He introduced the first sugar-cane in the Attakapas, and established that it could be cultivated successfully. His active and well informed mind, and inventive genius, was always striving to make improvements, and he first directed attention to the navigation of the Bayous and rivers, and was interested in the first boat that engaged in their trade. He traveled on the first two boats that made trips on the Mississippi, and subsequently on the first boat built by a company at Brownsville, Pa., and run by Capt. Gregg on the lower Mississippi and Red River. His suggestions in construction and navigation, his knowledge of the rivers and the country, contributed much to those enterprises.

It was with the view of carrying on a trade with the southern country that he located at Connelsville, and engaged in erecting machinery for manufacturing; and hence his deep solicitude for successful navigation of the rivers, to promote which he carried on correspondence, published articles, made investments, and labored industriously. The first Cotton Factory on the Youghiogheny he erected, and operated successfully, bringing the raw cotton from his old home in Louisiana. His lands in that country were of great value, and his business there for about a half century was faithfully attended to by Gov. Johnson, as his agent, who has informed us of his unsurpassed reputation as a business man. He never relinquished the idea, which he had entertained though life, of returning there to live, and which was only broken in upon by his coming to this county to marry, and being still further irresistibly attracted by the fine water power, fertile lands and beautiful prospects of Owl Creek.

The building of machinery and improving of mills and manufacturing establishments may be said to have been the ruling passion of his life. We find a petition presented to the General Assembly of Ohio, when it met in Chillicothe, by Daniel S. Norton, John H. Piatt and Herman Long, of Cincinnati, Asa Norton, of Kentucky, and Abraham Baldwin, of Pennsylvania, who had associated in manufacturing business, asking for encouragement of woolen manufactories, etc. The first complete carding machines, west of the Allegheny mountains, were put up by Daniel S. Norton, and our venerable townsman, Wm. Reeves, says that he first saw him, in 1805, at Tom Smith's mill, on Whitewater, setting up machines.

I have often heard father laugh about how his father caused him to trade a valuable lot in Cincinnati for a little sorrel pony, saddle and bridle, and leave there for his home in the Attakapas. Another trade that amused him very much was that of a set of machines, to a man named Lowrie, for a scholarship in Transylvania University, which his father, who had given him what he deemed sufficient education at Middlebury College, did not relish; nevertheless, he procured his books, and took out the value in Latin, Greek, and mathematics, &c. There he formed the acquaintance of many young men who have since become eminent in the country, and that friendship and regard for Henry Clay which caused him to cling to his fortunes through good and through evil report.

His career in this county—his efforts to promote education, home manufactures and internal improvements; his contributions to objects calculated to benefit the public; his assistance to old settlers in purchasing their farms and stock, making improvements, and providing for their families; his kindness to friends, and generosity to relatives—will long be remembered. His love of country was unbounded, and the blood of the Revolution never coursed through veins more determined to perpetuate "Liberty and Union." His liberality and patriotism in the War of 1812, the Texan Revolution and the Mexican War is on record; and were he living to-day, he would be faithful to the Union and true to the principles of the Constitution.

NOTE.—The cultivation of the cotton plant attracted his attention, and among his papers of 1810 are calculations as to its culture and manufacture. He planted the first black seed in the Southwest (it had been brought from the Bahamas), and he was the first experimenter with the hirsutum and the *herbaceous* in that locality.

CHAPTER L.

KENYON COLLEGE AND THEOLOGICAL SEMINARY.

THIS valued institution of learning and religion was founded in this county by the Rt. Rev. Philander Chase, first Bishop of the Protestant Episcopal Church of Ohio, upon Section *one*, Township *six*, and Range *twelve*, U. S. Military Lands. The preliminary steps to its establishment were taken at Worthington, by commencing a school, in 1825, under an act of incorporation for a "Theological Seminary of the Protestant Episcopal Church in the Diocese of Ohio." In pursuance of this purpose, Bp. C. visited England, and obtained very liberal donations for the cause; and the surpassing beauty of the present site secured its selection. In his annual address, 1826, he thus speaks: "July 22d. This day, for the first time, in company with a number of gentlemen, I explored the lands now rendered so interesting to us on account of their many advantages for the location of the seminary and college." Two of the gentlemen alluded to were Henry B. Curtis, Esq., and Daniel S. Norton, whose statements in regard to that "interesting" occasion we have; and that of the former, as published in the *Kenyon Collegian*, we had designed giving entire, but our limits will not permit. In fact, we can only allude to the establishment of the college, with the promise of giving at an early day a complete history of the institution, its founder and benefactors, for which we have now a large amount of interesting material in manuscript. The college lands, 4,000 acres, on both sides of the Kokosing, five miles below Mt. Vernon, were purchased of Wm. Hogg, Esq., of Brownsville, Pa., who made a generous donation in consideration of the object; and by a unanimous vote of the Convention of 1826 the site of Kenyon College was settled forever.

Views of Kenyon College, Ascension Hall, Bexley Hall, Milnor Hall and Rosse Chapel, the principal buildings of the Institution, appear in this work. They tell of the pious and devout labors of Bishop Chase, whose lithograph is also given, and of his very worthy successor, Bishop McIlvaine. They also speak, more than tongue can tell, the liberality and nobleness of the Christian people of Great Britain and of the United States, who have been graciously moved to give of their abundance to this noble object. To Henry Clay, whose influential letters gave Bishop Chase access to the British heart, we are also deeply indebted.

Kenyon College to-day stands erect, having passed through many periods of tribulation and gloom. With an able corps of instructors, trustees and friends, zealously devoted to her interests, a bright future is before it. In our forthcoming work, we will prove, by showing what it has done for the country, that the expectations of its friends have, in great part, been realized.

In 1827, the foundations of the work were laid

on College Hill, commanding the most beautiful view in the whole country. The place is noted for health, as the Institution has been for the thoroughness of its course of instruction. Among the very able officers at the present time are—Rt. Rev. G. T. Bedell, Rev. T. M. Smith, Rev. M. T. C. Wing, Rev. J. J. McElhinney, of the Theological Faculty, and Professors John Trimble, H. L. Smith, B. L. Lang, Francis Wharton, H. D. Lathrop and G. T. Chapman, of the College.

The Kenyon Grammar Schools in charge of Rev. A. Blake, at Gambier, and Rev. Peter S. Ruth, at Worthington, are valuable adjuncts, and well sustained.

The Libraries of the College and the Philomathesian and Nu Pi Kappa Societies, containing over 15,000 volumes, and an abundant supply of literary food, are ever accessible to the student.

The present Trustees of the Institution are—Rt. Rev. C. P. McIlvaine, D.D.D.C.L., President; Rt. Rev. G. T. Bedell, Vice President; Rev. S. A. Bronson, D.D., Rev. E. Burr, D.D., Rev. James McElroy, D.D., Rev. H. B. Walbridge, Rev. Lewis Burton, Rev. J. E. Grammer, Hon. J. W. Andrews, Hon. R. C. Hurd, Hon. C. Delano, Gen'l Kent Jarvis, Wm. Procter, Esq., Dr. J. N. Burr.

CHAPTER LI.

THE FAMOUS RACE OF SEELEY'S BULL *vs.* TOM'S HORSE.

ONE of the "phunny" characters in our county's history is our old friend Seeley Simpkins, who is now in his 70th year, and was born in West Jersey, the precise spot he doesn't know—nor is it material to the thread of this discourse. In 1804, when five years old, he was brought by his father from Morgantown, Va., and his recollection of Mt. Vernon runs from the time Capt. Walker lived in a little log hut close by the old sulphur spring. Seeley says that its water had a great medicine reputation with the Indians. He was a great favorite with the squaws and pappooses, by reason of his uncommon musical talent. He could mimic any sound of varmint or human, surpassed the lute of Orpheus, and out-whistled all creation. He furnished *the* music for early musters, and when it took four counties to make a regiment he gave a challenge to out-whistle any man within them. He recollects with much pride the encomiums of Adjutant Stilley, who, he says, was "the best judge of swill music then in the country." He frequented race tracks, and drew crowds and supplied hoe-downs on demand. For a long time he labored under the disadvantage of making his pilgrimages on foot, but having the good luck to hear at preaching that "Balaam took his ass and saddled him," he concluded to take the next thing to it—his bull—and saddle and ride him. He was a nice little muscular brute, raised by him, and being gentle, was trained so that he traveled right smart on Seeley's circuit. Often have we seen Seeley in all his glory ride to the mill with his grist, and while it was being ground he would take an airing around the town, whistling as he went. The races were usually on the flat front of Norton's mills, and there Seeley acquired "immortality and fame." On the occasion of a grand race, when the Critchfields, Sam. Arbuckle, and the Creek nation were in town in their strength, a race was gotten up by Hugh Neal, John Gregg, and John Kellifer, between Seeley's bull and Tom Irvine's horse. The stakes were up; judges took their stand; and expectation on tiptoe was soon gratified by the entrance of the steeds. At starting, the little bull's tail received a sudden and severe twist, causing him to bellow lustily as Seeley with "vaulting ambition pricked the sides of his intent;" and goaded to desperation, bull pawed the earth and sped on with all his might, while the air was rent with the shouts and yells of the spectators, frightening him almost out of his skin. The horse, altogether unused to such "noise and confusion," inclined to balk, shied to one side, and trembling from fear, could not be brought to the "outcome" in time, and the judges honestly pronounced in favor of Seeley's bull. Amid the applause of the large concourse, Seeley proudly mounted his charger, and as he stroked his neck, complacently took the wager, and rode home a happier man than ever in his life before or since. The poet says:

> "Honor and fame from no condition rise;
> Act well your part—there all the honor lies."

Seeley has done this, and his name is inscribed on the page of his country's history, to be remembered long after those who have laughed at his career shall have been forgotten.

TO THE READER.—We rest—not insensible to the fact that we may, in your estimation, "have done those things which we ought not to have done, and left undone those things which we ought to have done;" but there is no help for it now. Our field was entirely new, and but very few papers are accessible at this early day in our history—the future writer will have still less, and this work may prove advantageous to those who succeed us. We have not sought to embellish, but simply to give plain statements of old matters. Several thousand families have been named, and omissions of any of the old settlers have been unintentional. The multitude crowding upon us has caused us to give less notice to several of our best citizens than we designed. Errors, typographical and otherwise, may exist; attribute them to the peculiar circumstances that surround us in these days of war and excitement, and join us in prayer for a return of the good old times of peace, prosperity and happiness.

www.ingramcontent.com/pod-product-compliance
Lightning Source LLC
LaVergne TN
LVHW021147110826
845150LV00005B/1149

* 9 7 8 1 4 2 5 5 4 7 0 1 1 *